Your Guide to Wellbeing at University

STUDENT
SUCCESS

Your Guide to Wellbeing at University

Gretchen Geng
Leigh Disney

Los Angeles | London | New Delhi
Singapore | Washington DC | Melbourne

Los Angeles | London | New Delhi
Singapore | Washington DC | Melbourne

SAGE Publications Ltd
1 Oliver's Yard
55 City Road
London EC1Y 1SP

SAGE Publications Inc.
2455 Teller Road
Thousand Oaks, California 91320

SAGE Publications India Pvt Ltd
B 1/I 1 Mohan Cooperative Industrial Area
Mathura Road
New Delhi 110 044

SAGE Publications Asia-Pacific Pte Ltd
3 Church Street
#10-04 Samsung Hub
Singapore 049483

Editor: Kate Keers
Editorial assistant: Sahar Jamfar
Production editor: Sarah Sewell
Copyeditor: Jane Fricker
Proofreader: Christine Bitten
Indexer: Melanie Gee
Marketing manager: Catherine Slinn
Cover design: Sheila Tong
Typeset by: C&M Digitals (P) Ltd, Chennai, India
Printed in the UK

Library of Congress Control Number: 2022942680

British Library Cataloguing in Publication data

A catalogue record for this book is available from the
British Library

ISBN 978-1-5297-6321-8
ISBN 978-1-5297-6320-1 (pbk)

At SAGE we take sustainability seriously. Most of our products are printed in the UK using responsibly sourced
papers and boards. When we print overseas we ensure sustainable papers are used as measured by the PREPS
grading system. We undertake an annual audit to monitor our sustainability.

Contents

Contents

About the authors

Dr Gretchen Geng is currently the Deputy Head of School in the School of Education Victoria (Melbourne campus) at the Australian Catholic University. Before that, she was a Vice President (curriculum) in the International Educational Groups at Beijing Foreign Studies University, the Teaching Lead at the DVC (Education) Office of RMIT University, and an Associate Professor in Pedagogy and Learning at Charles Darwin University.

Before her tertiary career, Gretchen was a preschool and primary school teacher and had years of practising experience in teaching young children and school-age children. Gretchen has also been involved in using digital educational technologies in teaching school students in the global learning context.

Gretchen has a strong interest in curriculum development, technology use in students' learning, and students' health and wellbeing. Currently, she is working on developing a model to assist university teachers' teaching competencies development.

Dr Leigh Disney is an Early Years lecturer within the Faculty of Education at Monash University. Prior to this, he was an Early Childhood lecturer at Charles Darwin University. During this time, Leigh has worked with both undergraduate and postgraduate students across the field of initial teacher education.

He began his career in Early Years working as an early childhood educator in both preschool and school-based settings for over 10 years. During this time, he developed a detailed knowledge of the educative and care needs of children within the 0–8 age range, specialising in supporting young children's social and emotional development, as well as the curricular domains of science, technology and mathematics. Leigh has also spent time working in China on projects related to cross-cultural early childhood practices and the implementation of play-based learning within Chinese preschools.

Preface

Introduction to this book

The experience of higher education students has been the subject of research for many years. With the recent global impact of the COVID-19 pandemic, there has been more research focusing on higher education experience. Factors that have been identified as influencing higher education students' academic experience include: (1) prior academic performance (Corcoran & O'Flaherty, 2017; W. Lee, 2017; Scott et al., 2008); (2) social and academic readiness to collaborate with course lecturers and other students (Berman et al., 2020; Cox et al., 2005; Harmoinen et al., 2020); (3) technical readiness to use online technologies (Geng & Disney, 2010; H. Kim et al., 2019); and (4) conflicting work commitments (Long et al., 2006; Popoola & Fagbola, 2021). Furthermore, other researchers have identified the following specific factors leading to the attrition of higher education students amid their studies: course dissatisfaction; financial problems; transferring to another university; academic difficulties; family responsibilities; personal issues; and poor-quality teaching (Garcia-Ros et al., 2012; Pedler et al., 2022; Shah et al., 2021). Willcoxson et al. (2011) also found that having an apparent reason for attending university and knowing the type of occupation to which they aspired were significantly related to a lower likelihood of attrition. Many individual students frequently perceive tertiary study as an opportunity to achieve their life goals for themselves as well as their families (Pedler et al., 2022). In a previous project (Geng & Midford, 2015), we also identified several stressors for university students. These included university stressors, such as academic requirements and professional performance, and stressors beyond universities, such as outside work and family commitments.

The findings of all the above research indicate there is an urgent need to develop resources to educate potential and current university students on the issue of stress and create new supportive learning strategies for students that focus on their wellbeing. Thus, this book has been written to address these needs.

Stress is a normal part of life, and learning how to deal with it and maintain wellbeing is vital to achieving success within higher education contexts (Putwain, 2019). Yet, Henning et al. (2018) describe that in pursuit of academic goals, there is the risk that within the structures of higher education students may put their wellbeing at risk to attain those goals, which is actually counter-productive to achieving their goals and ultimately remaining within higher educational settings.

With the ease of the restrictions of the COVID lockdowns, it is expected that students in higher education will recommence their study on campus in many states and territories. However, although much research has indicated that the prolonged stress experienced during campus closures likely results in students with social, emotional and different academic needs after their return to campus studying or mixed-mode studying (Hoffman & Miller, 2020), there is minimal research focusing on strategies that students can use to manage their wellbeing and engage in their studying. Therefore, this book investigates current higher education students' strategies to maintain their wellbeing within the present, chaotic academic climate, particularly during the pandemic. Moreover, the strategies thus described have been analysed to identify suitability for use across disciplinary areas. The ultimate goal is to ensure a better understanding of higher education students' needs and how more personalised strategies can be developed and utilised to develop resilience and wellbeing. The book, therefore, is supported by an extensive overview of the literature and personalised strategies that promote wellbeing within the current higher education environment.

Theoretical background

The content of the book has been developed based upon the Neuman Systems Model and Engagement Theory.

Before we present the Neuman Systems Model, the General Systems Theory (GST) should be briefly discussed. The GST has been proposed and defined by many researchers and theorists (e.g. Boulding, 1956; Klir, 1972; van Gigch, 1974). Although their definitions are not completely aligned with each other, the theory's importance overall is that it provides a dynamic system that recognises the collective force of systems. In addition, it is acknowledged that systems theory offers an explanation for real-world systems, not just limited to the scientific world (K. M. Adams et al., 2014). Systems theory can invoke improved explanatory power and interpretation with significant implications for system users. Systems theory covers the philosophical, theoretical and methodological aspects and the techniques of educational sciences (K. M. Adams et al., 2014).

Evolved from systems theory, the Neuman Systems Model (Neuman & Fawcett, 2011) describes the open-system-based perspective that focuses on a wide range of concerns. In particular, it is an open system that responds to stressors in the environment from a physiological, psychological, sociocultural, developmental and spiritual perspective. This model identifies three relevant environments: the internal, the external and the created. Although universities can represent the internal environment in the model, university students' stress can also come from external factors and the created factors unconsciously developed to cope with stress. Thus, this model enables us to conceptualise thought and action with respect to university systems, understand the variety of academic disciplines and provide an improved understanding of students' stress and subsequent strategies to support wellbeing.

The Neuman Systems Model also discusses five different kinds of variables: physiological variables (people's own bodily function and structure), psychological variables (mental processes), sociocultural variables (relevant social and cultural expectations and activities), developmental variables (development processes throughout the lifespan) and spiritual variables (influence of spiritual beliefs). Similarly, Loehr and Schwartz (2005) developed a framework to convert stress by channelling energy into high performance and personal renewal in their Power of Full Engagement Theory. In their strategy, the process of converting pressure and managing energy was undertaken by using 'energy muscles' that included the physical, emotional, mental and spiritual. This energy muscle training system has been popularly used to manage stress effectively across many disciplinary areas (Loehr & Schwartz, 2005). This book, therefore, uses the Neuman Systems Model and Loehr and Schwartz's theory to investigate the current strategies higher education students use in the physical, emotional, mental and spiritual 'muscle' and 'energy' to transfer stresses and challenges into more efficient engagement in their learning and to support their wellbeing. This book also endeavours to identify a more personalised strategy that students can develop and utilise to build their resilience and wellbeing. The aims of this book include (a) using narrative methods to investigate the strategies that higher education students use to develop or maintain their wellbeing, and (b) evaluating which wellbeing strategies are suitable for utilising across disciplinary areas within higher education.

The innovation of this book and research methods of this book

This book has used a literature review and a case study approach. A literature review provides this book with a thorough understanding of energy building and its related theories.

This book also involves a collective case study approach. It uses a number of cases to understand and investigate a phenomenon, and studying multiple cases can provide a better illustration of particular phenomena (Ary et al., 2010).

An Interpretative Phenomenological Analysis (IPA) was used to collect case studies to understand and investigate a phenomenon, and studying multiple cases can provide a better illustration of particular phenomena (Creswell & Poth, 2018; Smith & Osborn, 2015). The IPA was employed to produce an account of lived experience without rationalising that experience (Creswell & Poth, 2018; Smith & Osborn, 2015) but rather to make sense of participants' lived experiences. IPA also allows researchers to take an extra interpretive layer into account to allow more or less empathy and the interview data could be analysed along the spectrum (Ary et al., 2010) of an insider's view. In accordance with IPA's emphasis on particular cases and small, relatively homogeneous samples (Reid et al., 2005), semi-structured interviews were used to explore the phenomena of the participants' lived experiences.

The related research has also obtained ethics clearance from an Australian university. Online semi-structured interviews have been used to collect the narrative studies on how higher education students build and maintain their wellbeing. The research used snowball sampling to gather participants for the study. A snowball sample is where potential sample groups are identified based on the particular characteristics to be studied, and whereupon those participants will be requested to nominate other potential participants (Ary et al., 2010). To begin the snowballing process, the authors contacted university-based students' associations. They asked them to nominate potential individuals who have studied or are currently studying in higher education to give insights into how they supported their wellbeing.

In line with the IPA method's focus on specific cases and small, relatively homogeneous samples, as mentioned above (Creswell & Poth, 2018; Reid et al., 2005), this book conducted a number of interviews to reach reasonable data saturation and to achieve a comprehensive overview of and guide to the strategies that help students improve their wellbeing whilst studying at university across various disciplines and further within their careers.

How to use this book

This book has four parts, starting with Part 1 (introduction and understanding of wellbeing in university life), Part 2 (university students and their wellbeing), Part 3 (developing personalised wellbeing strategies), and Part 4 (from university to beyond university). Part 1 has three chapters, including the common stressors of university life which are investigated in Chapters 1 and 2 to provide readers with a general understanding of the wellbeing of university studying. Chapter 3 of Part 1 provides different stress measurement instruments for readers to test their stressors. Part 2, comprising Chapters 4 to 6, starts with investigating the stressors experienced by the students across their different stages of studying (at the beginning, in the middle, or at the end) and useful stress management strategies. Part 3 of the book then helps students develop their resilience by using the personalised strategies of students to understand their academic, professional and personal needs and make use of various resources within and outside the university. Part 3 includes four chapters: Building physical energy (Chapter 7), Building emotional energy (Chapter 8), Building mental energy (Chapter 9) and lastly, Building spiritual energy (Chapter 10). Part 4 of the book discusses how to maintain wellbeing from university to beyond university in Chapter 11.

The interviews in the case studies include an investigation of current university students and graduates from different demographic backgrounds and various stages of their university life, including school leavers, mature age students, returning students, international students and research students. In each chapter, the book provides an outline of the book's structure and where this chapter is in the structure. Moreover, recommended activities, including readings and stress level measurement activities, are provided at the end of each chapter.

This book also includes three Appendices. Appendix A allows readers to either go to the PSS-10 diagnostic test first to measure their stress levels (Chapter 3) and then turn to the relevant chapter of the book in Part 3, or go to Part 2 of the book to understand the stressors before turning to build personal strategies described in Part 3. For example, a first-year student can take a PSS test and then investigate the stressors to understand their stress levels better, or turn to the section of the book relevant to their immediate needs. Appendix B provides readers with a strategic planning template to relate to the case studies and appropriate activities or strategies to develop resilience skills across the four areas of physical, emotional, mental and spiritual energies. Finally, Appendix C provides an overview of university support for their students. Authentic examples from the United Kingdom, Australia and the United States are included to acknowledge the differences and identify the similarities among the universities and countries.

Acknowledgements

We would like to acknowledge the contributions from the participating students and staff. Their strategies to achieve a healthy university life and wellbeing are highly appreciated.

WELLBEING IN UNIVERSITY CONTEXT

1

Understanding wellbeing

Part 1

Wellbeing in university context

- This part has three chapters, and this first chapter discusses the common stressors across different year levels in the university context from university students' social and emotional needs, and academic requirements to their personal and professional needs. Understanding the stressors helps you build energies and achieve greater learning outcomes and better wellbeing throughout your university life.

Part 2

University students and wellbeing

Part 3

Develop personalised wellbeing strategies

Part 4

Wellbeing beyond university

Figure 1.1   Chapter summary

Congratulations. You are now officially a university student, but are you prepared to start this challenging but rewarding journey?

We live in fast times, and the changes in the digital world have pushed us to work to our utmost to meet all different kinds of requirements or expectations. Our daily lives are crammed with bits and pieces of juggling study, family and work. Much research has shown that the first year of university study plays an essential part in a successful university life. For example, Coertjens et al. (2017), Harvey et al. (2006) and Meehan and Howells (2019) found that the first year of higher education is an important transitional experience that can lead to success or failure at university. Most of us are just trying to do the best we can. However, sometimes we race through our lives without taking the time to pause and reflect on how we will go further or who we want to be as we progress through our journeys. Therefore, the first-year transition to university life is a critical starting part of our future career and life. When considering the first year and planning for subsequent years of university life, we should not skim across the surface of days. Instead, we should use this critical time to build our resilience for our wellbeing and future life. Consider the following scenarios:

- You just found a part-time job (two days a week) working in a retail store starting from 1 p.m. straight after your lecture at the university, so once your lecture is completed, you need to rush to work. You have no time to ask your lecturer questions, nor can you have an academic conversation with other students. Once you come home after work, you are so exhausted that you cannot focus on your studies and assignments.
- You did not do well in one academic task, and you start to doubt your capacity and career choice. You start to overthink, and your sleep patterns are disrupted.
- You have four assignments from four subjects due around the same week in the semester. Each assignment requires you to write around 2,000 words. You become overwhelmed about where you should start and how to proceed.
- The examinations are fast approaching, but your family is planning a holiday during the break. You feel incredibly guilty that you have excluded yourself from the planning as you are trying your best to catch up with your study and other work.
- You know you are not well and feel tired. However, you have tried to stay up and meet the requirements and due dates. You start to wonder whether your degree is actually setting you up for the rest of your life.

We use day planners and to-do lists. All the universities will use curriculum management systems, in which pop-up reminders are designed to help us manage our time better. We are constantly feeling time-short and craving solutions.

This book is developed to show you how to understand the challenges of university life, to generate energy to the full, and to achieve high performance and success in your study at university and beyond. In this chapter we will show you some stressors encountered at differing university levels of study, grounded within the overarching context of university life, which will be discussed next.

University life contexts

To maximise the time and learning opportunities you have at university, it is useful to understand the concept of performance. To most first-year university students, performance refers to academic performance. That is, how well did you do in your studies? What is your grade point average (GPA)? And can you obtain an academic recommendation from your lecturers?

We have, however, seen many university students drop out from their learning during university study. Here we also refer to the students who change their academic course or career pathways during their studies. For example, you have taken science (chemistry), but you want to change to learn midwifery as you realise this is your future career. However, according to many universities' regulations, you have to stay in the science programme for at least one semester before transferring to the other programme. This then requires us to understand further the university system and whether it will impact on your study and future life.

To reach your expected academic performance, we refer you to the full energy framework throughout this book. Many studies have researched and identified several factors that influence university students' academic experience. The factors start from pre-transition and during the transition. They cover prior academic performance, social and academic readiness to collaborate with course lecturers and other students, technical readiness to use online technologies, and conflicting work commitments. Willcoxson et al. (2011) identified some specific factors, such as course satisfaction levels (including your learning experience and the quality of teaching and learning), financial issues, academic difficulties, family responsibilities, and personal issues. Evans et al. (2018) reviewed the transition from academic and psychological impact perspectives with reference to contextual constructs, including environment-level constructs, individual-level constructs and outcomes. Outcomes in university life include not only academic performance but also emotional wellbeing and social integration. Hence, based upon the study by Evans et al. (2018), we have developed the diagram shown in Figure 1.2 of university life's contextual constructs to show you the teaching and learning context and conceptualise the constructs across various levels.

For example, in the environment-level constructs, we shall focus on: (a) university teaching and the learning environment, including pre-transition academic attainment, academic goal orientation, student autonomy, course size (number of students); (b) the support provided by academic lecturers and administrative staff in universities; and (c) external community involvement.

Among the individual-level constructs, factors such as your prior knowledge, academic competence, learning experience and self-efficacy levels and motivation, and self-related needs and demands are focused on. These also include peer relationships, relationships with academics/lecturers, learners' own learning intentions and interests.

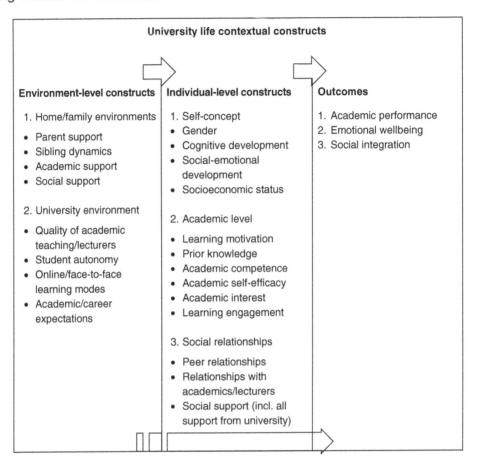

Figure 1.2   University life contextual constructs

Figure 1.2 emphasises the outcome of successful university life (and student retention): students' successful integration in an institution's social and academic systems. Although some research has shown that drop-out can be seen as a positive outcome for some students (e.g. Brunsden et al., 2000), there is undoubtedly a strong push for us to understand the reasons behind drop-out and consequently look after university students' wellbeing in recent studies (e.g. Arslan et al., 2020; Lee-St et al., 2018; Will, 2018).

In 1982, Bean developed a model of understanding student attrition via a balance between the organisational and personal/external factors. In this model, he emphasised the background variables of both environmental-level constructs and individual-level constructs. For example, he discussed the student's prior academic performance, socioeconomic status, distance from the parental home and hometown size. He also pointed out other factors, such as the degree's practical value, university teaching and learning quality, communication about requirements, fairness of treatment, work commitments, housing and social involvement in campus activities. In addition, postgraduate students have distinctive characteristics. For example, they might be studying part-time and have a different work commitment. This commitment places a perceived influence on their stressors and academic decisions. Then, the escalated stress also makes it challenging to identify and capture the significant interactions between personal and other factors.

Researchers such as Deeley et al. (2019), Doggrell and Schaffer (2016) and Douglas et al. (2015) found that commitment to academic work and the nature of interactions with academic and administrative staff were significantly related to the withdrawal rate of first-year students. In Australia, Dodd et al. (2021), Farrer et al. (2016) and Peel et al. (2004) reported that the factor of 'course dissatisfaction' was a crucial contributor to first-year students' drop-out. Willcoxson and colleagues (2011) studied first-year students' withdrawal in six Australian universities and found that they were at the greatest risk of drop-out. Other researchers (Saccaro & França, 2020; Williams et al., 2018) further investigated the principal reasons for this withdrawal among first-year students and found that commitment to their institution and learning, to their course and to study time were significantly associated with the likelihood of withdrawal. On the other side of the balance sheet, they found that having an apparent reason for attending university and knowing the type of occupation to which students aspired were significantly related to a lower likelihood of withdrawal during the first year. Therefore, to cope with the stress and maintain wellbeing during university life, we need to understand the everyday stressors. When working with stressors, most of us would view it as a negative term, as uncontrollable stress can lead to anxiety and depression. But it does not have to be so; rather, understanding how to deal with them leads to the development of techniques to work with stressors. In particular, strategies will be provided in this book to support communication skills and to guide students on ways to improve their own stress levels.

Possible challenges for university students

There are many factors causing stress for university students. Although sometimes we would like to avoid the stressors, often they are forced upon us. For example, many of us do not like to sit examinations; exams are prevalent assessments in many degree courses, such as science, engineering and mathematics. It is unavoidable for students to experience stress when sitting exams.

Back in 2014, we conducted a stress study among approximately 350 education students, and one of the key findings was that male students prefer individual work to group work (Geng & Midford, 2015). Some consider group work to be stressful as it involves academic contributions, communication skills and collaborative work. But of course this will not apply to every male. Therefore, for us to know the best strategies to cope with stress in university studying, it is important to understand the various stressors and which cause you the most stress.

Willcoxson and his team conducted large-scale research on retention and attrition factors across six Australian universities (Willcoxson et al., 2011). More recently, many other researchers (Akos & James, 2020; Naylor et al., 2018; Ortiz-Lozano et al., 2020) have also studied stressors for first-year university students and beyond the first year. We will now detail the various factors identified, analysed and studied in the research.

Commitment factors

- Commitment to university and to learning
- Commitment to course
- Commitment of time

Expectations factors

- Support for learning
- Expectations of teaching
- Commitment to university and to learning
- Expectations of facilities
- Academic confidence
- Travel requirements
- Teacher enthusiasm/passion

Support factors

- Support for learning
- Expectations of teaching
- Commitment to course
- Counselling
- Financial issues

Feedback factors

- Support for learning
- Expectations of teaching

Involvement factors

- Student interactions
- Engagement: Academic
- Engagement: Social

The chapter will now synthesise the common stressors for university students across the first, second and final year of your degree.

First-year challenges

The first year is a critical year for any university student as they embark upon university study for the first time in their lives. Some researchers have noted that first-year students are the group at most risk of attrition from universities. In 2009, Professor Sally Kift conducted a comprehensive study on the issue of Transition Pedagogy. This research-based pedagogy includes six first-year curriculum principles which underpin support for first-year higher education students: transition, diversity, design, engagement, assessment, and evaluation and monitoring. Kift's Transition Pedagogy provides a solid theoretical background for understanding the students' diversity, transition experience and full engagement for first-year university students. For example, Stallman (2010) reported from a large-scale research project involving 6,479 students in two large universities that Australian university students have significantly higher stress levels than the general population. Mooney et al. (2018) also reported the importance of transition pedagogies that are embedded within curricula in ways that are relevant for health and physical education (HPE) teachers. They found specific pedagogical features that were integral to inclusive, engaging and positive first-year experiences. In the following text, we are going to present some true cases of first-year university students to show you some stressors you may face.

Financial challenges

STUDENT
EXAMPLE

As a high school graduate, Jessica is 'ready' for her university life. She has just accepted the offer from a university to study nursing. She is the oldest child of a family who live in a small country town. She is excited and very keen to start her new life in an urban city. She is also nervous about whether she can find near-by accommodation. Her friends and family tell her, 'A shared house will be great, as it is not expensive.' She is also looking for a part-time job to support herself and not entirely depend on her family.

Financial problems and family responsibilities are common stressors for first-year university students transferring to another city to study. Moving away from home can be expensive and the realities of renting (even within shared accommodation) and the bills associated with independent living mount up quickly. Furthermore, shared accommodation also brings with it stressors of other kinds.

Cultural understanding challenges

STUDENT EXAMPLE

Aiko is an international student at an Australian university. She completed her first degree successfully from another university in Australia but has now transferred to this university to study. Although she does have studying experience at a higher education institution and has become more familiar with Australian culture, she now needs to adjust quickly to the new culture of another university. Interestingly and naturally, many first-year university students may feel awkward discussing learning tasks with academic staff. Aiko also found it difficult to talk to her lecturers, which impacted her academic and psychological readiness (Joubert & Hay, 2020; van Rooij et al., 2018) to study.

Having said that, we learn continually from each other in daily life, and in most cases, seek information from friends and colleagues, and do not rely on taking a course or consulting a teacher. Boud et al. (2014) state that learning from each other is a feature of informal learning. It happens in informal courses at all levels where students share their learning experiences inside and outside the classroom. Learning to work with peers collaboratively and being willing to discuss learning tasks with other students can be challenging for some people, particularly if they prefer to work alone or experience cultural differences in communication strategies.

Life and work balance challenges

STUDENT EXAMPLE

Julie is a mature age university student. She studied her engineering degree eight years ago when she completed high school. She worked as a civil engineer for a private company for a couple of years. After getting married and now with two school-age children, she is ready to restart her career. However, instead of going back to her engineering career, which requires her to travel constantly and work late hours, she wanted to find a job that allows her to drop off and pick up her children before and after school. She consulted with her husband and family, and decided to go back to university to study to be a school teacher.

Although Julie is not a traditional first-time university student, her last time study-ing at university has 'faded'. Now, she needs to study for a completely new degree and start a new career pathway. She is nervous about the academic workload, as well as other part-time work she has to complete to support her family financially, and, of course, the day-to-day household chores she shares with her partner and children. In recent studies, Garcia-Ros et al. (2012) and Logan and Burns (2021) found that perceived stress was common in the first year of university studies. The highest stress levels related to oral presentations, aca-demic overload, lack of time to meet commitments and taking exams. Julie's story is common, particularly among mature age students. Their stressors mainly come from a lack of time to meet academic commitments. Julie related, 'I am looking after my children, helping my children with homework, taking my children to after school activities, domestic duties, working in the family business. It is tough to find a time to have a group meeting for a group presentation, and I am a bit concerned that I would not contribute to my group as I should.' Researchers such as Deeley et al. (2019), Doggrell and Schaffer (2016) and Douglas et al. (2015) found that commitment to academic work and the nature of interactions with academic and administrative staff were significantly related to the attrition rate of first-year students.

Geng and Midford (2015) conducted a study to investigate pre-service teachers' stressors while on placement. Listening to their voices about the challenges of teaching, the study offered a solid base for pre-service teachers to share their stories with peers as entrepreneurial professionals during their studies and later into the teaching profession. One of the aims of the study was to understand better the barriers and enablers that face students in their journey to qualify as teachers and to develop practical strategies that enhance their success.

The findings provided a vital resource to understand different educational stu-dents' needs. Significant results include: (a) students' stress levels were much higher than the general population; (b) first-year students' stress levels were significantly higher than those of students in other years; (c) male student teachers had significantly higher stress levels than female student teachers (this finding contributes to understanding why there is a shortage of male teachers because when students are overwhelmed and stressed with their workload or completion of assignments, many either withdraw from the unit or even the whole course); and (d) a lack of development of reflective thinking and adaptive teaching strategies is a contributing factor for graduate entry student teachers.

Researchers (Darabi et al., 2017; Logan & Burns, 2021) have identified several factors that influence first-year tertiary students' experience. These include: (a) prior academic performance (Logan & Burns, 2021; Olvera et al., 2018; Swanepoel & van Heerden, 2018); (b) social and academic readiness to collaborate with course lecturers and other students (Ketonen et al., 2016; Swanepoel & van Heerden, 2018); (c) technical readiness to use online technologies (Geng & Disney, 2010); and (d) conflicting work commitments (Logan & Burns, 2021).

Second and following years' challenges

Although the second and following years have similar challenges to the first year, and although first-year drop-outs represent approximately half of all the attritions of university students, little attention has been paid to the challenges of university studies in later years. Yet, given the equal importance of the second year and following years, clearly support for these students and online services, for example, can also have a positive impact on their wellbeing. Furthermore, Johnson (2008) studied faculty differences in a Canadian university. He found that while science major students tend to withdraw from the first year, education and arts major students drop out mainly in the second year. Therefore, there must be a difference between the first-year challenges and the following years.

STUDENT EXAMPLE

Kevin is a second-year science student. He presented his stressors from the perspectives of academic satisfaction and other work commitments. *'I work as a Principal Policy Officer 3 days a week (22.5 hrs) for the government, and it has taken a lot of my time and efforts.'*

Like Kevin, many second-year students have found a stable study and work pattern; however, the requirements of work commitments can be demanding. Some students also participate in volunteer work or engage in community services to enhance their future employment opportunities, which may consume a lot of their energy. They may feel exhausted and find it difficult to concentrate.

STUDENT EXAMPLE

Roby is a third-year law student. She has had a placement in a law firm as an assistant and has been involved in many cases. She has become worried as she sometimes finds the study she is doing through university is not always related to her work, which may trigger a 'dissatisfaction' towards the academic work she is required to complete at university. She expected to have more practical feedback from her lecturers and when this occurred, found the detailed feedback of great significance to her.

Students in the second and following years have been found to have more frequent communication and interactions with academic and administrative staff (Zander et al., 2018). They have a clearer understanding of their studies and their future career. Therefore, they can explain their needs and seek support or clarification from the university. Meanwhile, they become more familiar with university policies and procedures and become stressed or dissatisfied if their needs cannot be met. In summary, the differences between the first and other years lie in that first-year students' stressors stem from their background, such as lack of academic preparation, inability to integrate into university social and academic systems and lack of academic goal commitment, while the other years students' challenges come from their management of the study balance, particularly related to the quality of interactions with academic and administrative staff.

Final-year challenges

We purposefully take final-year students' stressors individually in this section (and in separate chapters in this book), as they can be unique and completely different from other years. This year can also be stressful as it would be viewed as a transition year from university to work or to start a career.

STUDENT EXAMPLE

Hannah is finishing the final year of her teaching degree. She has been actively looking for teaching positions around where she lives. '*I prefer to have an ongoing position at a school.*' Job security has been labelled as a priority by many final-year students. While it is essential, it can also cause a certain level of stress. '*I have been waiting for over two months for my screening application to be approved. This has made life in general very stressful! The things I organised for the proper placement time have all been messed up, and I'm living in limbo. Where I'm living, there is no internet, so I've been worrying about doing my assignments while away* [no Internet and not at campus].'

Final-year challenges can also come from decisions about whether to continue further study or work. The stress is often due to the transition from the university environment and financial issues. Moreover, many students are now looking for career advice and interview tips from the university.

During this period, the stressors move beyond year level and the type of degree undertaken (we also focus on research students below) and the individual differences between students play a vital role in understanding what stressors impact student wellbeing.

Challenges for research students

In this book, we will also elaborate on the challenges faced by research students, as they are experiencing completely different domains to coursework students.

STUDENT
EXAMPLE

Sarah is a second-year PhD student. She has just had her proposal passed and is ready to commit to doing her fieldwork and data collection. Sarah is excited about her fieldwork. However, she is also nervous about whether the data she is collecting are appropriate and will be helpful in writing her dissertation. She has heard from some PhD students who had to re-collect their data as the first round of data collection was not successful. She is also wondering what else she needs to do to get better prepared.

Instead of doing assignments, taking examinations, or other group work, research students are required to complete a few milestones, including developing a research proposal, conducting fieldwork, data analysis, and finally doing their research dissertation. Some detailed work may include attending regular meetings with supervisors, attending university research workshops, learning data analysis strategies and writing skills.

Diversity of university students

While we have elaborated on the different year levels of university students, we have to acknowledge that every student can be different. Their gender, prior knowledge about their work and understanding of the profession and career they may be pursuing can all be very different.

For example, gender can play an essential role in stressors we encounter, with acknowledgement of the diversity of students including transgender/non-binary students. The stress response theory, developed by Horowitz (1976), has been used as a framework to understand how different genders react to stress: fight-or-flight in men or tend-and-befriend in women (Horowitz, 2001). While men report lower stress levels and are less likely to report anxiety symptoms, they are less likely to actively work at relieving or managing their stress (American Psychological Association, 2015). They also tend to respond in a more immediate, reactive fashion. Bendezú et al. (2021) and Owens et al. (2018), for example, found that adolescent girls rely more heavily on their support networks when stressed, while adolescent boys typically engage in activities that involve aggression and physical release. It was also found that women and men interact differently with others (Walsh & Bartikowski, 2012). Women tend to be more socialised for interpersonal interaction and provide more social support to others (Bendezú et al., 2021; Bonneville-Roussy et al., 2017). In contrast, men do not use emotional display as much as women (Bonneville-Roussy et al., 2017; Prowse et al., 2021). Consequently, women are more engaged in emotional regulation and focus more on feelings, while men regulate their emotions to a lesser extent (Graves et al., 2021; Kargin et al., 2021). However, it was also noted that men could feel a greater sense of achievement when engaged in their work (Simpson & Stroh, 2004). These findings may help us understand how to deal with stress among men and women.

As discussed earlier in this chapter, mature age university students and school leavers will have different stressors. In particular, their family commitments and other work commitments can put a level of stress among mature age university students. At the same time, school leavers have stressors related to the transition between school and university.

If we are going to investigate the diversity of university students, we might first understand the differences between different students according to their cultural-historical backgrounds. In addition, some disciplinary courses may require university students to meet unique requirements for course completion. For example, pharmacy students need to attend interviews and some other different prerequisites. Medical students have to complete placements in hospitals, and education students have to do placements at schools or childcare centres to graduate. Completing learning tasks outside university adds an extra layer of stress, as more collaborative skills are required.

STUDENT EXAMPLE

Isabel is a second-year education student. She has completed her first-year university studies successfully. Entering her second year, she knows she needs to start her teaching practicum, in addition to her theory study load. Her first teaching practicum is 15 days in total, carried out in several blocks. During her professional practicums, she is required to complete a range of experiential tasks, such as getting familiar with school culture, working very closely with her mentor teachers, and planning her teaching. She is assessed on her performance by both the university lecturer and her mentor teachers in her placement.

Lemon and McDonough (2020) and Rieg et al. (2007) state that the style of placement assessment, designing and developing lesson plans based upon their understanding of the national curriculum, teaching students and applying strategies and pedagogy from their theoretical learning, all within the tight timelines of teaching practice can be very stressful for education students. Research on the mental health and wellbeing of education students has indicated that this stress can result in students withdrawing from study and teaching as a future career (Rieg et al., 2007).

In this chapter, we have discussed the various challenges faced by university students, with some examples. We understand performance in university includes academic and other performances. In Chapter 2, we will guide you in how to develop skilful management strategies of full energy to achieve better wellbeing.

Mapping your journey to success

- University life contextual constructs have various levels, including environment-level constructs and individual-level constructs.
- Challenges for university students come from different aspects, such as individual students' personal backgrounds, year levels along the studying journey and the nature of the degree.
- Understanding the challenges will help us to build our energy and achieve greater learning outcomes and better wellbeing throughout our university life.

Recommended reading

This section recommends some useful texts, including newspaper articles, academic publications and other expert knowledge.

The article 'UK university students struggle with stress as uncertainty grows over return date' was published by *The Guardian* newspaper in April 2021 (Ferguson, 2021). You may find this text relevant to you as it discussed the stressors during the COVID period. Although it is an article about universities in the UK, the stressors and uncertainty were shared among all university students during the pandemic. Beyond the UK, the article 'Canada: Survey points psychological, academic and financial stress' published by Pie News (posted on January 28, 2022) presents findings from a survey among international university students in Canada (Stacey, 2022). The study found that 'Over 25% felt both financial and psychological stress but not academic stress; about 20 per cent felt all three kinds of stress.' Other than the news articles, it is recommended that you read some academic texts too. For example, you may be interested to know the gender differences in coping with stress by reading 'Motivation and coping with the stress of assessment: Gender differences in outcomes for university students' (Bonneville-Roussy et al., 2017). You may also be interested in finding coping strategies to manage stress. You will find a practical approach in the book by Lemon and McDonough (2020), *Building and sustaining a teaching career: Strategies for professional experience, well-being and mindful practice.*

2

Four areas of building resilience

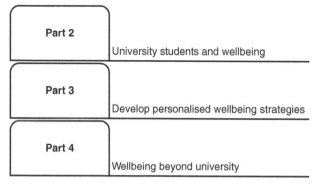

Part 1

Wellbeing in university context

- This part has three chapters. Following the first chapter, this second chapter helps you understand how to build energy muscles from phyiscal, emotional, mental and spiritual perspectives for overcoming challenges and stressors in university life.

Part 2

University students and wellbeing

Part 3

Develop personalised wellbeing strategies

Part 4

Wellbeing beyond university

Figure 2.1   Chapter summary

As discussed in the last chapter, university studying can be rushed, rapid, relentless, and our days in university are divided into many different areas. We have academic performance standards to satisfy; we have family commitments to fulfil; we also have our own social-emotional and mental health to look after. A human being can be very resilient, though. Sometimes people carry on through life, with or without enormous difficulties. In the end, be it celebrating all the little moments or the final graduation ceremony, we are acknowledging not only the work we have done but also the positive energy we put in throughout the studying journey. We reflect at each turning point and try to work out the deeper meanings in our life.

On the other hand, there are also moments where we react quickly instead of reflecting or deep consideration. Some students we have talked to told us that they were racing through their university time without having a moment to pause and consider why they really want to study and who they want to be. They said to us that university was just a preparation for the knowledge they needed for their future employment. They skim the surface; then, some of them dropped out in the middle of their studies or changed their career after completing their university studies, never using their degree for its intended purpose.

True, we are simply trying to do the best we can. We make choices, sometimes sensible choices, to get us through the days and nights of university life. We have interviewed and observed students who recount overloaded studying schedules, working day and night with little sleep, and being always on the run, with minimal awareness that this will take a toll on health and wellbeing over time. These students admit to fast food diets, fuelling up their energy on caffeine, sometimes alcohol and sleeping pills. In the end, many of them get so challenged that they become exhausted and easily distracted. They become annoyed with themselves and short-tempered and then do an about turn with regard to studies: a 'do not care anymore' or 'simply give up' mode. They may start to miss classes, fall behind in studying schedules, miss the due date for turning in their assignments, or fail exams.

Interestingly, we all find excuses for our behaviours. We have family commitments and other work commitments we have to attend to. Then the to-do list is simply overwhelming and is jettisoned out the window. We become short-tempered at our own 'failure' and find it even more challenging to find a source of joy and renewal of energy. However, we have found that the majority of students we have met take pride in their work, which brings strong positive attitudes in behaviour. For example, if we find pleasure in producing good quality work, we tend to put in the long hours of work required to achieve the desired outcome. Howe and Krosnick (2017) and Wallace et al. (2020) described attitude strength in their studies. They investigated the tremendous value of understanding attitude functioning and structure to effectively apply the positive attitude concept in a practical setting from a psychological perspective. Miller et al. (2016) and Ferrer et al. (2022) also confirmed the importance of people's positive attitude, which appears to enhance attitude-style behaviours.

However, in juggling work, family and study commitments, we may feel constantly overwhelmed and unable to bring sufficient energy and a positive attitude into everything we do. Consider the following scenarios:

- You need to attend a one-hour lecture in the morning, yet your tutorial doesn't start until 3 p.m. You are using the time between to work on a group assignment task and then catching up on other family and work commitments. When the 3 p.m. tutorial arrives, you feel tired and are dreading being stuck in peak hour traffic after class.
- You have spent your weekend working on your assignment due that Sunday evening. By 5 p.m. on Sunday, you still have one section of the paper to write. You start to be annoyed with yourself, short-tempered, edgy and feel defeated.
- You missed an important family outing because of a must-attend examination or a must-complete experiment. You feel overwhelming guilt and may question whether your commitment is worthwhile.
- You are completing the fieldwork for your research. There is a global pandemic, and you are unable to collect data for your research project. You feel frustrated and hopeless.

These scenarios have the potential to prevent us from achieving our goals in our work, family life and academic studies. Thus, the question then turns to how to build our resilience. This book will show you various ways to develop your own strategies to achieve wellbeing. In this chapter, we will also draw on the Full Engagement Model (Loehr & Schwartz, 2005; Zhang et al., 2018) to develop our strength and maintain our wellbeing in higher education, physically, emotionally, mentally and spiritually. The new paradigm shown in Table 2.1 was promoted to develop full engagement in high performance. More traditional paradigms focus on how to avoid stress and make the best use of positive thinking, while the new paradigm acknowledges the stress, but emphasises how to manage energy to achieve full engagement. Therefore moving away from stress is not building energy to manage stress appropriately.

Loehr and Schwartz (2005) developed a framework to convert stress and manage one's energy to achieve high performance and personal renewal, which they call the Power of Full Engagement. In their strategy, the process of converting pressure and managing energy entails using physical, emotional, mental and spiritual 'energy muscles'. This energy muscle training system has been popularly used to build strategies to achieve wellbeing effectively across many disciplinary areas, particularly management.

Table 2.1   New paradigm of building resilience

The new paradigm of building resilience	The traditional paradigm of building resilience
Energy management	Time management
Welcome stress	Avoid stress
Downtime can be productive	Downtime is a waste
The power of full engagement	The power of positive thinking

To help frame our understanding of how to manage stress and develop resilience for students in higher education settings, this book utilises a systems theory approach. As noted in the Preface, many researchers and theorists utilise General Systems Theory (e.g. Boulding, 1956; Klir, 1972; Lopreato, 1977; van Gigch, 1974). Their definitions may not be completely the same, but overall it can be described as a dynamic theory that recognises the collective force of systems. Furthermore systems theory provides an explanation for real-world systems, it is not just limited to the scientific world (Batt et al., 2021; van Assche et al., 2019). Using systems theory can offer improved explanatory power and interpretation with important implications for systems users. For the educational sciences it has philosophical, theoretical and methodological relevance (K. M. Adams et al., 2014). Based on systems theory, the Neuman Systems Model (Neuman & Fawcett, 2011) is an open system that responds to stressors in the environment from a physiological, psychological, sociocultural, developmental and/or spiritual perspective. Moreover, for our purposes here, it enables us to conceptualise thought and action regarding university systems, understand the variety of disciplines, and provide an improved understanding of our stress and subsequent strategies to support our wellbeing.

In this book, we have drawn upon the Neuman Systems Model and Loehr and Schwartz's Full Engagement Model to investigate the current strategies higher education students use, employing the concept of physical, emotional, mental and spiritual 'muscle' and 'energy' groups to transfer the challenges we face into more efficient engagement in learning and to support wellbeing. We will now outline the physical, emotional, mental and spiritual areas in relation to study within higher education settings.

Area 1: Physical muscles of resilience

Medical doctors around the world have proven physical health to be an important part of our wellbeing. It has been shown too how physical muscles can be developed and trained systematically. World athletic champions in different domains train in order to achieve stronger physical performance in their chosen discipline and to be at peak condition for their sporting events. Commonly these days, non-athletes have also developed a physical awareness to maintain a healthy BMI (Body

Measurement Index) in order to sustain their energy levels in life, work and study. For example, since the early 2010s, technology companies, Apple for example, have worked on technical devices to help people maintain their health and physical wellbeing. The iWatch, Fitbit or step recorders are common gadgets used by people in an attempt to monitor their physical routines and develop positive habits. Likewise, university students can utilise such devices to track their own levels of movement, which can be very helpful when faced with busy times, and provide a gentle reminder of when to move away from the desk and engage in physical activity.

Breathing patterns

Not surprisingly, we take certain things for granted, including such daily activities as eating, drinking and breathing. Particularly, the oxygen we breathe is never thought of as an essential energy source. Stress, anger and anxiety prompt fast breathing patterns. In fact, anger and anxiety make us use deeper abdominal breaths than our normal breathing patterns. Thus, we can see the importance of focusing on building our physical muscles for breathing, as they are closely related to mental and emotional equilibrium. Many resilience programmes promote how to breathe properly in order to relax. For example, Fitbit offers a 'relaxation function', including two- and five-minute breathing programmes. According to Fitbit, deep breathing is a common meditation technique that can help you let go of stress and maintain a quieter state of mind. Research (e.g. D'Agostini et al., 2022; Polychronopoulou et al., 2019) shows that taking a few minutes to relax each day can help reduce blood pressure and lower your risk of cardiovascular disease.

Extending exhalation prompts a relaxing self-regulation and a powerful wave of recovery from stressful moments. Deep, smooth, rhythmic breathing is a source of energy, focus, relaxation, stillness, and ultimately restores the pulse to a normal, steady state (Kahn et al., 2019). Thus, do not overlook the importance of breathing techniques and ways to enhance your practice. It can be a vital component of health and wellbeing.

Eating

Food is a source of energy. The food we eat provides different nutrition for our bodies. When we have an empty stomach, we will find it difficult to concentrate on our work. Much research has found (e.g. Bryce, 2019) that brain work consumes 20% of the body's energy use; that is a typical 320 calories per day are consumed from thinking. Your brain energy consumption is used to sustain your alertness, concentrate on important information and manage other related

21

study activities. University studying mostly involves brain work, which causes many staff and students alike to experience 'prolonged hunger' and 'chronic overeating'. Because of this 'prolonged hunger', people tend to eat food high in fats and sugar and other high carbohydrate food. These lead to overweight and obesity, and consequently poorer health and performance.

Thus, eating better can benefit weight loss and improve health, producing positive energy. This requires us to choose better sources of food, maintain steady eating habits and sustain a low blood glucose level. Unfortunately, owing to time constraints and external pressures, many university students pay little attention to developing healthy eating habits. A habit common among university students is to leave project work to just before the due dates, which, as those deadlines fast approach, means they do not have adequate time to think and work. Therefore, they live on caffeine and high glycaemic foods such as muffins or sugary spike food to sustain their studying lifestyle.

Our bodies don't magically tell us 'when to eat' or 'what to eat', but if we choose the wrong time and wrong food to eat, our bodies will let us know and perform poorly. Research has found eating five to six meals of low calorie and highly nutritious food a day increases the steady supply of energy needed by our body to perform at its best. Moreover, the waiting period between meals is essential as it takes some time for our stomachs to produce energy and be emptied. However, while working or studying, we can easily consume more food and more frequently than we should, thus gaining weight and having less positive energy. It is always advisable to seek support and knowledge from professionals such as doctors or nutritionists to evaluate what eating habits work best for your own body.

Therefore, forming healthy eating habits is vital for university students to satisfy our body's energy needs during our time in higher education, such as extended periods of concentration for study, as well as work and other life commitments. To maximise our physical energy capacity, we must become more attuned to the relationship that food has with our wellbeing.

Sleeping

It is widely acknowledged, by medical doctors and other researchers alike, that most of us require six to eight hours' sleep per night to function properly. Sleeping is the most potent part of our circadian rhythms, sustaining healthy body temperature, hormone levels and heart rates. We have met many university students who complain of significant sleep deprivation. Of course, this links to previously discussed notions of busy work schedules – yet sleep must not be overlooked. However, few of us have reviewed the effects of insufficient sleep on our studying, work performance and levels of engagement at university or within life at home.

Studies demonstrate that our mental health and performance is related to our sleep patterns: our reaction time, concentration and memory are associated with our sleep time and patterns. In particular, if we have severe sleep debts, our mental performance decreases accordingly. Current research has shown people can perform better at different times in the day. For example, some people will enjoy better performance or concentration in the morning, while others at night time. Try and find what your biorhythms are and frame your work times and commitments around times when you are most effective. However, this does not change the need for a sustained period of sleep each night, regardless of when you go to bed! In 2018, Linda Geddes conducted research on living without clocks or natural light. Her study showed that when human beings are put in an isolated context, they can still sleep approximately seven to eight hours per day, without clocks or natural light. You should aim for the same amount of sleep regardless of other contextual factors.

Given the benefits of adequate sleep, it is clear that healthy sleep patterns can be beneficial for university students to perform better and more efficiently in their studies. More physical training programmes and examples will be shown later in this book for you to follow.

In summary, to build physical muscles of resilience, you need to:

- Understand physical energy is fundamental for your ability to study, work and live.
- Develop healthy breathing, eating and sleeping patterns for better performance in your university studies.
- Remember that breathing, eating and sleeping can be trained to build physical capacity efficiently.

Area 2: Emotional muscles of resilience

Before we look into building our emotional muscles, we will need to understand what we actually mean by 'emotional muscles'. Essentially, people's emotions can be divided into two kinds: *positive* and *negative*. Positive emotions include enjoyment, challenge, adventure and opportunity, while negative ones include fear, frustration, anger and sadness. They are all associated with specific hormones such as cortisol. Emotional muscles refer to the competencies that are related to self-confidence, self-regulation, as well as social and interpersonal skills. They are also directly connected with our patience, openness, empathy, trust and enjoyment.

University life can easily drain our emotions as we are exposed to various challenges – our academic performance, our own personal needs, our health problems, how we adjust to new people and environments, how we cope with family issues. We have discussed some relevant concerns in the previous chapter. It is undeniable that we have to expend our emotional energy to meet these demands. Without properly exercising our emotional muscles regularly and seeking intermittent recovery, we will lack confidence, patience, or passion for maximising our university study.

The last section introduced physical muscles and discussed the importance of developing healthy breathing, eating and sleeping patterns. We should also understand that physical energy can be related to our emotional energy. If we lack sleep or struggle to eat healthily, we may become emotionally stressed, angry, defeated. We may also have low self-esteem or self-confidence. Therefore, from an emotional energy perspective, negative emotions caused by our physical health can be counterproductive and costly.

Moreover, there is a risk that we can become increasingly, and easily overwhelmed and walk in circles of feeling anxious, frustrated, defensive, or hopeless. Alfredsson Olsson and Heikkinen (2019) studied the emotional impact for adults when they engage in dancing activities. Their findings showed that successful physical activities such as dancing create positive emotional energy, such as joy and pride. Their study also found that these emotions may contribute to producing forceful energy to motivate people to try again after initial failure. If positive emotion fuels individual high performance more efficiently, it also has a profound impact on other areas of your body (McCarthy & Glozer, 2022).

As university lecturers, we have encountered students with high levels of engagement in their work or study. We have found that for these students, success tends to feed itself, reinforcing the positive emotions that activated the initial work or performance. When we interviewed these students, some commented on the 'supportive wind in their sails' they received from their academic lecturers or peers. More specifically, the care they received from their teachers or peers helped them grow more confident in their own life values and beliefs. Undoubtedly, they reciprocated this support in what could only be classified as a positive cycle for all. Thus, highly engaged students tended to be more confident and encouraged to recover from setbacks, with greater emotional energy.

Moreover, they also tend to reciprocate with care to others. Developing healthy friendships can also be considered a powerful source of positive energy and renewal and assist in developing networks and connections. A critical factor in sustaining higher performance is to develop networks at university. After all, many of these people may work in the same industry as you after graduation. Developing these networks whilst at university can open up new pathways and lead to strong, enduring friendships and relationships, giving you multiple outlets for emotional giving and taking, talking and listening. Most importantly, you will feel supported and valued in return.

Now we are going to ask you to think for a moment about your current life. How many hours a week do you spend on pure pleasure and energy renewal activities? Any activity that is enjoyable, fulfilling and affirming can promote positive emotions. Your hobbies, such as singing, dancing, gardening, playing a sport, or simply being alone and reflecting, can prompt positive emotions. However, some of us view these activities as a waste of time when we feel we have so much to do. We feel very guilty for spending much time on them. On the contrary, let's make room for these activities and invest adequate time in them. You will notice pleasure is not just its own reward but a critical source in sustaining emotional energy. Most of all, don't feel guilty for taking time to renew your emotional energy; it will sustain you in the long term.

In summary, to build emotional muscles of resilience, we will need to understand:

- Positive emotional energy results in self-confidence, self-control and empathy.
- Peer friendship or an effective interaction with your lecturers can summon positive emotions, particularly during times of intense stress and can support long-term networks.
- Downtime activities can bring joy, a sense of fulfilment and affirmation, and serve as sources of emotional renewal.

Area 3: Mental muscles of resilience

In addition to physical and emotional muscles, mental muscles can help us sustain concentration and internal and external focus. They provide us with a sense of optimism (Latham, 2020; Vierkant, 2013). Mental muscles refer to the competencies that are related to self-efficacy, self-awareness and self-development. The development of mental muscles can fuel and optimise our mental energy, including mental preparation, positive self-talk, effective time management and creativity.

During the busy schedule inherent to university study there can seem limited moments of 'downtime' and thus simply following routine schedules seems appropriate in terms of time management. However, it is also known that university work requires a certain level of creativity and innovation. Only being involved in what we deem to be routine work brings us slim opportunities to be creative thinkers. Ask yourself a question, When was the last time you came up with a great idea for your work or studying? What were you doing and what were your emotions at the time? In our experience, we often have flashes of creativity during times when we are not in the mundane, rather we are engaged in tasks beyond the everyday. During these moments, our minds tend to relax a little and all of a sudden creative ideas and theories appear to be generated out of a recess in our thoughts.

The 1967 Nobel Prize winner Roger Sperry contributed to our knowledge about the brain's two hemispheres (Pearce, 2019). We mainly 'live' in our left brain hemisphere as it provides step-by-step, time-conscious and logical perceptions. In particular, Sperry studied the right hemisphere, which was most underappreciated by many of us. Through his study, we are able to understand that our right hemisphere is less linear and time-focused than the left hemisphere, which can result in sudden insight or an intuitive leap in solving problems. So now we understand why our best ideas come forth when we are not consciously looking for ideas or solutions to some aspect of work. We can find 'magic' solutions while we shower, walk in nature, or just rest in bed. Interestingly, other than the function of being innovative, the right hemisphere of our brain provides a powerful ability to recover from the routine, rational, analytical work managed by the left hemisphere. That said, both hemispheres are equally important in providing innovative work, as the information our brain processes comes from either step-by-step multiple sources or seemingly irrational random elements.

When we discuss mental muscles, we cannot separate them from developing physical or emotional energy. If you are fatigued from too little sleep or bad eating habits, you will find it difficult to concentrate. Moreover, if you are frustrated, anxious or angry while studying, you will also struggle to focus your attention or remain optimistic. This could be more intense if you are working under great stress or during demanding times. Remember that our mind and body are inevitably connected, and research has shown physical activities can increase cognitive capacity. Training muscles, including brain muscles, can be essential to produce high-quality work or maintain performance and to support your ability to adjust to learning even more complicated new skills. Research has found that people who do regular exercises (e.g. jogging, yoga and other exercises) have better memory and performance. Thus, continuing to challenge our body and brain can help. As a university student, find what works for you, continue to work out your brain and body to learn new knowledge and skills, and trial different studying activities. This will push you to develop stronger mental muscles that serve performance.

Mental capacity also refers to what we use to organise our lives and attention. Time management is a capacity reflecting our mental energy. As a university student, with all of the commitments expected of you, you will feel time-poor. Particularly at the end of each semester, with a multitude of deadlines approaching, we find ourselves constantly working towards completion of a task or several. If you also have other work or family commitments, this will add to your time demands and you may feel overwhelmed and stressed. Whilst research has found moderate stress can motivate us to work harder and sometimes produce better performance, if the stress is not managed and lasts over a long period of time, we can damage our mental health, leading to negative outcomes. Therefore, the capacity to manage our time and recover our mental energy and prevent further damage becomes an essential skill in university students.

In our experience, university life requires every student we have ever met to have one essential skill: time management. Even though you might have experienced a similar structure while you were in high school, you will notice some differences between time management in high school and in life at university. The main difference is you will be managing your study schedule entirely independently. Some lecturers or professors may send friendly reminders about any learning tasks due and how to submit assessments; they probably won't be chasing you and ultimately it is up to you to perform at your best. We are all prone to momentary lapses in attention, which may result in us overlooking tasks or expectations. Thus, to rest and rejuvenate, mental capacity is derived from a balanced expending and recovering of energy. All this requires us to build capacity through systematic training of our mental muscles.

In summary, to build mental muscles of resilience, we will need to understand:

- Positive mental energy can help us with life organisation and achieve goals.
- Only with mental energy will we be fully engaged in realistic optimism.
- Brain development helps us to build mental muscles.
- Physical exercises can stimulate the development of cognitive capacity.
- Mental energy needs to be recovered to achieve innovative outcomes.

Area 4: Spiritual muscles of resilience

When we talk of spiritual muscle building, it does not simply mean religious spirituality. Instead, spiritual energy refers to the internal force to drive our work attitude and actions. Willcoxson et al.'s (2011) comprehensive research across six Australian universities found that having an apparent reason for attending university and knowing the type of occupation to which one aspired were factors significantly related to the success of first-year university studying. Moreover, according to Loehr and Schwartz (2005), spiritual energy is the most powerful energy in developing our resilience, and it is the power source for our motivation, perseverance and direction. It is about the energy of a human being to connect their values with a purpose beyond themselves. It provides the strength for a human spirit to bring full engagement and perform at their best to achieve work and life goals. It includes passion, a sense of commitment, integrity and honesty.

In one of our previous research studies, we surveyed over 300 pre-service teachers studying for a degree to become school teachers. The degree typically takes at least four years of full-time engagement and commitment in studying educational theories and at least 80 days of professional experience in schools. Some pre-service teachers drop out of the course, sighting a myriad of reasons as to why. Furthermore, when we look into the alumni data about teacher graduates, we also notice a number of teachers who decided not to continue within the teaching profession two to five years into their career. Yet, there is still a very high demand for teachers and to become teachers, which raises the question as to why people choose not to remain in their studies or the profession.

This needs reflection on balancing a commitment to others, including a career, with adequate self-care. However, this balancing does not come purely from building physical, emotional or mental energy, the development of which can be draining. Without spiritual muscles, we may feel physically and emotionally exhausted and mentally misfunctioning. Our spiritual energy is closely related to the deepest values held by human beings. Only with these values can we renew our spirit, seek out ways to rejuvenate and reconnect with the values we find meaningful. With powerful spiritual energy, we can challenge our complacency.

Getting back to our research on the teachers. When we followed up with the people who withdrew from their degrees or ended their teaching careers, we found that by and large they did not have a vision of what they wanted from their lives or where they were headed when they made the decision to withdraw. Many stated that they were literally in survival mode when they were conducting their studies or as teachers early in their careers. That's why their spiritual energy was compromised. Which is why it is imperative for prospective university students to consider their own life path and ensure there is alignment between what they want to achieve and an understanding of how to be successful and maintain it.

STUDENT EXAMPLE

Shannon Miller is a famous gymnastic athlete and cancer survivor. Published by American Cancer Society (2016), Miller spoke of how tough treatment was, both physically and emotionally. She was determined to do chemotherapy five days a week for nine weeks. However, by the end of the first week, she had such severe nausea and vomiting, she was unable to keep even water down and was forced to check into hospital. *'My next true moment was with God and me in that room thinking, "How do I do this?"'* said Miller. *'I kept coming back to the realisation that I don't have to do this alone. I have my faith, and I have my team around me.'* Today, Miller tells her cancer story and encourages women to take care of themselves. *'I use whatever voice I have from my Olympic career to encourage women to keep medical appointments, get more sleep, eat right, get and stay fit, and recognise the signs and symptoms of cancer'*, she says. The explanation for Shannon's case is simple. She built high spiritual energy to achieve her deep, focused purpose.

We cannot put Shannon's success all down to her solid spiritual energy. However, we can see a certain link with that energy and how she conquered this mission impossible. At times, there will be moments in your own university study where challenges appear insurmountable. It is during those times that your spiritual energy will fortify you and give you the strength to continue with your goals and purpose.

Many of us have religious beliefs. Prayer requires an effort of concentration and contemplation. It serves as a source of spiritual comfort. It offers us regular reflections on our deepest values and may be inspiring. Not all people are religious, but if you find spiritual nourishment through your faith, by all means it can be a wonderful source of purpose and direction.

Developing your spiritual energy can be seen as a devotion to your own purpose, the discovery of which will serve as a foundation for future goals and achievement. Developing your spiritual muscles is a rich source of renewal, emotionally and spiritually, and it can undoubtedly provide a profound source of meaning and deep satisfaction.

In summary, to build spiritual muscles of resilience, we will need to understand:

- Spiritual energy provides us with the force and power for routine activities and actions in our lives and meaning beyond the "everyday".
- Spiritual energy is the most powerful form of energy; it can renew other energies and rejuvenate us.
- Spiritual energy comes from a connection to deeply held values and a purpose beyond ourselves; it augments our passion, commitment, integrity and honesty.
- Spiritual energy can be demanding, but it can certainly make us overcome severe physical limitations.

Mapping your journey to success

- The process of converting life's pressures and managing energy is undertaken by using the 'energy muscles' – physical, emotional, mental and spiritual.
- Understanding energy is fundamental to your ability to study, work and live.
- Our physical, emotional, mental and spiritual energies are mutually reinforcing to help us overcome challenges and stressors during our university life.

Recommended reading

We would like to recommend you read Loehr and Schwartz's *The power of full engagement: Managing energy, not time, is the key to high performance and personal renewal* published in 2005. The authors begin with an observation about our daily life. Then the method they propose to improve energy management and obtain remarkable performance consists of three main points: 'find alignment with your personal values (a reason to expend energy), face the reality of your situation, and then develop a plan of action, based in particular on the power of rituals, to finally reduce the gap between the person we really are and our values and the person that we are in our professional and daily life' (p.18).

3

Test your wellbeing level

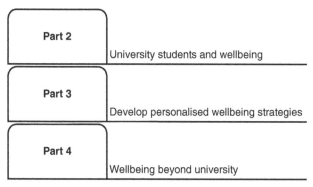

Part 1

Wellbeing in university context

- This part has three chapters. In the last chapter, we shared with you the four areas of building your resilience and maintaining your wellbeing during your university life.
  The four areas are physical, emotional, mental and spiritual. Before we share more information about how to build our full energy in the four areas, we would like to lead your attention to a further understanding of stress. It is important to know if you are stressed and how stressed you are.

Part 2

University students and wellbeing

Part 3

Develop personalised wellbeing strategies

Part 4

Wellbeing beyond university

Figure 3.1   Chapter summary

One of the important focus areas of this wellbeing book is understand and test your stress levels. This and the two previous chapters use various terminologies to introduce 'stress'. Stress levels can change from time to time, and day to day; therefore, if you have received a 'high' result from the stress test, it is best to read the next section of the book to learn effective ways to develop suitable strategies to build your wellbeing.

In 1936, Selye published an article in *Nature*, and the term 'stress' was used to define a response from our body to stressors that are believed to be harmful to our health and wellbeing (Selye, 1936). Since then, many studies have tried to investigate the impact of stress on people's psychiatric disorders, such as anxiety and depression. For example, one line of study has found a strong correlation between childhood adversity, stress and depressive symptoms (e.g. Eyice Karabacak et al., 2021; Harkness & Hayden, 2018; Newhouse & Albert, 2015; Sawatzky et al., 2012). There are multiple causes of psychiatric disorders and without proper management, chronic stress can lead to mood fluctuation, a feeling of worthlessness, and even self-harm.

Why do we need to test our stress levels?

Stress can have a significant impact on our physical or mental fitness. Stress symptoms can be different among different people. You may 'detect' stress when the examinations are approaching, or a thesis is due the next day. Sometimes, you may also notice you are experiencing symptoms of stress when you are managing your finances or dealing with a challenging relationship. In fact, stress is everywhere. For example, in 2015, the Australian Psychological Society conducted a survey among the general population, and the results showed that many Australians reported that stress was impacting their mental health (64%) and physical health (17%). Globally, the *World Happiness Report* (Helliwell et al., 2021) indicates that as we adjust to a COVID-19 normal world, there continues to be a range of disruptors to everyday life, further providing stress to mental and physical health.

Some stress can help you accomplish tasks. For example, stress can be a stimulator for you to study before examinations. However, too much stress can lead to damage to your health – physical and mental. Physical damage can include exhaustion, severe headaches, dizziness, increase in or loss of appetite, or problems sleeping (Föhr et al., 2017; Lines et al., 2021). Mental damage can include anxiety or depression. In addition, our body is not equipped to handle long-term or chronic stress. This can lead to serious consequences. Thus, it is important to understand our stress levels so we can make the best use of them to better manage university life.

Most stress can be managed by yourself; however, if your stress is high or you are concerned, it is always important to book an appointment with a counsellor within your university or external medical practitioners or family doctors.

Stress measurement tools

Perceived Stress Scale (PSS)

There are various stress measurement tools, and one of the most common is the Perceived Stress Scale (PSS). It is currently the world's most widely used instrument to measure perceived stress and has been continuously applied in much empirical research across a variety of cultural contexts (e.g. Klein et al., 2016; Siqueira et al., 2010). The original PSS is a 14-item scale that measures the degree to which the participants believe events in their lives are currently unpredictable, uncontrollable and overwhelming. It is a self-reporting, reliable instrument that measures the level of perceived stress during the last month, using a 5-point response scale for each of the 14 statements (0 = never, 1 = almost never, 2 = once in a while, 3 = often, 4 = very often). The higher the score, the more stressful the participants perceive their current life situation to be. Summarised by Cohen et al. (1983), the PSS does not raise the possibility of psychiatric problems; rather it is a well-regarded tool, used by many researchers to measure work-related stress (e.g. Cohen & Janicki-Deverts, 2012; Cohen et al., 2007).

PSS-14 was used in China, for example, in a 2010 research project studying a sample of 1,860 cardiac patients who smoked (Leung et al., 2010). Back in 1992, the PSS-14 was applied in Canada to study 96 psychiatric patients (Hewitt et al., 1992). PSS-14 was also used in Japan to compare local students undertaking postgraduate programmes and students from the UK (Mimura & Griffiths, 2004). More recently, researchers in Australia also used PSS-14 to analyse the data from the 'State-of-the-Nation' Stress and Well-Being Survey (SWBS) from 2011 to 2015 (Santiago et al., 2020). These studies highlight the cross-cultural applicability of the PSS scale.

The PSS-14 has displayed adequate reliability in different samples. The internal consistency reliability (Cronbach's α) was higher than .70 in 11 of 12 studies, for example, while the test-retest reliability was higher than .70 in two out of three studies (E-H. Lee, 2012; Santiago et al., 2020) – showing that the PSS is a valid and reliable instrument for its intended purpose.

Later, the 10-item PSS-10 was created to estimate students' current psychological stress associated with their completion of theory unit assessments and their teaching practicum. The PSS-10 can be administered in less time and is easily scored (Remor, 2006). It provides a slight improvement in total explained variance and internal reliability over the longer PSS-14 (Cohen & Williamson, 1988). A PSS-4 was also developed, as a shorter version. Both versions have also been used widely since their development. For example, PSS-10 was applied to 479 adults in Thailand to study collectivist Eastern culture (Dao-Tran et al., 2017). PSS-4 was used to evaluate stress among 217 pregnant women in Canada in 2012 (Karam et al., 2012).

Depression, Anxiety and Stress Scale (DASS)

The DASS is a 42-item self-report scale measuring the negative emotional states of depression, anxiety and stress (Lovibond & Lovibond, 1995). Its value in a clinical setting clarifies emotional disturbance, and it is part of clinical assessment. It can be used to determine the severity of the core symptoms of depression, anxiety and stress. Owing to its high validity and internal consistency, many clinical researchers use this scale to measure people's current state and change in state over time. However, this tool is more focused on the negative emotional states, and it has been used commonly in a clinical environment rather than the general population.

Multidimensional Scale of Perceived Social Support (MSPSS)

This MSPSS scale has 12 items, measured on a 5-point scale (1 = strongly disagree, 2 = disagree, 3 = neutral, 4 = agree and 5 = strongly agree), and a three-factor structure, including family (FA), friends (FR) and significant others (SO). The MSPSS scale was developed by Zimet et al. (1990) to further understand people's social and emotional support (Pushkarev et al., 2020). Although the MSPSS has been shown to have internal and test-retest reliability, validity, and a fairly stable factorial structure, it is a short research tool designed to measure perceptions of support from three sources: family, friends and significant others. It does not present fully about one's mental status and stress levels.

Thus, in this chapter, we focus on the Perceived Stress Scale (PSS) to measure our stress levels. The following section introduces the PSS-10 and how to use it.

Why Perceived Stress Scale-10 (PSS-10)?

The PSS was designed for use with community samples with at least a junior high school education. The items are easy to understand, and the response alternatives are simple to grasp. Moreover, as implied above, the questions are quite general in nature and hence relatively free of content specific to any subpopulation group.

The PSS-10 is not a clinical measurement instrument; rather it uses 10 questions to estimate the extent to which recent events in your life are appraised as stressful. The scale taps into the degree to which you believe events in your life are currently unpredictable, uncontrollable and causing overload. The scale is appropriate for people in a variety of situations – scores on the PSS range from 0 to 56. The higher the scores, the more stressful your *current* life situation. The PSS measures the issues you are experiencing, such as your current psychological stress associated with your completion of university tasks.

Additionally, as the PSS is not a diagnostic instrument, so there are no norm tables; González-Ramírez et al. (2013), however, developed norms and a factor structure based on a large-scale sample in Mexico. They found that the average score for their population on the PSS-10 was between 14.52 and 17.73. Thus, if your score is over 18, you can consider your stress levels are higher than the average of the general population.

Theoretical basis of PSS

The PSS was developed based upon the work of Richard Lazarus (1966). Lazarus focused on external environmental stressors, and the perception of such may determine different stress responses. According to Lazarus, external environmental stressors include life events such as losing a job, having or losing a family member, and divorce. In addition, stress can also be caused by feeling 'threatened', and believing that you have no coping strategies or available resources (e.g. I do not have another job, and I do not know who will employ me). Based upon Lazarus's work, various psychological perspectives have been used to measure stress levels in PSS.

Structure of the PSS-10

As stated before, the PSS has been used and evaluated in multiple countries, including Brazil, Canada, China, Germany, Japan, Mexico, Spain and Australia. The PSS has a two-dimensional structure: comprising negatively worded and positively worded items. For example, the question '*In the last month, how often have you felt that you were unable to control the important things in your life?*' is a negatively worded item. Other questions, such as '*In the last month, how often have you been able to control irritations in your life?*', is a positively worded item. These two dimensions are aligned with Lazarus's theory based upon perceived stress (negatively worded) and perceived control (positively worded).

PSS-10 use among university students

The PSS-10 has also been used widely among university students. Since 2010, there have been many studies using the PSS-10 to understand stress levels among university students. You can use them as a reference for your own score in the PSS-10.

For example, the PSS-10 has been used in the studies conducted by Geng and Midford (2015) to study the stressors experienced by first-year education students in completing teaching placements as well as studying theory units in Australia. The aims of the research were to investigate the nature and level of stress experienced by first-year education students compared to the stress experienced by education students further along in their studies. In their study, the authors found among the 282 participating education students, the average score of the first-year education students was over 22, while for education students in the later years the scores were about 20.

In 2017, 94 UK university students aged (average age) around 28 years old were asked to complete the PSS-10 and scored between 10 and 25. It was found that despite the different context in which students studying in a further education college complete their university study and the 'untraditional' demographic from which they come, levels of perceived stress appear to be comparable to those of the 'traditional' undergraduate (Shaw et al., 2017). For example, there were no significant differences between employed and unemployed students, and between those students working part-time work or not. Recently, in 2020, a study was also conducted to assess the psychometric properties of the PSS-10 among 192 healthy Saudi university students (Anwer et al., 2020).

The PSS-10 has also been used in various studies of stress levels among university students during the COVID period. For example, in 2021, Kostiè et al. published a paper about perceived stress among university students in South-East Serbia during the COVID-19 pandemic. There were 434 participants and the study examined the students' experiences during emergencies and crises, with the aim to develop online stress management programmes. The average level of perceived stress is moderate (between 14 and 26). Therefore, as a tool to evaluate university students' self-perceived stress, the PSS-10 appears well formed as an adjunct to considering your own stress as you navigate your path through your university studies.

What's next?

This chapter has provided you with a lot of information about stress and how to measure it. It is a mostly theoretical chapter. Now we know how to understand our stress by using the PSS scales. Appendix A provides you an example of how to use it. It is recommended to use the scale monthly to assess your own levels of stress. To look after your wellbeing, the next chapters will help you to understand stressors in university and present various strategies to manage them.

Mapping your journey to success

- Unmanaged chronic stress can lead to anxiety and depression.
- It is important to understand the stress and how to measure it.
- Many clinical and non-clinic measurement tools were developed and tested by researchers worldwide. This book recommends PSS-10.

Recommended follow-up activities

If your stress levels are high or you are concerned with your stresses, please book an appointment with a counsellor or student wellbeing tutor in your university, or consult your family doctor or a general practitioner.

UNIVERSITY STUDENTS AND WELLBEING

4

Getting started in your university life

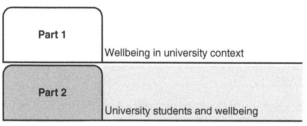

- This part includes three chapters. This first chapter begins to expand on the transition to university studies, be this as a high school graduate, mature age entrant, international or research student. The chapter gives you insight into the expectations of you as you commence your studies and the levels of support that will be available, dependent on your institution. This chapter raises some issues that you will need to address in order to successfully commence your studies. By giving consideration to the factors raised in this chapter, you greatly enhance your potential to reduce your stress and positively impact your wellbeing not only at the commencement of your studies, but throughout the journey.

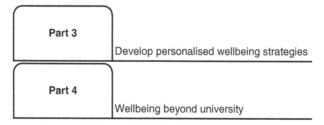

Figure 4.1   Chapter summary

No matter if it is the first time or not when you receive an offer from a university, you should be feeling proud and fantastic! To start a new learning journey could mean the beginning of your time in higher education, turning a new page within your career pathway, or an exciting opportunity for further professional development. This chapter in your life can be taken at different points in your life, dependent on what situation you find yourself. Offering unique perspectives from high school graduates to mature age students, as lecturers ourselves we have taught teenagers through to people approaching their seventies and we appreciate that higher education taps into what it means to be a lifelong learner.

It is absolutely an exciting moment for most high school students to receive your first offer letter. It could mean 'freedom' to leave home, move into a dormitory and make new friends – in many ways, a brand-new life in another city. Even if you did not do well in your university entrance examination, you might also find an alternative way to work on your university goal as well. Nevertheless, when the emotion of excitement starts to settle, the reality check will kick in. 'What shall I do to get started?' 'Is there any checklist I can use to start my preparation?' Some high school graduates choose to have a 'gap year' to connect to the community or society by starting work as a trainee or understanding different cultures and histories by travelling around to gain a 'world view'. There is no right path to finding your way to university after school graduation; rather you will find the best path that works for you and those closest to you.

But when you do start your studies, you may find that some of your high school friends have gone to other universities in other locations to study. Therefore, you may start to feel a bit daunted at the prospect of beginning your new journey. This section will show you how to make a connection with the university step-by-step.

For some mature students, starting or re-starting university study can be a different story. You may have been in the workforce for many years already and have achieved much of what you were hoping to in your current work and are looking for a career boost leading to more significant opportunities. You may have spent a lot of your youth being a parent, and now your children are starting full-time schooling, and you are beginning to look at your own career development. You may have worked in a profession for many years and decided that you are ready to make a career change, eager to investigate new passions or expand on interests in your working life. Whatever your reasons and background, you will also be looking at changes and new challenges in your further studying.

High school leavers

From a high school leaver's point of view, university life can be mysterious, fun and challenging. Some may receive specific family support, including financial, social and emotional support. In the end, it is you yourselves living life and facing different challenges. That said, though, starting university life can also mean you start to be 'independent'. High schools tend to be quite structured environments where the school administration will take a great deal of care to ensure you are 'meeting your potential'. The beginning to university can be liberating experience, but also one that if you are not used to that level of independent living and thought, can be somewhat over-whelming if you do not manage your transition well. Let's have a look at the following checklist.

Academic preparation

The first step of having a successful start to university study is to be very well prepared for your academic work. Generally, universities will have some form of orientation package (sometimes in hard copy, at other times digi-tally) you will need to read. Whilst the general welcome is obviously important, in our experience it is really vital to focus specifically on the courses you will be studying.

The course pamphlet should include the following important information: the course learning goals, the core subjects, campus tour, career pathways, com-munity engagement, special events and offerings, key contacts and other requirements (e.g. professional examinations) for course completion. Make sure you are really familiar with your course and what the university is trying to achieve by offering this course. This will maximise your time in the course and ensure you are fully aware of all of the potential benefits for you.

Attending Orientation Week

The majority of universities will offer an Orientation Week (often referred to as o-week), which is a five-day continuous programme, including academic preparation and university activities to prepare you better for your studies. In our experience most students find this week helpful in getting to know the university, the course requirements, and other facilities and support they have access to. First-year students obviously gain a wealth of knowledge and expe-rience and returning students will often use the week as a springboard into their new academic semester. On the first day during Orientation Week, you should take the opportunity to visit the campus, lecture hall, tutorial learning areas/classrooms, and most importantly, your lecturers and academic and administrative staff you need to get to know. This section will concentrate on the academic support and other facilities you will go through.

Walking on the campus will generally give you a reality check about university life. Joining a campus tour can be a pleasant experience in getting to know the environment you will be studying in. Usually, a campus tour includes the library, students' clubs, student services facilities, canteens and sometimes your course department buildings. If you can, try and have a campus map with you. The digital maps available, which can be downloaded from the university website for your reference, make it easy to navigate your campus. Many universities have put virtual campus tours online due to the pandemic period. For example, a university in the UK has developed a virtual tour on its website, and students can access and get acquainted with the campus without physically being onsite. The following introduction of the university virtual tour (see Figure 4.2) offers prospective students opportunities to know more about the university courses.

The university website provides a Virtual Tour for prospective students. It uses a Youtube video as a platform for its students to navigate their campuses. In addition, newly enrolled students can watch the warm addresses "Welcome to the Virtual Open Days" from its Vice Chancellor.

On the website, two subject areas, including undergraduate and postgraduate subjects, are listed with dropdown menus for its students to choose and explore.

Figure 4.2   Introduction of a university virtual tour

Another example includes Swintopia, an app developed by an Australian university. In this app, visitors can be guided by walking around through an interactive tour of its major campus (see Figure 4.3) using a personalised avatar and interacting with features of the environment to support orientation.

Orientation Week can be your first step in building a connection with university life.

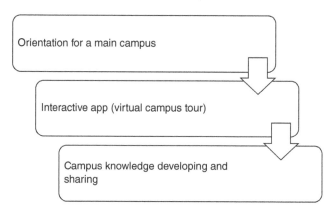

Figure 4.3   Swintopia (www.swinburne.edu.au/news/2020/08/swinburne-unveils-swintopia/)

Knowing your course

Many areas in your course need your immediate attention to be academically prepared. These areas include a course map or structure and additional course completion requirements.

A course map or structure (some universities also call it a study plan or module guidance) provides clear recommendations for you to follow. Most course maps divide your learning journey into what units/subjects you will need to learn over the semesters. The course map contains all the compulsory sub-jects you need to complete, and it also provides a sequence of the learning process for you. If you are a full-time student, it is suggested you follow the course map to ensure you complete the course on time.

Other than the course map or structure, you will focus on the career pathway for your course: what job will you do after your graduation from your course? This is also related to the possibilities of a relevant part-time job you may be able to do while still doing your studying. We have heard from many students who work in the field they are studying, suggesting it provides them with invaluable insights which make their transition to the field much easier after graduation. Some courses may require students to do fieldwork, work-related or integrated practice. This requirement can demand you to have a part-time or full-time commitment, which of course will impact other elements of your life.

Sometimes, you can have the 'freedom' to choose an elective unit or subject. Electives are of two kinds: specialist electives or general electives. Specialist electives allow students to select one unit from a few listed units, while general electives allow students to choose any unit offered in the semester or academic period. Knowing your career goal may help you decide what electives you would like to do, as they may be beneficial while you are applying for jobs after graduation. To avoid regret later in your course, take the time to get to know what the electives can do for you and subsequently if you feel you could benefit from specialising in a particular field of study from your educational discipline.

Knowing your course also includes understanding assessments. Examinations are commonly used in sciences degrees. You will be required to answer questions in a set period of time. Experiments reports are also used as an assessment in science studies. Essays and reports are used very often to test students' reflections, reviews and exploration based upon your understanding of the content knowledge of the courses. There is no 'perfect' assessment, rather, become familiar with the styles of assessments used within your course and invest time in learning strategies to assist you in how to maximise these tasks.

According to learning sequences, you will find your first year of study mainly focuses on understanding and knowing your learning areas. Second- and third-year study moves onto more critical thinking, evaluation and applications in your practice. Some courses have a fourth or fifth year, which involves a higher level of critique, review and applications skills. In detail, during the learning process, you start with reading other people's work to develop your knowledge based upon previous people's research and theories. Then, you evaluate these theories and research knowledge while reflecting and practising them in your own assessments and work. You may find theories useful and develop a further understanding of the knowledge; you may also find other theories dated or not beneficial for current practices. These understandings are built with reading, experience and debate. Excellent graduates establish their own 'theories' of knowledge based on their learning and practices. These developments are also closely related to your full energy building and set different milestones towards your career.

Students' Union

As a new student in university, you may feel eager to participate in your hobbies or life interests which you had before university. Almost all universities in the UK, Australia and the United States offer a number of opportunities for students to join students' unions or societies (see Appendix C). If you have an interest in a sport, arts, community or political activity, you can go through the students' unions and join the relevant club or society.

Pathway students

Having a passion for your career can always bring you to a higher level of success, regardless of your entry point. Therefore, to achieve your career goal, there is no one 'set' pathway. If you are motivated to achieve a rewarding career you can enter higher education through different pathways and as the saying goes, 'all roads lead to Rome'. You might have been eligible and are currently doing a transition course – this will also lead you to your career goals. Most degrees recognise pathway courses. For example, students who have completed a Diploma in Early Childhood and Care can have it recognised in their higher education degree. That is, the diploma they have completed can be credited into their teaching degree at the bachelor level. Most courses also provide detailed course structure/maps for pathway students to achieve outstanding academic learning goals. So, if you are a pathway student, be aware that you may or will have a different course structure than some of the other students. Ensure that you are aware of what your altered course map means for you and investigate what structures exist in the university to support you with your specialised entry.

Online learning preparation

Since early 2020, with the pandemic, most universities have started to move to online learning. Students do not need to attend campus face to face for learning. Instead, they have been studying through online learning. Although there is a global hope that the pandemic will dissipate, online learning has become a critical course delivery method. It is highly likely you will encounter some form of online learning during your studies and for some, they may do their entire course online. Which begs the question, what can you do to be better prepared for online learning as a new university student? You will need to have access to a *reliable* computer and broadband Internet. As lecturers we have had many a panic-stricken late-night email from students whose computer crashed whilst completing an assessment. Ensure your technology is reliable and treat your technology well! Most of you may be used to having a smartphone with a wi-fi connection, such technologies are useful for staying connected to your studies whilst commuting and away from university/home.

Besides these hardware technologies, you also need to pay close attention to the learning platform or Learning Management Systems (LMS). Some most commonly used LMSs include Blackboard, Canvas and Moodle. These systems or platforms provide lecturers and students with a space where (a) lecturers provide learning content knowledge and other information to students to learn, (b) lecturers deliver online lectures and tutorials to students, (c) announcements are made by lecturers passing important information to students, (d) exchange forums are set up for students to communicate with each other, and (e) students submit their assessments to be marked and lecturers provide feedback on students' assessments.

When interacting virtually, many universities use either Zoom or Adobe Connect to deliver their tutorials or lectures to students. These technologies provide synchronous and asynchronous (recorded) content knowledge. You need to download these tools to attend live lectures and tutorials. Take Zoom as an example: you should be prepared to turn on your video and audio to participate in live discussions with the lecturers and other students in breakout rooms. Some practical subjects also require purchasing or renting some tools/instruments to practise at home. More detailed information of various support from the university will be provided later in this chapter.

Lifestyle preparation

Starting a learning journey in university also means a change in lifestyle for many people, particularly high school graduates. Many of you will move out of your family home where you have spent the last 17 or 18 years. Some of you will even move to another city or a country to live. These changes include changes in housing, living habits, work and life balance, and developing a sense of community.

Housing changes

If your university is in another city from where your family lives, renting is the first thing you may consider about lifestyle preparation. If you have a friend who lives in the same city, you may rent with them. Depending on your financial budget, you choose your rental conditions, including the house location, house quality (a flat or shared house room), and other related bills (e.g. electricity, Internet and water bills).

When you are a student, you may share a house with other people or live in a university dormitory or student accommodation. Student accommodation is popular among first-year university students. Student accommodation or dormitories can be a shared house among students or a building with many students living with each other. Traditionally a student dormitory offers a shared room between two university students. These two students have their bed, study desk, wardrobe and private space. They may share a bathroom, a living or common area, and a kitchen with more students in the same building.

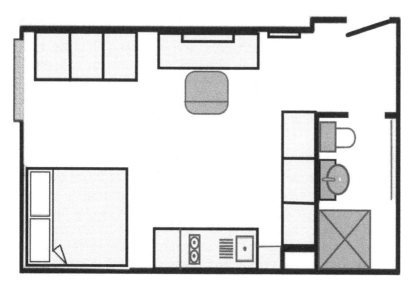

Figure 4.4   A single room of student accommodation in Melbourne, Australia (www.unilodge.com.au/student-accommodation-melbourne/royal-melbourne/rooms-apartments)

Many university students choose to live in houses other than the university dormitory. This means they need to rent other dwellings. If your university is located in a big city, you will find the houses close to the university generally are more expensive to rent than the houses farther from the university. The advantages of living close to the university are numerous. For example, you will save the time of travelling, and cost of transportation. You can walk to the university and do not need to worry about purchasing a car or taking public transport. Some universities offer their students escort services to their rental house if they live close to campus. If you do not live close to your campus and need to commute, try to make use of your commuting time and find habits that support your wellbeing. You may listen to a pre-recorded lecture or conversely you may just like to do something that relaxes you, such as listening to music.

Whether you live in student accommodation or rent a private house, you share the place with other students or people. This means you will share house bills, such as electricity, gas and broadband. Other than these, you will also share household chores, including cleaning duties and timetabling schedules to use the shared kitchen or bathroom.

Living habit changes

When you start living with new people, you will make changes in your living habits. For example, you may have a 'social' or 'anti-social' flatmate, a 'messy' or 'clean' flatmate, or just someone who has a similar habit as you. Household chores are shared among all the people. It is a good idea to set 'rules' of living together and be mindful of following these rules yourself.

Other than sharing with other people and household chores in a shared house or dormitory, other lifestyle changes include moving to another city. Most universities are located in large cities, but not everyone grows up in big cities. Moving to a city can mean complete living habit changes. These changes include driving on busy roads, paying higher rental prices for rooms, transportation costs and longer commuting times. Living habit changes can manifest in cognitive changes because of life experience, with some of these experiences being perceived negatively and others positively. Some students find moving to a city stressful as they lose the sense of community. As one of the authors of this book, Leigh, acknowledges, growing up in a small city or country town means knowing all your neighbours or everyone in the community and moving to a bigger city can lead to an initial loss of the sense of community. But give yourself time and acknowledge that there is no 'set time' upon which you will feel truly settled and that a gradual adjustment will occur as you become more familiar with your environment and the people and landmarks within it.

Many university students have part-time jobs, which means you are busy juggling between study and life. Much previous research has found financial issues are stressors in university life.

Due to the COVID pandemic, online studying involves lifestyle change as well. Besides learning styles, your university living habits also need to change. Instead of using transportation to attend face-to-face lectures or workshops/tutorials, you need to study at home. This means your room will be used as both study room and living room. Keep things organised and try to maximise the space that you have.

Peer learning or peer support

Living habit changes also include sharing interests. Research shows that long-term friendships can develop in your university life. During your time in university, your class colleagues can become your future colleagues in your working career and may form a very valuable part of your social networking within your industry relationships. Within the university classroom environment, peer support is a crucial part of the learning process, especially through modelling

(Bowers-Campbell, 2008), and peer rapport can help promote active learning (Sherman & Kurshan, 2005). This peer support and communication are crucial for university learning.

Peer learning has been studied across the world. For example, in 2013, a peer review assessment tool was developed by Gutknecht-Gmeiner to improve the provision of vocational educational training in Finland. Back in 2006, Sanchez and colleagues worked on peer-mentoring programmes for first-year students in US universities to achieve higher satisfaction levels, commitment and retention in their courses. In 2015, research in Ireland found Irish students valued peer mentoring as massive support in transitioning smoothly into higher education (Egege & Kutieleh, 2015). In Australia, Boud et al. published related books and articles on the effects of peer mentoring, such as *Peer learning in higher education* (2001) and 'Peer learning and assessment' (1999). Heaney et al. (2006) used action research to evaluate peer learning in marketing courses. All these researchers have proved that peer support can be instrumental in university students' successful transition into higher education.

Peer learning includes learning from the same level of students, for example, learning with your class friends. You may learn with them in the same class in the same course. You can help each other by previewing what will be understood, discussing the best way to complete assessments, or reviewing what you have learned. While it is argued that peer learning may not always include the most accurate information, it does provide the same level and informal, convenient learning opportunities to learn from each other or in the same situation (Aderibigbe et al., 2015; Holland et al., 2012). Peer learning also includes listening to previous learners' learning experiences. You may consider joining a social media learning platform. Nowadays, many students create private learning communities on Facebook, for example. This kind of learning community is managed by the students studying on the same course, and university lecturers or other administrative staff generally do not have access to this page. It can be a convenient way of getting a quick answer to a question. That said, because the community is managed by students themselves, you cannot control or manage the atmosphere or culture of the community. Some students may express some of their negative feelings on the page, and you, as a member, may be influenced by the comments. Therefore, if you are looking for official and formal feedback or answers to your questions, it is best to contact the relevant university staff directly.

Talking about using social media to learn, you are also encouraged to learn in professional groups. These professional groups include such organisations as LinkedIn. If you haven't registered yourself in LinkedIn, you may consider doing so. LinkedIn was established in 2003 and is a platform for professional networking in professional communities. By registering and connecting with other professionals in your field you may learn about new work opportunities or be exposed to the current issues and directions of your field.

Besides using social media, you can also register on various professional associations. These associations usually offer considerable discounts to student members and welcome students in their profession. You will receive the most updated information on your profession and future employment opportunities in the association. The following picture is an example of a teacher education association in Australia. Here, student teachers, school teachers and university teacher educators are the key member bodies. They exchange information and the most up-to-date knowledge in teaching and learning in their membership journals and annual conferences.

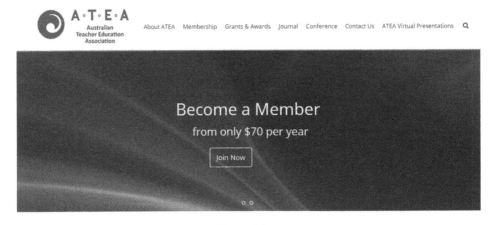

Figure 4.5   An example of professional association: Australian Teacher Education Association (https://atea.edu.au/)

Know your support

Having discussed the many areas you need to pay attention to, this section will show you the various support facilities in universities.

Although the most contact you have during your university life is with your classmates and your lecturers, many other people are also involved in your journey.

Student services

Student services are an important department in the university. They are in charge of your profile, ensuring your name, student ID and contact details are all synched together. Suppose you have any issues in relation to administrative processes, such as enrolment problems, technical issues, the trouble of locating a lecturer and locating different application forms. In that case, the first contact person is student services. They act as a hub in the university or the faculty, and they provide extraordinary assistance to you in the first instance. Student services are usually located in the university, and students have access to them in person or online.

For example, the following picture shows what the student services in a campus of an Australian university look like. Staff in student services provide various support to students, including course advice, assistance in making an academic decision, helping sorting through the administrative process and requirements related to your course, enrolment and re-enrolment assistance and guidance for managerial procedures. It is suggested before you visit the student services, you read your course requirements carefully and write down your questions. If you have an urgent need, it will also be helpful to include your student ID for immediate assistance. Don't forget to contact student services for your student ID collection.

Figure 4.6   Student services at an Australian university

Health and wellbeing

Your health and wellbeing are crucial areas at university. The university's mission is to produce high-quality graduates to service communities. This includes producing physically and mentally healthy graduates. Your health and wellbeing include medical/physical health, mindfulness and counselling. If you are not well, you can contact the medical centre in the university, as most universities offer onsite medical clinics (see Appendix C). Other than physical sickness, you can contact student counselling services when you are stressed or experience any mental difficulties. Most universities offer free student counselling services and ensure that you utilise these services when you feel you require them. In our experience, many students are not aware of these services and don't access them when needed – please remember that you are well within your rights to do so as a university student.

Statistics show many people experienced high stress levels during the COVID period, not least university students (Helliwell et al., 2021). In November 2020, *The Conversation* published an article entitled 'For university students, COVID-19 stress creates perfect conditions for mental health crises' (Hellemans et al., 2020). In the article, Canadian academics comment on the mental health of the young population (ages 18–25) affected by COVID. During the COVID-19 pandemic, university students have faced social isolation and a loss of social support. The required physical distance has made many students feel disconnected from support. Some traumatic events were involved, including the anxiety of coping with different issues, symptoms of depression and thoughts of suicide. It is predicted in this article that higher rates of depression among university students, particularly female students, may be exacerbated. Therefore, universities are offering online or phone counselling services for students. For example, Monash University offers students counselling using the Counselling Help Online form. Once students complete the forms, the service will get back to them within three business days, and a telehealth appointment can be organised for the students if it is urgent. Asking for mental support does not mean you are weak. Instead, it is an important and very common process for anyone who needs help.

Disabilities services

If you are registered with government disability support services, you will have access to disabilities services provided by universities. This service helps both students and academics to understand the needs of the student and help them to participate productively and independently in their studies. As lecturers we often work in consultation with support officers, who we find are very helpful in providing information that support us to ensure that we can create teaching activities that incorporate equality in learning for all of our students. All the information will remain private, and only with the student's permission can any detailed information be shared or released to other parties. However, if you choose not to share your data or disclose your medical condition to the university, that is totally fine as well.

Financial support

Starting university life, you begin to live more independently. This means you are in charge of your budget, your spending and finances. You may have already started a part-time job with some savings, but if you have to move to another city to attend university, you may have to quit that job and use your savings to start your new journey. Thus, managing your financial costs can be stressful.

Many people face financial challenges and getting support as soon as possible can help you manage financial stress. The financial support provided by universities can include interest-free study loans, emergency grants, scholarships, and there may be government financial support. It is advisable to look into what your institution offers, as this may support you during times of need.

Additionally, if you encounter any financial difficulties or want to manage your money better, you can seek financial support services. They provide support in budgeting, dealing with debt and managing costs and finances.

Spirituality

We discussed the energy for spirituality in Chapter 2 (and we will discuss how to build spirituality energy in later chapters). It is not only the students who have religious beliefs who need to build spiritual energy, but also students who are not religious but like to engage in personal reflection. For these students, universities provide prayer and quiet rooms. Students in need can go to the rooms to pray or reflect.

Childcare services

If you are a young mother or father, seeking a close-by, quality childcare service can be a top priority for you before you pay any attention to other requirements, including academic requirements. Thus, most universities provide childcare services. As a student in the university, you can be put on the priority list for childcare services. These services are staffed by highly educated teachers who have met relevant childcare regulations. In addition, most of these childcare services also offer play spaces, quality library and other spaces. These childcare services costs are similar to such services outside of university.

Sporting/arts performance services

Some universities offer sports and arts performance facilities to students to combine their academic success with sporting/arts success, or simply to take a break from studying and build physical energy through sporting activities.

All students can benefit from using these facilities and continue to perform at an elite level in their academic disciplines. Such services can also help students balance their studies with their non-disciplinary needs. Moreover, students' unions in universities also provide many sports and arts clubs and societies for students to join.

Student complaints and advocacy services

During your university journey, some of you will encounter difficulties and challenges, and these problems may include a dispute between you and your lecturers and other students. An example we have encountered where there has been dispute is during group work on an assessment item. Let's say another student's inactivity has impacted your grade. This frustration may disturb your mood and desire to continue your learning. Thus, if you feel unfairly treated or not satisfied with your mark, you can contact your lecturer to discuss your feelings and perspective. If, however, you do not find the resolution you seek, you can contact student complaints and advocacy services to complain and appeal. These services can provide you with guidance on documents you need to attach to your complaint application and who you need to consult before your submission.

Besides making a formal complaint, you can apply to the Student Ombudsman. This service will work with you to get independent legal advice, for example, and recommend changes to university practices to prevent similar complaints.

Other than these services, there are also other 'invisible' departments in the university involved in your studying journey. These include the admissions department, course administration department and enrolment department. The admissions department is in charge of your application to the university. They will work on your application documents and determine whether you will be successful. The enrolment department is in charge of your enrolment, including withdrawal, enrolment and re-enrolment. The course administrative department is in charge of your course progression, grade entry, grade change and course completion. You will not contact them directly, and most of the time, they will work with the student services to solve your issues.

Returning students and mature age students

It is very common to find students returning to university to study. These mature age students include (a) people who have already completed a diploma or a degree and want to continue further study to improve their career opportunities, (b) people who decide to make a career change, and (c) people who may have missed a studying opportunity when they were younger, and now it is a time for them to start, to pursue a new career for example.

These returning students also comprise a significant proportion of the university student population. For example, a person graduated with a Bachelor of Business and has worked in a bank branch for five years. There is now a manager position available in the department, and whilst eligible to apply, the person lacks the leadership experience. Although they have years of working experience, a deeper understanding of the role of leadership would support the application to take on a manager's role. Thus, returning to university to study a Master of Business Administration (MBA) as a returning mature age student is seen as a positive step within the application process.

Many master's degree courses are offered to people who want a career change. For example, the teaching profession can involve either a four- or five-year bachelor's degree or a two-year master's. Some countries, such as Canada, require a three-year bachelor's degree plus a two-year master's degree. Nevertheless, many bachelor's degree graduates can study a two-year master's degree in teacher training to become a teacher. For example, a person with a bachelor's degree in science can return to university and study for a two-year master's degree to be a school teacher to teach general science, chemistry, physics or earth science in schools, depending on the content they completed in their bachelor's degree.

Within our experience working in teacher training in higher education, we have found many mature age women are also included in returning mature age students. Many of them had taken the role of stay-at-home parent when they had young children to raise. When their children start school, these mothers want to either start or return to university to study and appreciate the opportunity to work in the field of education. They need to establish or update their skills and knowledge to prepare for a career as a teacher.

For some returning mature age university students, university life is not strange. Many of them have already completed their first degree in universities, and thus they know the studying journey quite well. However, they may also have noticed differences from their first learning journey. The returning journey can be very different. They may experience the stress of financial pressure from having a family; they may lack social and emotional support; their physical wellbeing may change as well; or they may have to work out a different schedule for their learning (e.g. part-time studying). If you are a returning student, you may find your university life completely different from your last time, which may take some adjustment and life reorganisation. Let's have a look at the following checklist.

Academic preparation

In this section, you will also find some different strategies of academic preparation for returning students or mature age students. Unlike school leavers, in our experience, many returning students or mature age students found preparing for academic performance either easier or more difficult, rarely similar. The length of the gap between the previous and current studies plays an essential role: the longer the gap, the more complex the returning students find it; on the other hand, the shorter the gap, the easier students tend to find the return.

If you have completed your first degree, and you have returned quickly to conduct further studying, you can resume your 'previous' study habits a lot faster. It also takes a shorter and smoother period to readjust to your work and study life balance. You will notice the differences between your current and previous studying habits pretty quickly. For example, you will have to enrol in some evening classes to study, if you are working in the daytime. However, you can still find the 'study patterns' balance. For example, you still have the knowledge of understanding and completing various assessments, using library resources to find important information, understanding the use of learning platforms and other university facilities. However, if you have a gap of several years between your first degree and your current studying, you may find it challenging to adjust your work, study and life balance. Time management could be a stressful task. Other academic tasks can include finding updated information about your subject, group work management, and in-depth higher-order thinking. If you are a mature age student, who has not been in professional work for a few years, you may find it more challenging to study, particularly perhaps if it is still your first degree. You may find yourself studying with young school leavers. All these can be a concern or hinder your success in learning.

It's certainly not all doom and gloom though for mature aged students; you may have an advantage in your study owing to your life and work experience. For example, you may have first-hand work experience. You can share your experience in classroom discussion or implement your knowledge and first-hand professional experience in your understanding of theory in your subject. Many first degrees require university students to conduct their placement in their profession to better understand the profession. In contrast, master's or higher degrees provide more in-depth theoretical understanding and knowledge and require students to critique and evaluate their learning and working experience. Many returning students are also involved in new knowledge development and contribute to new content in the community and add to the human knowledge bank.

Therefore, how can you be better academically prepared for returning to study as a mature age student?

One, understand your course and attend Orientation Week.

Two, browse your course map and get familiar with the requirement of the course structure.

Three, start developing relationships with your lecturers by sending them emails with questions, if needed.

Four, be familiar with the course delivery methods, such as online learning methods, and finding resources, such as using the library and e-books. This may take some time, but there should be support provided by the university to assist you.

Five, utilise your strengths and trust in your life experience to help you gain per-spective within your study.

Lifestyle preparation

Unlike school leavers, returning or mature age students have a different expec-tation of lifestyle changes. The most significant change you may notice is the demand to develop a new family, work and study balance.

Firstly, some mature age students are either in a relationship or have already started a family and have young children. You may also have a regular job. This means you have many other responsibilities such as housework, caring for young children and earning a regular income. Thus, you may find adding 'extra' studying responsibilities can also be very difficult to 'juggle'. In addi-tion, studying does not involve simply sitting down and working straight away. Instead, it means focusing time, developing the ability to start concentrating quickly after a tiring day, or completely changing your living habits. Many returning students change their lifestyle by waking up early in the morning (some get up at 3 or 4 a.m.) before their families wake up to spend the 'pre-cious' time studying. However, the 'longer' hours of work can burn people out, causing high stress levels, high anxiety, or depression. The COVID pan-demic has made things even worse. Without a regular income, being stuck in one place and home-schooling if you have young children to educate can also make your life busier and more stressful. Thus, some mature age stu-dents find it very challenging to focus on their studying and apply for an interruption or break from their studying. If the situation worsens, some mature students may drop out of their studies altogether, which can be a significant retention issue for universities and a loss to mature students. The following chapters will show you how to build your full energy to continue and complete your studies.

Peer learning

Peer learning is a valuable tool to be used among mature students. With their various learning experiences and working background, they can help other students to see events from different perspectives. In our experience, during tutorials we have observed many mature age students taking leadership roles during class and often facilitating discussion. We have found that school leavers tend to appreciate this form of leadership and it allows them to feel more comfortable to share their own perspective when the mature aged person shares theirs first. It might be that mature age students are more aware of their own strengths and weaknesses and can help others to consider their own professional practice. As mentioned earlier, some returning students or mature age students come back to university to study for a higher degree (e.g. master's or doctorate). These higher degrees require students to write, critique and evaluate literature or theories; this requires higher academic understanding and writing skills. Therefore, keeping abreast of such academic skills (in between breaks from study) is important to maintain a flow to academic writing and thought.

Know your support

In the previous sections, the various support provided by the university has been introduced. Returning and mature age students will have access to this support also. When we spoke to them about their experiences most returning and mature age students found both academic support and counselling support useful. In this section, academic support is elaborated in more detail.

Amanda is a mature returning student. She has completed a degree in business, but now she is returning to university to do her Master of Business Administration (MBA). When we interviewed her about when she started her master's degree, she indicated the importance of using academic writing support.

STUDENT EXAMPLE

The most useful support I found when I started my MBA is the academic writing support. They provided the support to help me write an essay at a master level, and how to implement my working experience into writing my report.

Another example comes from Jamila, a mature aged mother of three returning to study to complete a PhD in Education. When we interviewed her, she spoke of the challenges of writing and thinking academically at a doctoral level.

STUDENT EXAMPLE

When I first came back to study after almost five years away, I found it incredibly difficult to get started. In particular, writing academically and synthesising information at the level required for a PhD was very tricky. It was almost like I had forgotten how to write! Luckily my academic support advisors gave me some simple, yet effective activities and this supported my academic writing.

For example, an Australian university has an Academic Skills Unit, which has a team of educational experts to support your transition to academic work and throughout your degree (see Figure 4.7).

In details, the unit helps you develop:

- **Study skills:** Strong study skills lead to academic success. We can work with you to develop better time management strategies, set study priorities and improve your planning and reading skills.

- **Academic writing skills:** Writing is central to success in your assessment tasks. Explore the different kinds of writing required at university and find ways to improve your writing.

- **Academic referencing skills:** Referencing is a complex, essential skill that new students may not bring with them to university. We can help you understand the different referencing systems used at ACU to be more confident in your assignment preparation.

- **Maths and numeracy skills:** Maths plays a vital role in your university learning, so it's good to be proficient in the core concepts. We have many resources to help you build your numeracy knowledge.

- **Exam skills:** Don't let exam stress prevent you from doing your best. Our tools and tips can help you maximise your preparation time.

Figure 4.7   Support from Academic Skills Unit (www.acu.edu.au/student-life/ student-services/academic-skills-development/academic-skills-unit)

Besides the expert sessions, the unit also offers the Peer Assisted Study Session (PASS). In these, senior university students who have already completed the degree with a high grade are named PASS leaders. They provide the university students with an opportunity to learn from their peers in a 'relaxed, supportive, interactive and fun environment'.

In detail, through this kind of support you can (a) discuss lecture content to consolidate and deepen your understanding, (b) develop effective strategies for learning and studying, (c) engage in activities that encourage active learning and improve academic performance, (d) have access to additional study materials specific to your course, and (e) develop your confidence, make new friends and feel part of a learning community (see www.acu.edu.au/student-life/student-services/academic-skills-development/peer-assisted-study-sessions---pass).

International students

If you are an international university student, you may encounter different situations and stress. This section thus will show you the stressors and learning context you will meet and the support many universities can provide.

Unlike domestic students, international students come from other countries and cultures. If you are an international student, you will consider many factors before starting a new university life. For example, you will consider renting a place to live in a new country, getting used to a 'new language' and 'new culture', attending to a different academic or grading system, making new 'friends', paying more attention to your 'social and emotional needs', such as homesickness.

Academic preparation

International students may have to pay more attention to academic preparation for their university learning journey. This preparation includes (a) language preparation, (b) understanding academic grading systems, (c) knowing the assessments and (d) knowing the university academic facilities. Let us go through all four aspects one by one.

Language preparation is the key and initial step for international students. Take English as an example. As most English-speaking countries' universities have English proficiency requirements, such as TOEFL or IELTS, international students need to meet these standard English tests. If you have passed the requirement, you will also need to prepare for the professional language of your course, such as getting to know the academic terminologies and jargon used in the profession. If you have not passed the requirement, you may receive a conditional offer of a place, which means you can meet the language requirement when you come to university to attend the specific English language preparation workshops. Once you pass or complete the workshops, you will be considered as meeting the language requirement.

Besides language requirements, international students may also need to prepare for their courses. It is recommended you send an email to your academic lecturers to request face-to-face individual meetings. During the sessions, you may ask for some suggestions about the textbooks and other tips for academic preparation.

Although most academic lecturers are very busy, they are happy to work closely with students who seek academic support. Academic preparation for international students does not only mean meeting the standard university language requirement, but also academic terminology preparation.

Grading systems can be completely different from international students' home countries. Thus, this may also be essential preparation for them. For example, universities may use A, B, C grading systems, Pass, Credit, Distinction grading systems, or percentage grading systems. Thus, understanding the grading system is vital for your studying journey. Many universities that use a pass credit grading system, for example, like to use shortcut 'C' to represent Credit, which will confuse international students who are used to the ABC grading system. It is not difficult to get used to the grading system, and once you are used to it, this will not be an issue. Universities will have policies around assessment and grading and these should be publicly accessible to students, so they are aware of assessment and grading expectations.

Regarding understanding assessments, you should go to the previous sections about getting prepared academically. In addition to this, international students must understand how to refer to literature. We have encountered a few circumstances where international students have come up against the dilemma of not understanding what plagiarism is and then later encountering the stress of redoing the assessments or failure. This issue can be managed by introducing international students to university referencing styles and library resources or tips for why and how to use reference styles according to different requirements.

Lifestyle preparation

For international students, starting university study in another country means a dramatic lifestyle change. In addition to academic preparation, a lifestyle change for these students includes cultural preparation, residential preparation, living preparation, and social and emotional preparation.

Cultural preparation does not mean simply understanding the differences between cultures. Cultural differences do not happen in just a few areas in your life, but can involve many and various aspects. Your daily lifestyle, including clothes style, food habits and currency use, can be influenced by cultural differences. For example, every country will have their own currency, and you are not allowed to use currency from your home country. Thus, you may need to prepare for the 'foreign currency' you will use before you leave your home country or use bank transfers after you open a bank account in the new country. We have already discussed language preparation in the previous section – an essential task for international students. Other than academic language, it is suggested you also get used to using everyday language. Language use is not just for writing essays; it is also required for grocery shopping, bill payment and communication with friends. This point was expressed to us by Zoe, an international undergraduate student doing a teaching degree.

STUDENT EXAMPLE

My first year in Australia was very tricky. I thought my English skills were quite good, but when dealing with people in different places, it made me need to rethink my own level of English. It was like every new place I visited had its own special sayings and words I needed to consider. I still struggle sometimes, even three years later!

You can use the various Internet resources available to get to know the city you will be living in while studying, checking to ensure that the suburb you choose to live in suits your needs and requirements. Also be aware of seasonal differences between your new city and your own hometown. What do people usually wear, commonly used transportation, and just as importantly, the courtesy and customs of people resident in the city. You can look at the previous sections which discuss student accommodation. We recommend international students start living in university student accommodation when beginning your learning journey and branching out once you feel comfortable and know your environment. It might take you a while to get a driving licence or private transportation. Further, transferring a foreign driving licence to a local one will take time and effort. Therefore, try and choose accommodation that has public transport routes that you know how to navigate and if possible, close to university campuses.

Know your support

Even though we have tried to show you some tips and critical areas for preparation in the last two sections, some universities will provide an international student advisor and a specialised administrative counsellor for international students. These advisors offer multiple layers of support to international students, including language support, administrative support, campus life and social support, employment and career support, health support, safety and security support, and academic connection. Administrative support can include explanation of letters, visa application support and financial scholarship applications. International students can also join their cultural related student unions to seek support and develop a greater sense of belonging in the new country.

In addition, international student advisors work closely with the student services departments to refer international students in need to the right person (including academic lecturers or academic advisors) through the fastest and most efficient channels.

Research students

Research students, or higher degree by research (HDR) students, come to university to strengthen their theoretical understanding, conduct a research project, and write a comprehensive research dissertation. During this process, there are a few milestones, such as completing the proposal and other related requirements, fieldwork and data analysis, and thesis writing. Some HDR students are also required to complete coursework-based study to start their research journey. This section introduces research students to the specific areas they will encounter in their studies.

Academic preparation

Choosing to be an academic can be an exciting pathway for many people. This means you may make significant contributions to knowledge in specific areas and continue researching in the disciplines. Unlike coursework-based studying, research does not have a single set schedule for everyone. Depending on your discipline, you will have completely different research schedules. For HDR students in science subjects, such as physics, chemistry, biology or engineering, their research journey may involve many experiments and lab work. For other HDR students in social science subjects, such as arts, education or law, their research typically involves many interactions with people. Chapter 5 will look into your needs in detail in the middle of your journey.

Preparing for the academic journey at the beginning of HDR studies means understanding the studying requirement. If you are a new HDR student, you will need to first look into the milestones and their due dates. The first milestone you will meet is the confirmation of your candidature, which means you will need to work closely with the supervisors, but also independently on your proposal. Your proposal includes some key components, such as research questions or hypotheses, understanding and knowledge of the critical content or literature, understanding research methodologies and choosing the appropriate research methods. These tasks involve higher-order thinking and very hard work. You will be preparing yourself to search and locate the most up-to-date, authoritative and highly impactful research articles. This means you will understand how to use the library very well. It does not simply refer to borrowing or lending books from the university library. It includes further understanding and use of library databases. Wikipedia or other social media knowledge platforms are generally not considered appropriate academic references. Moreover, you will find many books are not as up-to-date as journal articles, and thus, it is recommended to search and read journal articles in high quality journals.

Setting up initial contact with your supervisor(s) is a good step for a successful learning journey. You can include a short agenda with your supervisor(s) in the meeting: (re)introduce yourself, your research topic and why you are interested in studying under their supervision. Most importantly, take notes of what your supervisors suggest. The questions you prepare can include some books you can start reading and journals you would like your supervisors to recommend. All these steps in a healthy supervision relationship can help you have a smooth and productive HDR journey.

Lifestyle change

The biggest challenge in terms of lifestyle changes during your HDR studying journey may be the organisation of your own timetable. Whilst certainly you have milestones to work towards, for the most part you will be working on your own during most of your journey and reporting to your supervisors about your progress and asking specific guidance from them when necessary. As you do not have a timetable to follow, it may be a good idea to develop your routine according to your biological clock. For those of you who are early birds, you may get up in the morning to read and write and use the afternoons as the time to have meetings or communication with your supervisor(s) or peers. On the contrary, if you are a late person, you may make the best use of late morning or late nights. You will know which of these two lifestyles suits you best. Remember also that you may find you can be very productive some days, but not so much on others. As long as you are on track to reaching the milestones, you can consider your lifestyle routine to be effective.

Know your support

In addition to the other types of support discussed earlier in this chapter, there is further support for new HDR students.

Firstly, there are various scholarships offered to HDR students. As HDR students develop themselves as academic and knowledge builders, governments and society provide various scholarships. These scholarships include academic support (e.g. waiver of tuition fees, women scholarships for studying PhD in science), travel support (for your conference attendance), and other external scholarships.

Secondly, there are many professional development workshops for research students. As a first time HDR student, you should focus on any seminars about relationship development with supervisors, proposal writing, literature review (how to use library resources; see Figure 4.8), understanding research methodologies and so on.

Figure 4.8   An example of learning resources provided by a university library

Mapping your journey to success

- University students come from different backgrounds, such as school leavers, returning or mature students, international students and research students.
- Starting a university learning journey will include academic preparation, lifestyle change, and knowledge of the support provided by the university.
- Better prepared and knowing your university can set a pathway to success.

Recommended activities

Please go through your university website page and find the links or phone numbers for the following:

- Orientation date and time
- Student services weblink and phone number

- Course/programme enrolment website
- Course coordinator/programme director's name, email and phone number
- Research supervisor's name, email and phone number

Check the university students' union and join the clubs or societies that you are interested in.

5

What to expect in the middle of university studying

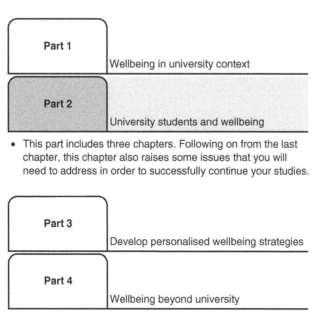

Figure 5.1   Chapter summary

Once you reach the second or third year of your studies, you are considered to be in the middle of your university degree. You may have already established sets of routines and good learning rhythms at university. This might be based on university guidelines or protocols – for example some universities provide their recommended daily study routine (see the example in Figure 5.2).

		EXTREME study productivity over the long run
Morning	7:30–8:00am	Wake up, dress, meditation
	8:00–8:30am	STUDY: review and re-test what learned yestorday
	8:30–9:00am	Breakfast
	9:00–12:00pm	STUDY: (55 minutes per block, and 5 minutes break in between)
Afternoon	12:00–12:45pm	Lunch
	12:45–1:15pm	Check emails
	1:15–1:30pm	Exercise (e.g., walk around)
	1:30–3:30pm	STUDY: (55 minutes per block, and 5 minutes break in between)
	3:30–4:00pm	Afternoon break
	4:00–6:00pm	STUDY: (55 minutes per block, and 5 minutes break in between)
Evening and night	6:00–7:00pm	Dinner
	7:00–9:30pm	STUDY: (50 minutes per block, and 10 minutes break in between)
	9:30–10:15pm	Shower, wind down, meditation (clear head for sleep)
	10:15–10:30pm	Get ready for sleep

Figure 5.2   A daily study routine in EXTREME Study Routine Secrets for Ambitious Students (Wadsworth, 2020)

Although this template does provide a structure of daily study routine, it does feel a bit robotic for some. You may also find when the novelty of starting a new university life begins to fade, you start to feel a bit bored or stagnant. You may ask yourself 'What if I cannot concentrate on studying between 9:15 a.m. and 12 p.m.? What if I received some critical emails in the middle of the morning that I had to attend to but did not? What if my family are not feeling well that day and I need to call a sick day or care leave day?' These scenarios might be rare but not impossible. This perfect schedule can add an extra layer of stress, make us feel guilty about not fulfilling the plan, and, most importantly, reduce our positive energy level to continue studying.

In Chapter 1, we used research data to show that many students drop out in the middle of their university journey. Thus, retention is always an important issue for university managers to investigate. Many factors are involved in a student's decision to withdraw from their studies or drop out. These might include: (a) not meeting the expectations or the standards of academic performance, (b) losing interest because of limited engagement in the course of study, (c) low satisfaction with the university support and standards, (d) confusion and stress about future job opportunities, and (e) change in one's personal situation, such as new family commitments or changes in one's life situations. All these stresses can be related to individual constructs, from socioeconomic status, gender and academic competence level to the awareness of the social support provided by family, friends or university.

Take 2020–2021 as an example. With the closure of countries' borders due to the COVID pandemic, many international students had to apply for interruptions to their study or had no other option but to drop out of university because of high financial stress and homesickness. As discussed in Chapter 4, international students must take extra steps and care when they decide to start a university journey outside their home country. Being prohibited from the flexibility of travelling back home can be devastating. Some international students only go back to their home country once or twice a year. The closure of borders meant they had to either stay around their university instead of their planned travel home, or return home but not come back to their university to study in person. This happened to many international students and delayed many of their studies. Some of them unfortunately had no choice but to drop out of university.

This chapter discusses the stressors that can be encountered during the middle of the studying journey for undergraduate students, postgraduate students and research students.

Undergraduate students

An undergraduate degree typically has three or four years of full-time study. Thus, it takes a while to complete your degree. Once you have settled into studying during the first year of learning, you will feel your stress level may be lower in the following years. Research shows the stress levels of the middle years of the higher education journey is the lowest compared with the first year and the last year studying (Barker et al., 2020; Geng & Midford, 2015; Maymon & Hall, 2021). The reasons could be that you have developed good learning habits, understood the requirements of assessments, and formed a good relationship with your lecturers and peers in the course you are studying. A successful transition into university life leads you to the successful completion of your degree. However, lower stress levels do not mean there is no stress at all; it has been acknowledged that there may be new and other stressors that emerge during the middle of higher education. These stressors are also related to academic performance, career pathways and social-emotional needs.

Academic preparation

Although you have successfully eased into your new life, settling into daily university life may be challenging. University courses will require you to meet different learning outcomes and achieve your best in your future career. Unlike high school studying, in university you will find your time scheduling can be *flexible*, and you might be able to choose the timeslot to attend your classes. For example, you may have over 300 students enrolled in one subject, and you are required to attend the large group lectures and then the smaller tutorials or workshops. Before 2020, you may have come to the university to participate in a large class with many students in a lecture theatre (see Figure 5.3). Some large theatres can hold more than 500 people, and lecturers use this space and time to deliver fundamental content knowledge to students. During lecture time, lecturers can also interact with the audience by having a vote, introducing quizzes or surveys or simply walking around the room and asking questions randomly. Since the COVID pandemic, many lectures have been moved online to avoid large gatherings. Many universities have also adapted to using other tools (e.g. Zoom, AdobeConnect, or PowerPoint) to record their lectures and upload the recording to students to listen or watch at any time.

Figure 5.3   Attending a traditional lecture at university

With more classes being recorded and uploaded online, you will unfortunately have fewer opportunities to meet your peers, listen to live lectures and ask live questions. You will, however, have more flexibility to be able to watch/listen to key content knowledge at any time or any place.

Universities are aware of this reduced interaction time, and that's why they still offer live tutorials or workshops. Tutorials or seminars refer to smaller scale classes in which you will have a tutor to work with you and go through the vital knowledge delivered in lectures, and sometimes you will need to complete hands-on activities. Take a nursing degree as an example: your tutorials can be conducted in a simulated classroom with *fake* patients lying in bed. Most tutorials will have 20–30 students per class, and each tutorial lasts two to three hours. In addition, in live tutorials, you can have more significant opportunities to ask detailed questions concerning the subject topics, and your tutors will work with you on any related issues. Group work is a prominent feature of tutorials or workshops. A tutor might divide the tutorial into small subgroups or teams of three to five students. Group work can help university students develop their collaborative working and negotiating skills, which can be very helpful for a future career. When you are involved in group work, you will find your own personal, collaborative strategies to work with your team members. For example, if you are a *natural* group player, you can use your skills (including ice breaking, humour or leadership skills) to participate in group work. However, suppose you prefer to work alone and are *scared* to participate in group work. In that case, you will still find a comfortable position for yourself, be a good listener and contribute with concise wording or provide an excellent conclusion at the end of the group activity. It is often a good idea to create a plan or agreement with your group mates to ensure everybody is aware of their roles and responsibilities. Group work time can also help you find a long-term peer to work with, who may provide you with needed social and emotional support.

Now you have started your learning journey, you may have developed a strong relationship with your academic lecturers. You may have already found a new learning friend or partner; you have had regular and frequent visits to the library. You are on the right track in attending the lectures and tutorials face to face or online and starting your assessments. Assessments of course are a vital component within your studies, and regardless of your year level, finding what works for you is very important.

In the first year of your studies, it was essential to understand the nature of assessment and work diligently to achieve the grades you aspire towards. All universities will have grading systems and assessment policies. The most common policies and procedures around assessments include the nature of assessment tasks (e.g. essays, examinations, reports, experiments, or work-integrated assessment), late submission procedures (e.g. late extension requests and late submission penalties), and dispute procedure (e.g. review process). Here are 10 tips to get better prepared for completing your assessments.

1. Understand the assessment policy and procedure. The information is usually accessible on the university website.
2. Know the nature of your assessment in each subject. Put the due dates into your calendar.
3. Start early on your assignments. Even if this is just mind mapping or framing your assessment task at this stage.
4. For group work, assign work to each member of the group fairly and work towards a final goal. Sometimes this might involve collaboratively documenting each person's role and sharing this document with the group.
5. Understand the plagiarism policy and reference styles required.
6. Understand the rubrics of your assignments and the weighting of each criterion or task.
7. Ask your colleagues or friends to check your work if needed.
8. If allowed, send your draft to your lecturer to have a pre-check. Or, send your outline to your lecturer for feedback and advice.
9. After grading, if you are confused or not satisfied with the feedback from your lecturer or marker, you can ask for further feedback. It will help you be better prepared for the following assessments.
10. Use your time wisely. If you need to apply for an extension, check the policy and use the correct forms with supporting evidence.

Some other assessments include work-integrated assessments. For example, medical students need to complete their placements at a hospital successfully to complete their degree. This work-integrated assessment for medical students means they need to go to a hospital (instead of university) for a period of time. This integrated work can start earlier in the studying period and last the whole course period. At the beginning of the course, the student may only need to observe and learn the other staff's roles at hospitals. Later, closer to completing their degree, the student will work as a practitioner and conduct responsibilities in line with their future career for a few months or year(s). This work-integrated studying provides authentic assessment opportunities for university students to understand their learning in-depth and have hands-on practice in the professional industry to better prepare themselves for their future work. For students who need to do work-integrated study, it means they will be prepared not only to complete their university assessments, but also to complete their practicum outside the university. It may be stressful for some people, including people who may eventually be your future work colleagues. The following 10 tips help you to prepare for your integrated work practice.

1. Understand the nature and schedule for each work-integrated practice. This can include basic issues such as travel and parking.

2. Once you are assigned to a practicum, contact the staff you need to liaise with promptly.
3. Contact the professional experience placements for help or clarification immediately if you have any issues.
4. Understand all the forms needed by going through assessment items one by one.
5. Work out a schedule with detailed timelines. Write each task into the programme (make sure your plan allows flexibility for any changes).
6. Write down your emergency contacts and enter these contacts into your cell phones.
7. Every night after your placement day, reflect on each task by writing down a few sentences or paragraphs to record your feelings.
8. Build good life habits (get up early and do not stay up late if possible) to be physically prepared and adhere to the routine throughout the placement.
9. Share your emotional moments with your lecturers or friends if necessary.
10. Don't feel ashamed to ask for help if needed.

If you feel you need extra support, you may also consider approaching Personal Academic Tutors (PATs). PATs are support personnel offered in many universities, and they are there to help you reach your potential in the classroom or work-integrated activities. PATs provide advice and feedback on your university assessments, future goals and help you find other services if needed. You will progress more successfully academically with the help of your PATs.

Other than the academic preparation, for many university students, some other challenges during the middle of their studying also include understanding your career pathways.

Understand your career pathways

It is not rare for university students to drop out of their course in the middle of their studies. One reason might include confusion about your career pathway. Understanding your career pathway is very important during your studies because it helps build your spiritual energy during the course (see Chapter 10).

Sometimes, the titles of the courses can be confusing and misleading. For example, a teaching degree and education degree can be completely different in the professional field of education and have different career pathways. A teaching degree means the graduates can be registered as teachers and go into schools to teach. In contrast, an education degree can help graduates be involved broadly in academic areas, such as educational consultants or teaching assistants. These are entirely different career pathways. Thus, it is suggested you understand your career pathways clearly to avoid frustration when you are close to your course completion. That said, many courses allow transfer from one to another, and some of the units or subjects that have been completed can be credited or transferred into the alternative programme you would like to enrol in and complete. In the next chapter, we shall investigate what career pathways support universities provide for their students.

Social and emotional preparation

The previous chapter discussed the life changes you will encounter when transitioning into university studying. We emphasised accommodation changes, and in this section, we will present the possible social and emotional changes you experience after your first time of living in a dormitory or shared house.

If you consider yourself a social person, you will find transitioning into a shared space easier. You will feel socially and emotionally prepared for your new learning life in university. However, even if the shared room is more natural for you, you can still feel socially and emotionally drained. You will spend time getting to know your roommates and peers by finding common interests. You may also feel pressure from your peers and other people, especially if you come from different socioeconomic, cultural and historical backgrounds. Here are some tips for you:

1. Choose a comfortable way to introduce yourself to your peers, including a formal introduction or an informal way.
2. Talk about your hobbies and be open to embrace friends who have similar hobbies.
3. Talk about your living habits (e.g. whether you are a morning or an evening person) with your peers.
4. You might find some peers who come from a closer geographical location to build your sense of belongings and feeling of security.
5. Don't forget your previous friends. They may also need your support just like you do from them.
6. Consider your family as a source of social and emotional support for you.

Maxi is a student enrolled in teacher education and will become a primary teacher in a few years' time.

STUDENT EXAMPLE

I have a friend of mine who likes reading. Thus, when we are stressed, we build a 'book club' ourselves. We use a couple of hours per week to share our thoughts on books and take our minds away from stressors. We found it very helpful in taking our stress away for two decent hours per week to enjoy fun moments from the books. We also found by doing this, we have read more books per year, and it helps us to maintain our sanity in some ways.

Vivian is an economics student and shares a house with multiple people.

STUDENT EXAMPLE

I live with three other people. It works well. We are all really respectful of each other's time and space. I'm an evening person, so I know not to make too much noise because I know my roommates are sleeping. Which goes the same for them in the morning. So, if I want to play my music at night to help me concentrate, I do so with my ear buds. Respect is important.

These are valuable strategies to help you maintain your wellbeing and build your resilience during your studying journey.

Returning students

As discussed in the previous chapter, returning students or mature students have different needs and thus other stressors when you restart your university learning journey. This section, therefore, is to show you what you may encounter while you are in the middle of the journey.

Meet academic requirements

For most returning or mature age students, time can have the most significant impact on your studying. Thus, excellent time management strategies can help you to meet academic requirements. We will show you a few energy building strategies in later chapters to help you have better time management and higher energy levels (see Chapters 7–10).

As also discussed earlier, many returning and mature age students are undertaking postgraduate studies (coursework). Thus, another area in academic preparation for this cohort of university students is developing your conceptual knowledge about your disciplines. Many postgraduate studies involve higher-order thinking and, indeed, a greater deal of study about theories. Such studies may require you to connect your working experience with your learning concept. The following shows a student's mind map. Catriona Fox is in the third year of a Bachelor's in Midwifery. She developed a mind map for herself. Although it is an undergraduate student's work, it shows a high level of understanding and mapping across her learning content (see Figure 5.4).

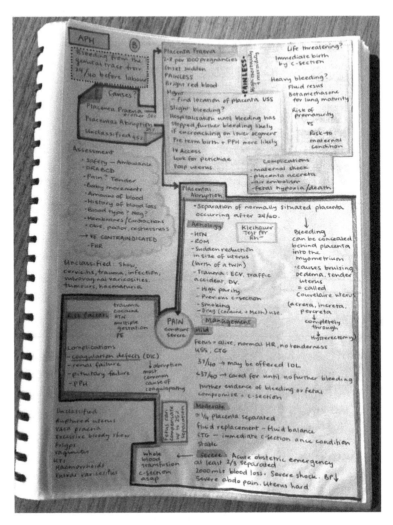

Figure 5.4   Catriona Fox's poster (mind map)

In this mind map, Catriona uses a colour scheme to demonstrate her understanding of the crucial key knowledge of APH (antepartum haemorrhage), and its key concepts, including definition, causes and assessment. In particular, it shows how to diagnose the reasons behind the assessment. This poster demonstrates the paths she was using to try to understand the concept. This handwritten map helped to create Catriona's portfolio towards a successful career pathway.

'Course websites, lecture notes and tutorial PowerPoints have posters and lecture notes that I use to help me study', said Catriona. Other than this mind map, she also showed us some of the lectures notes her lecturer provided for her (see Figure 5.5).

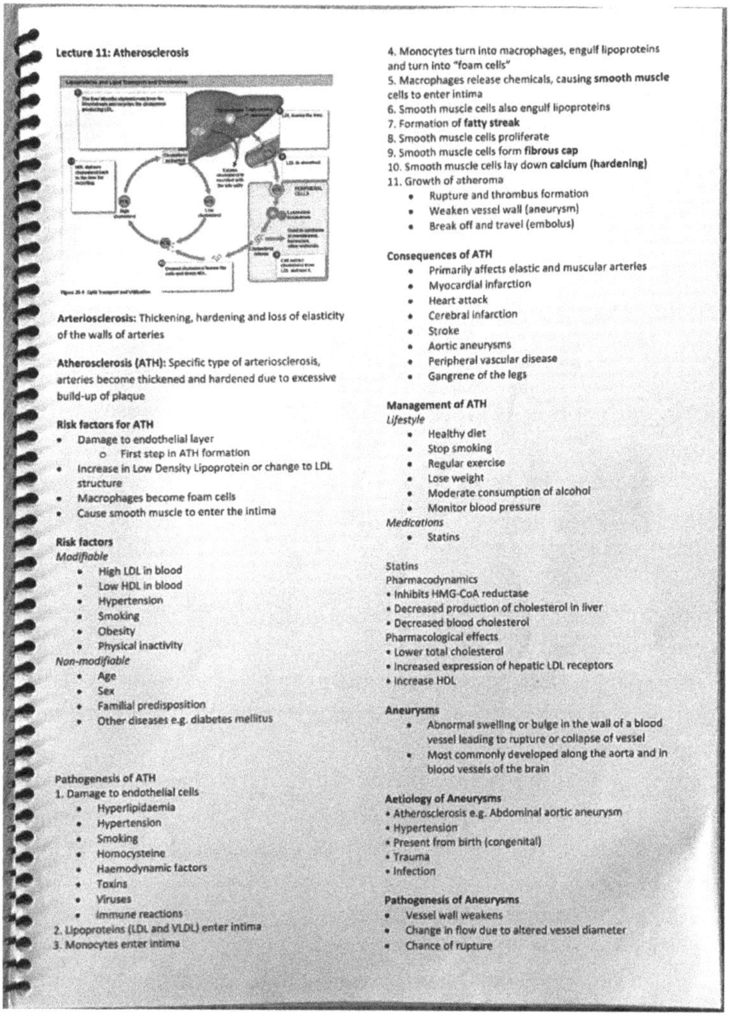

Lecture 11: Atherosclerosis

Arteriosclerosis: Thickening, hardening and loss of elasticity of the walls of arteries

Atherosclerosis (ATH): Specific type of arteriosclerosis, arteries become thickened and hardened due to excessive build-up of plaque

Risk factors for ATH
- Damage to endothelial layer
  - First step in ATH formation
- Increase in Low Density Lipoprotein or change to LDL structure
- Macrophages become foam cells
- Cause smooth muscle to enter the intima

Risk factors
Modifiable
- High LDL in blood
- Low HDL in blood
- Hypertension
- Smoking
- Obesity
- Physical inactivity

Non-modifiable
- Age
- Sex
- Familial predisposition
- Other diseases e.g. diabetes mellitus

Pathogenesis of ATH
1. Damage to endothelial cells
   - Hyperlipidaemia
   - Hypertension
   - Smoking
   - Homocysteine
   - Haemodynamic factors
   - Toxins
   - Viruses
   - Immune reactions
2. Lipoproteins (LDL and VLDL) enter intima
3. Monocytes enter intima
4. Monocytes turn into macrophages, engulf lipoproteins and turn into "foam cells"
5. Macrophages release chemicals, causing **smooth muscle** cells to enter intima
6. Smooth muscle cells also engulf lipoproteins
7. Formation of **fatty streak**
8. Smooth muscle cells proliferate
9. Smooth muscle cells form **fibrous cap**
10. Smooth muscle cells lay down **calcium (hardening)**
11. Growth of atheroma
    - Rupture and thrombus formation
    - Weaken vessel wall (aneurysm)
    - Break off and travel (embolus)

Consequences of ATH
- Primarily affects elastic and muscular arteries
- Myocardial infarction
- Heart attack
- Cerebral infarction
- Stroke
- Aortic aneurysms
- Peripheral vascular disease
- Gangrene of the legs

Management of ATH
Lifestyle
- Healthy diet
- Stop smoking
- Regular exercise
- Lose weight
- Moderate consumption of alcohol
- Monitor blood pressure

Medications
- Statins

Statins
Pharmacodynamics
- Inhibits HMG-CoA reductase
- Decreased production of cholesterol in liver
- Decreased blood cholesterol

Pharmacological effects
- Lower total cholesterol
- Increased expression of hepatic LDL receptors
- Increase HDL

Aneurysms
- Abnormal swelling or bulge in the wall of a blood vessel leading to rupture or collapse of vessel
- Most commonly developed along the aorta and in blood vessels of the brain

Aetiology of Aneurysms
- Atherosclerosis e.g. Abdominal aortic aneurysm
- Hypertension
- Present from birth (congenital)
- Trauma
- Infection

Pathogenesis of Aneurysms
- Vessel wall weakens
- Change in flow due to altered vessel diameter
- Chance of rupture

Figure 5.5 Lecture notes used by Catriona Fox

Thus, during the middle of your studying, you can find helpful strategies or tools to learn and review new and previous learning content or knowledge. The mind map also shows Catriona is a visual learner. The cause and effect are demonstrated in how she drew the mind map using arrows, colours and lines/boxes.

Returning and mature age students may be quick to provide an overview of the scheduling of learning, lecture rooms and assessments as they may have already gone through them before (e.g. in their first degree). However, as we discussed, some mature age students may find using new technologies complex and find studying online tricky. At the same time, they may have to learn online at home, as experienced during the pandemic in 2020. In 2014, Thomas and Herbert, two academics from Australian universities, published an article on *The Conversation* entitled '"Sense of belonging" enhances the online learning experience'. The article emphasised the impacts from a mix of personal, institutional and circumstantial variables.

Most importantly,

> The personal variables include previous academic experience, self-efficacy, ability to organise their study and motivation. Institutional variables include the balance between the learner's needs and the institution, the availability of support and the nature of university processes and systems. Circumstantial variables cover the learner's interactions with the institution as well as the changing circumstances of their lives.

You'll find the following tips for studying online at home will help you manage your online learning experience.

1. Locate a bright and quiet room (if possible) with good lighting. If there is no specifically allocated study room, you can certainly use your living room or bedroom.
2. Be familiar with the learning platforms you are required to use and check your technologies (e.g. microphone, cameras and speakers) are working properly at least 24 hours before the online class.
3. Negotiate your studying time with your family/roommates; let them know you need some concentration time and ask them to accommodate you. If you have young children living at home, you may need to study whenever you do not have child rearing commitments.
4. Take regular breaks and drink plenty of water. Even when you are super busy, you should remind yourself to take a break every hour or two. You may get up from the table, stretch your body and have a five-minute break away from your work. Physical energy is essential for your success in completing academic work.
5. Participate in the online subgroups. Treat them the same way as in a real classroom. Turn off your email and mute your phones. Your tutors will 'move' among individual online subgroups to check on your discussion as usual.
6. Finally, do not forget to reflect after class. Just as in a traditional learning style, you should also reflect on what you have learnt and record it in your reflection journal or notes. If you have questions, write them down and make sure you ask them before you forget.

Returning students or postgraduate students will have to complete assessments as required. For postgraduate students, the assessments for their studies can have higher learning volume standards. For example, the volume of learning for higher education studies in Australia was defined as follows in the Australian Qualifications Framework (2015):

The volume of learning is a dimension of the complexity of a qualification. It is used with the level criteria and qualification type descriptor to determine the depth and breadth of the learning outcomes of a qualification. The volume of learning identifies the notional duration of all activities required to achieve the learning outcomes specified for a particular AQF qualification type. It is expressed in equivalent full-time years.

As a reality check, most university students studying for a postgraduate degree will write over 100,000 words or equivalent per year if they study full-time. In comparison, most undergraduate students only need to complete 50,000 to 80,000 words or equivalent per year if they are studying full-time. If you need support, we suggest you contact PATs for advice and support.

Social and emotional preparation

Returning or mature age students may have different social and emotional needs from recent school leavers or new university students. Quite often returning students will be in a relationship, or are also a parent, which may act as the inspiration for their return to study. Some returning students are also providing care for their elderly parents. In the previous chapter, we discussed some aspects of these students' transitioning into university life; however, it must be noted that they may have other social and emotional stresses during their studying.

Consider the following scenarios:

1. You are a single parent; you are in the middle of a tutorial on the university campus, when you receive an urgent phone call from your child's school, and you have to pick them up from the local school.
2. You have planned to work on your assignments this weekend, but your partner wants to have a weekend break, and you have to forego the planning.
3. You start a practicum in your subject areas. However, it feels different from what you expected before (i.e. from what you had experienced in your previous degree).
4. You are working as a group member in a collaborative assignment, but one of your group members has missed the last two routine meetings. You are not sure whether you are on the right track to completing your assignment, which you have spent a lot of time on.

To better socially and emotionally prepare yourself for your learning journey, particularly in the middle of your studies, here are some tips.

1. Record all emergency contacts and phone numbers in your phone.
2. Form a good relationship with a peer or a few peers in your class. You can share your lecture notes, work together on your assignments, attend classes together, and most importantly, reflect collaboratively on your studying and work.

3. Discuss and share your schedule with your family. It helps when you need to be involved in family activity organisations and allows family members to understand how they can support you within your collective family journey.

Please remember it is not easy to study as a returning or mature age student, and the kinds of support we discussed in the previous chapter can also be used during your studying. Moreover, we will show you how to develop emotional and mental energy in later chapters.

International students

International students may meet other stressors during their studies. In this section, we look at these and how to make connections to complete your studies successfully.

Meet academic requirements

For international students, each year, you will meet different academic requirements. For the first year, international students work hard to familiarise themselves with the educational systems, know the lecturers, and understand assessments. From international students' perspectives, assessment tasks can be viewed differently. For example, international students may view examinations as the only assessments. You may also not understand references and referencing styles. These first-year stressors have been explored in Chapter 4. If you feel you need more support, you may also consider contacting PATs, as discussed earlier in this chapter.

In this section, we discuss group work activities and group work assessments. Group work activities in tutorials include group work discussions and presentations. When participating in group work discussions, at times international students, particularly new international students, are quieter than the domestic students. Depending on your personality and learning style (Abouzeid et al., 2021; Keshavarz & Hulus, 2019; Seyal et al., 2019), you will choose your own way to participate. For example, some international students prefer to learn from observing other students' performances, while some would like to participate more actively in group work. Either way is acceptable: being a listener is as vital as being a speaker, and participation can be conducted by working on different tasks. Taking notes for the group can be a good idea for international students. You can use the opportunity to practise your listening and write down the key points as much as you can. Let your group member know if you did not understand something that was said or if you missed anything. It also allows you to practise your summary skills.

Sometimes group work includes group presentation, which, in our experience as lecturers, stresses many international students. The reasons can be (a) you are worried about your language accuracy and fluency, (b) you are concerned you are repeating other people's opinions, and (c) you are worried that your opinions will not be accepted and your confidence can be damaged. To overcome such concerns, you should put your learning goals first. Remind yourselves that it is a learning process. Let another group member know your concern and if needed, ask them to help you pick a familiar area to present. Please note many people, including your peers, are also keen to understand your ideas or opinions from your 'international' perspective. Work with your team to ensure the presentations of each area are combined well and follow a proper order. Deliver your presentation loudly and clearly. Remember it is not language or your grammar skills that are being assessed. It is your ideas and your understanding of the concept that are being evaluated. This should be clearly articulated in your assessment criteria.

But as noted already, most international students may need to spend extra time to settle into their new life, such as making new friends and getting involved in the new community. This can take a bit more time away from your studying time. It is also normal and important for international students to spend time exploring and becoming comfortable with their new cultural environments. However, once you are settled, you will feel you can concentrate more on studying and other activities.

During the middle of the learning journey (e.g. the second or third year), international students cannot help but compare what they have learned in this country to the prior knowledge in their home country. It can be considered a privilege to be an international student because the reflection on your life this brings can be valuable to you. Thus it is suggested you conduct regular reflections during your studying. It will bring together your in-depth understanding and knowledge about what you have learned from your home country and what you are learning in the host country. It will form part of your education experience when you consider your future career pathways. We will go through career decisions in Chapter 6.

International students may find it most challenging to conduct work-integrated studying, e.g. medical students need to work in a hospital. Student teachers need to work at schools or early childhood sectors; engineering students need placements at construction sites. The experience provides insights into your knowledge and understanding of the professional industries. For international students, doing work-integrated studying may involve more preparation. In addition to the academic work you need to complete, you must also understand the new work environment. This includes understanding work stress, including knowledge about work structure, culture, policies and regulations.

Thus, international students might have to pay more attention to the work environment as it may differ from their previous experiences.

Tina, an international student studying in Australia for an early childhood degree, expressed her feelings towards the need to embrace more than just the outward culture of the host country when embarking on work-integrated studying.

STUDENT EXAMPLE

I thought I was really comfortable in my study, actually, really confident, especially in my English-speaking skills. Then, when I went on my first placement, it was like they were talking a different language! So much jargon and different ways of communicating. It took me a while to get used to the workplace, but I'm so glad I did.

Yu is an international student currently studying for a four-year undergraduate degree to be a secondary school teacher in Australia. In the course of her degree, she is required to work in primary schools. Her first placement is in the middle of the second year of her degree. After a first year of successful theory studying, Yu feels confident and comfortable continuing her studying. However, she is also concerned about her first placement in a school and keen to keep her studying pace. Thus, she has done a few steps to prepare for her placement experience.

STUDENT EXAMPLE

I did a Google search about the school to find the location and the school's structure. I have also studied the school's homepage and its principal's statements. I then go through the website about its curriculum and school information. I also explore the communication tool: Compass. I have used this tool before, so I feel a lot of relief.

By doing preparation work before the placement, as an international student you will be preparing yourself for a successful placement (of course this is good advice for all students). Besides this preparation, following the steps outlined by the university will help you complete your placement successfully. It is also essential to bring all the forms and understand 'at-risk' placement procedures.

Social and emotional preparation

As discussed in Chapter 4, international students need extra support socially and emotionally, preparing for their successful learning journey. The previous section of this chapter has also discussed some social and emotional preparation tips. This section includes cultural preparation for international students in the middle of your learning journey.

Here are some scenarios to consider:

1. You need to complete group work, but you may find it challenging to participate in group work as an international student.
2. The living costs are more expensive than your home country, and you may have to find a part-time job.
3. During the holiday period (e.g. Christmas), you may feel lonely as your peers or friends are staying with their families. Or you may miss your own country's local holidays and festivals.

To get yourself ready socially and emotionally to continue on your learning journey, here are some tips:

1. Plan a long-term holiday. For example, you can plan the Christmas period earlier by either going back to your home country, making a travel plan with some friends around the country where you are studying, or just working to earn some money to ease financial stress, according to local work regulations.
2. Make new friends. It can be good for you to make a friend who comes from your home country or the same cultural, historical and religious background. They can provide good emotional and social support for you. You may go to class together, share social and emotional experiences, or go out together occasionally. In addition, you may provide each other emergency support.

Research students

For research students, you encounter different stressors during the middle of the learning journey. For example, after you pass the research proposal, you enter the middle of your research candidature. Then, what are the primary milestones during the middle of your research journey? This section will discuss these.

Meet academic requirements

During the research candidature, one of the most crucial elements and time periods is when you are submitting your ethics application and getting ready to conduct data collection or research fieldwork. If you have never completed an ethics application before, you may be curious about the background and reasons we are required to complete this before starting data collection. From conversations with many research students (e.g. PhD candidates), it seems most have learned the procedure and process of ethics application with support from their research supervisors.

STUDENT EXAMPLE

Linda, a PhD candidate studying social science, says: '*I have heard of ethics applications from other PhD students in the same office. However, I haven't done it before. I just passed my proposal stage, and during my interviews with my examiners, I have been asked about the ethical application, so I did study the ethics procedure. I understand why ethics is so important, to protect the rights of participants at all times.*'

When asked about her ethics application experience, she also comments: '*It was more complicated than I expected. I had a few questions about some sections, such as qualitative questions, interview proformas and consent forms, but I am sure my supervisors will guide me through this stage.*'

Like Linda, you may also feel a bit overwhelmed, particularly if the questions on the application are new to you. Thus, to better prepare you to pass this milestone successfully, we provide the following tips.

1. Go to your university ethics application committee website and study *why* we need to complete the ethics application. Understanding *why* we need to complete ethics applications will ease any stress and help us realise the importance of the tasks (see the example below). It is to make sure the participants' rights, including safety, ethnicity, culture and confidentiality, are protected and looked after.

STUDENT EXAMPLE

Tim Wardle's 2018 documentary film *Three identical strangers* looks at the lives of a set of identical triplets, Edward Galland, David Kellman and Robert Shafran, who were adopted as infants by separate families. They discovered by accident that they were involved in a research study on 'nature versus nurture', investigating the development of genetically identified siblings raised in different social-economic circumstances. During the future investigation, it was also found that these infants were intentionally separated and placed with families having different parenting styles and economic levels (e.g. lower, middle and higher social economics status). In the documentary, it stated that ethics were 'not evident' and many research documents were 'confidential'. It was also shown in the documentary that the three brothers' lives had been impacted cognitively, socially and emotionally by being separated. One of them committed suicide ultimately because of the lack of connection among them when they were young.

---

2. Understand the structure of the ethics application. Ethics applications can be divided into human and animal sections, and the university ethics committee usually assesses the application at differing levels of risk. For example, the Australian Medical Association's (AMA) (n.d.) Code of Medical Ethics Opinion 10.7 states:

    In making decisions about health care, patients, families, physicians and other health care professionals often face difficult, potentially life-changing situations. Such situations can raise ethically challenging questions about what would be the most appropriate or preferred course of action. Ethics committees, or similar institutional mechanisms, offer assistance in addressing ethical issues that arise in patient care and facilitate sound decision making that respects participants' values, concerns, and interests.

3. Treat ethics applications thoughtfully and carefully. Consider all the possible hurt or discomfort participants might incur.
4. Find some examples from your peers. They can provide you with first-hand information if you are confused.
5. Use plain language, as the assessors of your ethics application may come from another jurisdiction area from yours.
6. Prepare your participant information sheet and consent forms. Understand why they are needed and how to prepare them. Look into the detail.
7. Discuss your research instrument's reliability with your supervisors (e.g. survey, experiments and interview proforma).
8. Make careful changes or provide clear justifications when you receive feedback from the committee.

A standard ethics application process will take 4–12 weeks to complete, depending on the complexity and risk levels of the research. Moreover, research students' ethical applications can be assessed by ethics committee members from different departments. Sometimes you have to submit several applications for different stages of your research data collection.

We found the most exciting part of conducting a research project lies in the fieldwork or data collection stage. Once you have clearance from your ethics application, it's time for you to collect your data!

Depending on the nature of your research, your data can come from different areas, such as science experiment data, human tissue samples, people survey data, interview conversation data, case studies, focus group discussion and so on. This book is not a research book so we won't be discussing where these data might come from. Rather our aim here is guide you on what kinds of factors or stress you might encounter while collecting your data. In this section we describe the context of your research data collection by sharing some PhD students' learning experiences.

STUDENT EXAMPLE

Philip is a PhD student in agriculture. His research is to develop a formula to help crops grow faster and better. He has spent two months working on his 'field'. However, that year was unexpectedly cold, and all his data 'died' overnight. Although his data 'died', it does not mean his research failed. It does provide another angle of how to grow plants. Having said that, it was a very stressful and unfortunate moment for a PhD student, and it means he had to start again to grow his plants.

STUDENT EXAMPLE

Shuang is an international student studying a PhD in early childhood education. She is researching a model for teaching STEM education in early childhood. She needs to do an educational experiment on preschool-aged children and support teachers' pedagogical knowledge of implementing play-based intentional teaching strategies. Shuang was planning to collect her data by pairing with another PhD student in their home country and comparing the differences and similarities of children's play contexts. Due to the COVID pandemic, Shuang cannot collect research data from the childcare centres in her current university city, while her peers can still collect data from their home country. This caused stress for Shuang as she could not progress her PhD studies because of the restrictions of the lockdowns, and thus, she needed to work out an innovative way to collect her data.

They were initially planning to use technologies to record children's play and data analysis. Later, her supervisors and herself came up with an innovative approach by twisting the technology tool and making the best use of the 'duo research methods'. Instead of Shuang and her peers recording their 'own' children participants' play, they embedded both pieces of research into one educational setting in their home country. Her peer can conduct her data collection as planned, and Shuang became a 'magical fairy' zoomed on a screen. She was zoomed in and interacted with the same group of children. She 'dressed' herself up as a 'fairy'. Children communicated with her as the 'magical fairy' by asking questions, treating her as a fairy instead of research. In the end, Shuang had collected her data successfully by recording her conversation with the children in a playful context.

This is an excellent example of working collaboratively with your peers to overcome some unexpected difficulties in your data collection, and it certainly worked out well for Shuang and her peers.

Most HDR students feel excited and 'in high spirits' when they are collecting data. The previous paragraphs discussed some 'tense' cases about data collecting. However, sometimes, data collections also include repeated or laborious work in science labs, repeated interviews or trying to send out your survey questionnaires to as many participants as possible. These activities involve effort, time, commitment, and sometimes networking skills. Data collection takes most of your candidature and can last several months or a couple of years full-time, depending on the phases of the research projects.

During the middle of your research candidature, you are also recommended to continue your literature review. A literature review should be conducted throughout your HDR journey. Some research students or candidates treat the literature review as part of the proposal stage. Then they will not do much more on the literature review until after the completion of the data collection stage. If this happens, they will find it difficult to review 'new' literature while analysing data. This can add a lot of stress to the data analysis stage. Some research students may even do a 'rushed' job, and when they start drafting their dissertation, the literature review can look very 'patchy' and dated. Thus, we recommend you always pay attention to reviewing the literature throughout your candidature. It will provide you with an up-to-date view of your research topics, keep you up to speed in the theory development of your research and provide an excellent underpinning for your data analysis and dissertation writing.

In summary, here are some tips for your study in the middle of your research journey.

1. Continue your literature review even if you have passed your research proposal. Use your resources wisely through the library and rich databases. Creating email alerts to journals and topics can be very useful.
2. Understand the ethics requirements; pay attention to details in your ethics application.
3. Plan carefully for your data collection stage and be innovative with your research methods.

This chapter has discussed everyday stressors in the middle of your studies and how to overcome them with proper support and energy building. In the next chapter we will focus on the final stage of your university studies and how to prepare for your career development.

Mapping your journey to success

- You may encounter different stressors in the middle of your studies.
- For school leavers, everyday academic preparation stressors include understanding university assessment policy and procedure and knowing the nature of assessments.
- For returning or mature age students, everyday stressors include balancing life and study, time organisation and energy development.

- For international students, everyday stressors include more involvement in the cultural and historical aspect of the host community.
- For research students, everyday stressors can cover ethics applications and data collection.
- No matter which group you belong to, academic, social and emotional preparation is always essential to maintain and develop full energy levels to overcome any difficulties during the middle of the work and towards meeting the final academic goal.

Recommended activities

Reflect on your current studies, and write down 10 things you will need to complete during the next week in your studies.

6

What to expect close to graduation

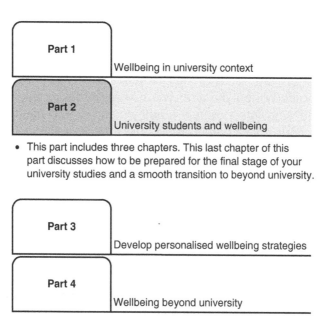

Figure 6.1 Chapter summary

You have now studied for your degree for a certain period (e.g. two or three years in an undergraduate degree, or one plus years in postgraduate degree), and you are close to the end of your studying journey. It is an exciting moment! However, it can also involve many uncertainties about the future. Some university students may also have higher stress levels during the final period or final year of studying. Common stressors can include a break from the routine of studying or future studying or finding a job and starting your career or even starting a new career. Some courses may even have final assessments or requirements which act as an 'accumulation' of study over the period of the course.

Moreover, for international students, completing your degree means you may need to go back to your home country and start a new career or stay in the country where you have spent the last few years. This decision can be stressful for you as it means considering what comes after your degree in terms of living arrangements and future work or study plans.

For research students, completing your studying involves data analysis, thesis writing, publications and potentially oral presentation for the final procedure. This stage can also be very stressful for you. This chapter, therefore, examines the stressors encountered along the differing university pathways and shows you the support universities offer their students and how to be included in the university alumni.

Undergraduate students

During the final semester or final year of your degree, you may start to think about what your life will be like after you complete the degree. You may have already begun looking into possible employment, or you have volunteered in work related to your future career. If you have done so, congratulations! You have found a great way to reduce your stress during your final years of studying. If you haven't done so, we will show you some tips on how.

To find a proper post after your graduation, you should start considering working in the profession or field a bit earlier during your studies. It does not mean you have to work full-time. Instead, you can start as a volunteer in the profession. It is a good way to get to know people within your field and build your networks. These networks may know of work opportunities and provide key information and contacts. Some professions require university students to have placements or practicum throughout their studies. These placements may help you develop your practical areas of knowledge; however, they will not guarantee you a job after graduation. Nevertheless, again, they are a great way to network with people in your chosen field.

The uncertainty about finding employment after graduation is certainly a real issue for many soon-to-be graduates. In an article published in *The Conversation*, Small et al. (2021) find that one in four unemployed people in Australia have a degree. More than 30 years ago, the Australian government initiated a plan to give more Australians access to university education. However, graduate jobs are more challenging to find.

In May 2019, 12,921,100 people were employed in the Australian labour market. Of those, 4,317,500 (33.4%) held a university degree. In February 2020, 13,048,200 people were at work, and 35.13% held a degree. By November 2020, the impacts of the COVID-19 pandemic had reduced the labour force to 12,909,000. However, 4,763,400, or 36.89%, held a degree.

In May 2019, the number of unemployed was 694,900, but the number of unemployed with a university degree was 129,900, or 18.7%. In February 2020, just before the pandemic hit Australia, there were 761,100 unemployed. Of those, 22.45% held a degree. By November 2020, the percentage of unemployed with a degree had risen to 23.29% or almost one in four.

However, the 2021 graduate survey (Quality Indicators for Learning and Teaching, 2021) shows Australian university graduates' full-time employment rates are increased significantly three years after completion (Table 6.1).

Table 6.1   Employment percentages four months and three years after graduation

	Four months after graduation (percentage)	Three years after graduation (percentage)
Undergraduates	74.3	88.9
Postgraduates	86.6	93.3
Research graduates	82.5	90.3

These graduate survey data show more than 25% of undergraduates were unemployed after completing their degree. Therefore, securing a job or a great job will probably be a focus in the final year of your degree. Thus, it might be a good idea to find an internship position first. An internship can provide you with a long-term opportunity to practise your knowledge in a working context with reasonable payment. Although internship payment is lower than contracted or full-time employment, it provides a clearer view of your current work and again can provide valuable networking opportunities.

In addition to work-based employment opportunities, Small et al. (2021) state in their findings that university graduates need to be resilient, determined and adaptable, and graduates have to 'take advantage of any opportunities and professional networks that their universities and alumni provide'. Moreover, the COVID pandemic has clearly had impact on employment rates, including those of university graduates. However, university graduates are still popular in the labour market. For example, the Australian Bureau of Statistics (2021) shows that employment increased to 13,156,400 in July 2021, including mid-year university graduates.

The final year is thus a critical year among undergraduate students in universities. The last year stressors can include that the third or fourth year academic performance standards are higher than the first and second years. The final year can be a transition year between university life and your career. The following section discusses the academic performance standards over the final year of studying.

Academic performance requirements

If you look at your learning materials, you can see many first-year or second-year subjects mainly cover knowledge sharing and theory understanding. The third-year and fourth-year subjects involve knowledge application and practice, critical evaluation and peer assessment. Thus, most of the first- and second-year subjects include demonstrating understanding of your knowledge and examinations. In contrast, most third- and fourth-year subjects include literature reviews, practice reflection and peer review of other people's work. Thus, the third and fourth years of a degree require students to review more literature beyond the required texts. You will also show your understanding of the subjects and apply what you have learned in theories into practice. As are the case, assignments for first-year and second-year subjects are generally 4,000 words, and assignments in final-year subjects can be 5,000 words or more. However, it is not simply the addition of 1,000 extra words. Instead, the differences cover your critical thinking and reflection.

The following shows an example of a final-year assessment from an Australian university's third-year or final-year creative arts unit. The assessment includes the following:

1. Research presentation
2. Studio research documentation
3. Body of work for submission to the graduating exhibition or an extensively researched written study

The three assessments are closely related to 'research work' and project-based learning. We discussed the importance of literature reviews in academic work in the previous chapter.

Monash University (2022) defines the 'review' in research work as follows:

To review the literature means to be able to identify:

- what has been established, discredited and accepted in your field
- areas of controversy or conflict among different schools of thought
- problems or issues that remain unsolved
- emerging trends and new approaches
- how your research extends, builds upon, and departs from previous research.

A review of literature presents much more than a summary of relevant sources. The act of reviewing involves evaluating individual sources and synthesising these sources to gain a broad view of the field. At this 'field level', a literature review discusses common and emerging approaches, notable patterns and trends, areas of conflict and controversies, and gaps within the relevant literature. When you can clearly observe these things, you will situate your research and contribute to ongoing debates within the field.

In other words, when reviewing the literature, 'not only do you need to engage with a body of literature, you also need to be able to compare, contrast, synthesise, and make arguments with that literature in ways that indicate a readiness to contribute to the literature itself' (O'Leary, 2010, p. 81).

Although the aim of this book is not to instruct university students on how to work on academic tasks, we are trying to show you what level of academic work you will be working on in the third or final year of your undergraduate degree.

To make it clear, the tasks in the final year will ask you to evaluate and synthesise various current and updated sources instead of simply summarising the references in your disciplinary areas. The sources include similar patterns, controversies and common themes. This literature review process requires higher-order thinking and identifying gaps within the relevant literature.

To sum up, the third and final year of undergraduate studying involves evaluating and critically applying the theories you have learned. Therefore, completing these academic tasks requires more time, effort and contributions from the university students. And especially when you are concentrating on your future work opportunities, this may add more stress to students, especially when the course completion is close.

Having said that, even though they require higher contributions and cause more stress for final-year students, successful completion of these tasks can provide you with an excellent opportunity for your future employers to view your work or know how you perform in your final placement. For some final-year university students, showing capacity in completing the final year of academic work will act as a stimulus for future employment. For example, the final-year placement for many courses is not just about completing your course, but also an opportunity to demonstrate the professional practices you have been developing over the course of your degree applied within the professional context. Employers may offer job opportunities or internships for high achieving final-year students, thereby giving the graduate security moving into their post-university career. In our experience of working in education, we have seen many cases where final-year students have future teaching opportunities presented to them, which is certainly an elating experience for both the student and staff who have worked with the student for many years.

However, to make this transition period smoother for yourself, here are some tips for final-year university students:

1. Pay more attention to where and what future employers you would like to work for.
2. Work out a good schedule to balance work and studying.
3. Work assiduously on your final-year academic tasks and focus especially on the areas in which you can excel.

During this transition period, you will also need to update your résumé and look for advertisements for your future employment. Some university students leave their résumés to the last minute. Thus, they are rushed and not detailed enough. In addition, some students never thought about asking for references, and therefore, when it comes to reference checks, they do not know whom it would be best to contact. If you are planning to nominate a university staff member or someone from your professional practice settings as a referee, you should advise them well in advance and ask their permission. If you do not have these relationships already set, you may be hindered in your application processes and you may miss employment opportunities in your dream job. Therefore, you need to liaise with student advisors from your university as soon as possible for graduation preparation.

Most universities provide career support to their students. For example, universities have career advisors who provide career counselling to their students. They also hold various events or webinar series to link the industry with their graduates. Other than this, they provide one-to-one counselling for students in need. Always take advantage of these services and attend as many events as possible.

Take the University of Sydney as an example. Its website (www.sydney.edu.au/careers/students/career-advice-and-development.html) encourages its students to prepare for their future careers from their first year of university. The Careers Centre provides guidance and support to its students' career journey across four areas: (1) career planning, (2) starting a new job, (3) professional associations and (4) employability skills.

They have also listed a few questions for students before deciding what kind of support to seek. We believe these are great strategies for you. The questions include:

- How do I start planning my career?
- What can I do with my degree?
- What can I do at each stage of my studies to improve my employability?
- What should I expect when starting a new job, and how do I make an excellent first impression?
- How do I explore alternative options, such as taking a gap year or starting my own business?

How do I start planning my career?

Career seeking is and should be the focus of your final year of studying, with universities recommending that you figure out what you want to do straight after graduation. Some of you may be confused about work and career, and therefore, instead of trying to find a career pathway, you may prioritise 'just finding work'. We recommend that whilst immediate financial security is important, giving special consideration to career planning is just as important. Research found that five years after graduation constitutes a milestone of whether you will stay in your profession or move into another profession. This may be in part due to the diligence given to career planning whilst at university. It is a pity that some of you will decide to change careers after you have completed your bachelor's degree, but it is not uncommon. We believe it may be because some university graduates are confused about their careers and work. Therefore, it is essential to think (again) about your work interests and research different career pathways after graduation. For example, if you graduate with a finance degree, it does not mean you will have to follow the same career path as your peers. A road map for yourself is thus recommended. To make your road map, the first step is career planning. It is not as simple as finding a job after you complete your university. Instead, it is a comprehensive process in which you use your time, networks and effort to reflect and make multiple decisions throughout your degree and professional life. Take for example the career planning advice offered by the University of Sydney (2022).

STUDENT EXAMPLE

Steps to planning your career

Self-awareness

Interests: Think about your recent endeavours (for example, subjects you have studied, work experience, volunteering, travel, sports, arts, hobbies) and the aspects you found most enjoyable. Understanding what holds your interest will steer you towards career options that keep you motivated and engaged.

(Continued)

97

Values: Your values will often significantly influence the kind of work you find fulfilling. What is important and meaningful to you in life, and how might that relate to your career choices? Values that influence career decisions can include helping others, prestige or status, autonomy, intellectual challenge, money, work-life balance, and work environment.

Skills: What are your strengths? Identify and clearly articulate the skills you have developed or utilised during your studies, work, extracurricular activities, volunteering and life experiences. E.g., communication skills from university presentations and resolving customer complaints at your casual retail job.

Personal attributes: Your personality will often inform your role preferences, and the working environment which suits you. E.g., analytical minds may enjoy a role that involves identifying and solving problems, and creative minds may thrive in environments where they can explore new ideas or try different things.

Explore your career options

Use job search websites as a research tool: Type keywords relating to your industry or interests into a job search portal and see what job titles and employers come up. Aim to simply understand the roles in your field and the type of recruiting employers seek.

Research your industry: Read industry journals or magazines, check news sites for information or new developments in your industry and follow organisations and people of interest on social media. Talk to employers at careers fairs or on-campus information sessions. Check the career resources of any professional associations in your industry and find if they offer any assistance to students.

Talk to people: Draw on the expertise of your networks and discuss your career ideas with friends, peers, colleagues or academics. Consider arranging an information interview with someone who does the kind of work you think you would enjoy. You can also book an appointment with the Careers Centre [the University of Sydney's career portal for students] to discuss your career plans or learn more about your options.

Decision-making

Evaluate your options: It's common to feel still unsure about your direction. Narrow down your choices by:

- Ask yourself if a career path reflects your interests, skills and values.
- Writing a 'pros' and 'cons' list.
- Talk to your friends and family or a career advisor about your ideas.

Remember that you don't have to have your entire future mapped out by your final year. Many people change their career direction more than once.

Take action

You've set your goals, and now it's time to work towards them! The action you take will depend on what stage you're at in your career planning: positive steps could be writing a polished application for a graduate job or identifying skills developed during your part-time work and adding them to your resume. Even joining a student society or researching career options on the internet can help move your career planning in the right direction.

The university offers career and employment services for students. The above information is advice in regard to career planning from the university and as they suggest, 'you don't have to have your entire future mapped out by your final year'. But we also suggest it is a good idea to have a plan and to take proactive steps to ensure you are putting yourself in the best position to achieve a positive career start. One way to do that is through a career officer. We talked with a career officer in the career and employment services at another Australian university, who gave us a more detailed insight into the support a career officer can provide you in a university.

STUDENT EXAMPLE

We offer career consultations to all years students; it was pretty standard that most students come from the final years. Approximately 90% of the final-year students are involved in a job application and interview practices.

The one-to-one, face-to-face sessions (now virtual sessions because of COVID) are offered to all year students. Every student is entitled to have six sessions per year (30 minutes per session) to develop their portfolio or résumé.

She further discussed the detailed sessions and other partnerships she developed with faculties.

STUDENT EXAMPLE

The busiest time is around June and July, and most of my student clients come from health science majors. The reason is that there is a deadline for application in public hospitals in mid-July. To apply, they need to list four preferences for four hospitals. As the deadlines are the same as they graduate (and still complete their degree), it can be stressful for students majoring in health science.

Different from health major students, other students also have their busy periods. For example, education students usually come for a consultation about September or October, as most schools start advising their positions for next year's staffing needs.

(Continued)

We also work very closely with the staff in the faculty of education. For example, we work closely with the staff or lecturers in their final placements. We are invited to deliver a session, usually 30–40 minutes, to the final-year education students.

We provide extensive support to all university students, including mock interview opportunities and provision of a bank of sample interview questions and answers to selection criteria.

She also talked about getting feedback from a student's interview experiences as useful for updating questions or recommendations for students. In addition, many students who used the services found them very useful. Examples of evaluations include:

STUDENT EXAMPLE

Hello and Merry Christmas!

I am writing a quick email hoping that this will reach you before you enjoy a Christmas break, and if not, this can be a little welcome back to the work year letter, I guess. I am excited to announce that I am commencing work with a Health organisation in February. This was my second-ranked preference behind Barwon's mental health program. I know we spoke about applying for the Royal Children's Hospital, but my indecisive nature had other plans. I am going to be working in Oncology and Haematology for the first six months, but I am not sure what will follow. However, I am still ambitious to work in mental health and will be working hard towards this goal.

I need to thank you wholeheartedly for your assistance this year in aiding my transition from clueless novice to clueless graduate. I always left our virtual meetings with more clarity and confidence. When the time came for interviews, I felt as prepared as possible, and I have you to thank for that. With this in mind, I wrote down and reflected on how the interviews went and the questions they asked, so if you would like any help with telling next year's final students what to expect, I am happy to assist!

This student's correspondence highlights another vital component of the job preparedness, which is the interview process. For many, this can be quite a harrowing experience. However, there are many different strategies that can be followed. The example in Figure 6.2 provides a practical STAR model to support how to answer interview questions.

STAR Model

The best way to package up your employability stories is to use the STAR model as outlined below. This technique is also very helpful when answering behavioural interview questions.

Situation	Describe a situation/context/background of where you developed/used the techniques
Task	Describe the specific task/problem/projects you were working on when you developed/used the techniques.
Action	Describe the actions/steps/processes you took (You can be a team member of a project, and talk about your actions specifically
Result and **R**eflection	Results or outcomes of the situation, actions and tasks you took. You may use an example. Reflect on what I learnt from this experience.

Note: commence response by introducing the criteria being addressing and elaborate on them by writing down your opinions.

Figure 6.2   An example of how to answer interview questions (Belludi, 2008)

In summary, most undergraduate students will experience some stress during their final years of studying, mainly because of the transition between university and post-university life. If you came straight out of high school, like many undergraduate students you haven't had a full-time position before, and thus your transition to post-university is crucial during the final year in university.

Postgraduate students

Unlike undergraduates, postgraduate students are more likely to be older and have had some working experience before starting their postgraduate studies. Thus, the stress between transitioning from university study to starting a career post-university is different from undergraduate students. This section describes some of the unique stressors for these students.

Academic performance

Other than the nature of the assessments of final years' studying, the stressors for these students are different as, in our experience, many of them are working full-time while studying part-time. Yet, completing their academic requirements during the final years is similar to other years (see Chapters 4 and 5).

The transition between postgraduate studying to after university

As stated above, postgraduate students may already be working full-time. However, many of you may be working in different professions (from your first undergraduate degree) or the same profession (perhaps you are doing the postgraduate degree for professional development or promotion opportunities).

If you are changing your career through your postgraduate study, you are going through similar stress to the undergraduate students as we discussed earlier in this chapter. You will feel unsettled. You will be planning for a new job, such as understanding interview questions, preparing for academic work, and building your network within the new profession. You might even be working in your old profession for financial security reasons, in which case finding time to under-stand your future career and build your new work network can be challenging. If this is you, consulting a career officer would be recommended (for detailed information see the previous main section in this chapter).

If you are working in the same or similar profession to your postgraduate degree or doing it as a professional development opportunity, you may be very familiar with the career and have a clearer understanding of your professional goals. These professional goals can start to be achieved earlier, such as in the final years of your postgraduate study. Figure 6.3 shows a professional teacher association website.

This Australian teacher association website has three main sections for teachers, students, and partners.

- The Teachers section provides teachers resources connected with curriculum, teaching materials and resources, conference information, research journals and grants information.
- The Students section covers professional teaching programs, mathematics summer school, talent quest, and other related activities.
- The Partners section involves employers, donors, and sponsors.

Figure 6.3 Introduction of an Australian teacher association website. (https://aamt.edu.au/)

This website provides a valuable resource for professional mathematics teachers in Australian schools. On the site, final-year university students planning to be mathematics teachers will find helpful resources for teachers and students.

University students can subscribe to the discussion board and access the professional online community on this website. By doing this, you will have access to the current school issues related to mathematics education. You will have the opportunity to discuss with other people in the field their experiences in teaching mathematics. According to the website, this online community:

> ... provides online communities to be used by its members and others in the broader mathematics education community. These online communities align with the Association's aims:
>
> • supporting the work of mathematics teachers;
> • promoting the learning of mathematics;
> • representing and collaborating with stakeholders in mathematics education.
>
> AAMT intends that these communities should be supportive learning environments. Users are encouraged to ask questions, engage in debate, share links and resources, offer opinions and suggestions, contribute experience and expertise and share knowledge.

Thus, it is recommended that final-year university students get to know the professional networks within their own chosen discipline area. These professional bodies can guide students as to their future careers and build future professional employment opportunities. Chapter 11 provides case studies of how professional associations can help develop final-year university students' career pathways.

International students

We discussed in previous chapters the transition period for international students between pre-university in their home country and university life in another country. During your final years of university life, the transition can also be stressful. Unlike local students, international students will encounter different stressors during their final years. This section addresses academic, career pathways, and social and emotional needs.

Academic performance

Academic performance requirements are the same for all students, including for international students. To meet a high academic level across your university studies, you are required to read a lot of literature relevant to your professional major. With the years of progression into studying, there is the need for 'higher-order' work by university students. We have discussed this already in this chapter; however it means a lot more reading and reflection for international students. Unlike local students, reflection for international students can involve further understanding from a cultural-historical perspective. While some international students may find it difficult, other international students would like to use their knowledge to form cultural comparisons. Suppose the home country and the university country have similar cultures (e.g. international students coming from the UK to Australia to study). In this case the international students may feel at ease in understanding the cultural and historical literature. However, suppose the cultures are very different (e.g. a student from China or East Asia studying in Australia). In this case, it may be more challenging for the student to understand and infer cultural differences. For instance, one assessment in an Australian university final-year English unit requires students to learn analysis, synthesis, writing and research skills. Students need to construct an evidence-based argument on an aspect of digital literary culture, in one example. This can be 'easier' for local students or students with similar cultural backgrounds as they are very familiar with English literature from an early age. Local students may investigate the digital literacy culture and develop an argument based upon their years of knowledge and experience. However, it could be more difficult for international students, particularly those whose first language is not English. Their literacy skills will have developed based on their home language. Their experience and knowledge of English use or English literature might be limited. Thus, an assessment task such as this:

> The fundamental purpose of this assessment is to foster skills in analysis, synthesis, writing skills and research. The task will encourage students to construct an evidence-based argument concerning an issue within digital literary culture while demonstrating an understanding of competing positions and approaches.

may take a more extended period of your studying time to achieve the grade you are working towards. Therefore, factor in extended periods of time for study and assessment writing.

In summary, the final years of international students have stressors from an academic performance perspective. Detailed strategies will be discussed through case studies in later chapters to help mitigate this. That said, we have also seen some great examples of how international students use their own unique experiences to develop a strong piece of assessment concerning their understanding of teaching practice. For example, Carmen Ferreira Gomes do Rosario (2017, p. 190) shared her opinion about strategies to engage ADHD and other students in the mainstream classroom:

In Timor, where I am from, we have children with special needs, but unfortunately, they do not get the opportunity to go to school; their parents ask them to stay at home. ...We even do not diagnose whether students have ADHD or not. After I came to study in Australia, I learned different ways of thinking while teaching. In Australia, schools need to diagnose children with ADHD to get medication and treatment, and teachers can manage their behaviour accordingly. ... I want to share the information with people in Timor, especially teachers, to change their thinking and see how important education is to all children in the world.

After discussing her observation of her placement and understanding what special education teachers are, she continued:

Unfortunately, in Timor, we do not have Special Educational Teachers. It is sad because I believe that all students have the right to learn and get a good education in their lives to have a bright future. I want to write down these words so that when I go back to Timor, I can share them ... with other colleagues that work as teachers. I want to change their thinking, and I want them to see how important education is to all children in the world. It will be worthwhile to see the different criteria levels for ADHD students in mainstream schools. (p. 192)

We found this reflection of this student's personalised account and research compelling and authentic. Carmen's reflection was marked higher and later included in the book *The challenge of teaching: Through the eyes of pre-service teachers*. Carmen's example illustrates how she uses the context of her own country (Timor) to consider the educational practices in the country of her study (Australia). She frames her experience in a manner that reflects learning and a willingness to embrace her learning and support her community when she returns after her studies – a wonderful goal.

Career pathways

We know, not least from our conversations with international students, that final years can be stressful because of different career pathway development than domestic students. You may have already started to consider career pathways from early on in your studies. Career services in universities also provide detailed support for international students. For example, the University of Sydney's Career and Employment Services offer a career development programme for international students. The programme gives international students advice on résumé development, job searches in Australia and overseas, writing a cover letter, developing interview skills, career planning, transitioning to the Australian workplace and building one's professional network. Universities also provide employability forums as well as face-to-face or individual virtual sessions with career officers. The following example (Figure 6.4) shows the various platforms offered to international students by career services at the University of Sydney (2022).

---

1. **International Student Employability Forum**

The International Student Employability Forum provided international students with critical insights into building employability skills in Australia during university and transition into graduate employment. Previous Forum Q&A panels have consisted of international student alumni and industry representatives.

2. **Building Your Networks in Australia and China**

The panel of successful Chinese alumni shared their experiences and practical advice on the importance of networking in launching their careers in Australia and China.

3. **Returning Home Careers Session**

This workshop provided final year international students with information on preparing for the job market back home.

4. **Fair Work Australia presents Your Rights at Work**

An opportunity for international students to learn about their rights and responsibilities in the Australian Workplace and gain important information on different employment statuses, national minimum wage, payslips, termination of employment and referral to free online resources. Fair Work Australia presents them.

5. **Visa Pathways for International Students**

Based on current research, experts in migration law present information on visa pathway options for international students who would like to begin their careers in Australia.

6. **Interchange**

Interchange is an exclusive 4-day entrepreneurial skills program that leads international students through an action-packed learning journey. You will work on real-world social issues, working in multi-disciplinary teams with international students from other universities.

Figure 6.4   Career services for international students at the University of Sydney (www.sydney.edu.au/careers/students/careers-support-for-international-students.html)

Social and emotional preparation

For international students, transition during the final years can be stressful, not simply because of the change from studying to work. This transition can be very emotional for many international students as you will be making the critical decision to either make a career back in your home country or start a career in the country you have been studying in for the last few years. Thus, completing the final years of your course means social and emotional preparation for international students, and less so among local students.

Suppose you are close to completing the final years and decide to stay in the country where you are studying. The stress arising from your social and emotional preparation will mainly involve deciding to have a long-term 'separation' from your home country. Some separation periods can be a few months, or longer, such as a year or even a few years. This means you may not be able to see your family, your old friends or other important people in your home country.

STUDENT EXAMPLE

Si is an international student, and she is doing a teaching degree in an Australian university. She is in her final year of the degree, and after spending almost four years in Melbourne, Australia, she decides to stay in Australia and work as a school teacher. At the time we interviewed Si, the COVID-19 epidemic was still causing countries to close their borders. During our conversation, she said, '*it is really difficult, as I will leave my parents at home and may not be able to see them for a few years*'. Owing to the lockdown and closure of borders, Si has not been able to go back to her home country and can only hope for the opening of the border and that travel can recommence. Not seeing her parents is stressful to Si as her family means much to her: '*I haven't found a way to solve this problem, but I am committed to making phone calls and face times as much as I can.*' To Si, virtual meetings are connections between herself and her family: '*We do not know when the border will be open yet. I guess we have to be patient and wait and see.*'

If, unlike Si, you decide to go back to your home country after completing your degree, you will face other issues. The transition from study to working in your home country means you will leave all the 'new' networks you have developed already and all your new friends. Therefore, it can be traumatic for some international students, particularly those who value the connections they have created. Even when career services provided transition support for international students, it is understandable why social and emotional stress can still cause anxiety for international students.

STUDENT EXAMPLE

Naomi, an international student and a friend and studying peer of Si's, is also close to completing her studies. She has decided to go back to her home country after her studying. '*Different from Si, I think I would like to go back to my home country to work,*' she said, '*I have a young*

(Continued)

family who is waiting for me.' Naomi is a mature age student, and she is doing her postgraduate degree in the university: *'My husband and my families have been supportive, and I cannot wait to go back to see them and support them when I finish my studying.'* When asked about her social and emotional stress around leaving Australia, she said, *'Yes, it is also not easy to just leave. I have made some great friends here, like Si. We are like families … we look after each other. For example, we discuss assignments, help each other with life issues. So … yes, it will be not easy to say goodbye later.'* She added, *'but I will value this experience absolutely and will use what I have learned back in my home country'*.

In summary, many international students experience this stress, like Naomi and Si, each with their own unique story and experiences. We will share more case studies in developing social and emotional energy later in the book.

Research students

This section addresses the stressors in the final years/months of research candidature. We have shown you some critical steps during your research candidature earlier in your studying in the previous chapters. In this section, we would like to focus further on what the everyday stressors are for research students in the final years/months of your candidature with regard to the following areas: data analysis, thesis writing and career pathways.

Data analysis

Whether you are a quantitative or qualitative research student, you will conduct data analysis after you collect your data. It is an essential part of your research journey. Shamoo and Resnik (2009) state that data analysis allows drawing inductive inferences and distinguishing the phenomenon of interest from statistical fluctuations present in the data. Thus, data analysis includes using different tools, understanding data and transferring them into new knowledge. Many websites related to data analysis describe the process in five steps (see Figure 6.5).

It is not the aim of this book to introduce you to the data analysis process and instruct on how to conduct data analysis on your research topic. However, we are trying to provide some guidance for you to learn about data analysis and what support universities can offer in this regard.

Data analysis happens after the data collection, and many research students find this stage an emotionally 'low' stage in their candidature. It is not surprising that data collection, as discussed in previous chapters, includes busy schedules and interactions with multiple people, such as ethics committees and

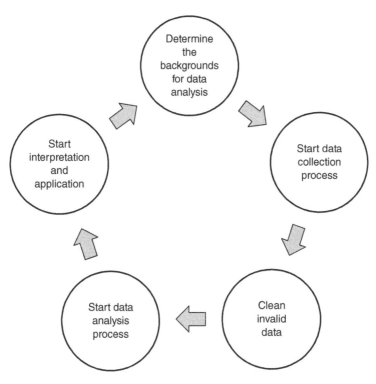

Figure 6.5   Data analysis process (Pickell, 2021)

discussions with supervisors and fieldwork stakeholders. It can also mean attending various meetings or going outside your studying office; thus, we consider the stage 'data collection' emotionally 'high and fun'. However, data analysis means 'hiding' yourself in your research office, unlike the data collection stage. It could also mean dealing with data, including printed surveys, online survey results, observation notes, experiment data, interview notes, focus discussion recordings, and so on. Compared to data collection, data analysis can be tedious. Sometimes, you are required to acquire further understanding of research methodologies, such as positivism, empiricism, modernism or post-modernism research methods, and different analysis skills, such as transcription, and the use of statistical tools (e.g. SPSS) or other analysis tools (e.g. NVivo).

Moreover, data analysis can also be done alone or collaboratively. In the last chapter, we provided an example of a research student - Shuang - who collected her data with her colleagues; however, when she finished the data collection, her data analysis was individual work because she and her data collection colleague looked at the data from differing perspectives using alternative concepts. However, some research students may use similar methodologies when collecting data, thus data analysis may become a collaborative process.

For example, Peter and Raya use positivist research paradigms, both utilising survey questionnaires. Thus, they can work closely together, making sure their design of the survey was aligned closely to their research questions. They asked each other and ensured the research questions (and sub-questions) were linked with the questionnaire design. Then they learned how to use the Statistical Package for the Social Sciences (SPSS) software together. It can make the learning journey more collaborative, as SPSS learning involves reading and understanding statistics and how to use them to find helpful information and answer the research questions.

Research students learn to use quantitative and qualitative data analysis methods. For example, Peter and Raya use quantitative data. The data analysis is based upon numbers, probability values and relationships among variables and the generalisation of the findings to the larger population. On the other hand, qualitative data analysis involves more subjective understanding from the researcher(s) and their ability to categorise themes, topics and theories. In addition, some research students include both quantitative and qualitative data analysis in their research, which makes you a mixed-methods researcher. It may add extra workload for you to study and master how to analyse quantitative and qualitative data.

Thesis writing

Nevertheless, however difficult or easy your data analysis stage is, all research students will come to the final stage of their research candidature: thesis writing. Maybe your supervisors have already advised you to keep writing at the beginning of your research journey, and you have been writing literature reviews or reflections now and then. When it comes to your research's final and prominent product, you will be required to produce a thesis, a published book, or equivalent publications. While we acknowledge that various media forms may be used as a research output, such as a painting, a programme, an artistic sculpture, the most commonly used research output is your thesis or a relevant published book.

Thesis writing can be lonely and tiring. Ewing (2012) published a fascinating article on the six psychological stages of thesis writing:

First, Elation: You're pumped, thrilled. Your idea is the best ... You are a creative mastermind.

Second, Despair: After about a week of pure joy, you begin researching in earnest. The more you read, the more you become aware of what you don't know and what is left to write. You may spiral into a very dark void of despondency and hopelessness.

Third, Acceptance: Sometime around week 3 or 4, you come to realise that this will never end unless you start writing. So you do. Feelings of hopelessness turn into plain old overwhelmedness, a familiar and more comfortable place for most grad students.

Fourth, Bargaining: While you're writing, you play mind games with yourself. I'll write two pages after I bake this cake, wash the baseboards, write this other piece I'm freelancing, alphabetise my bookshelf, paint this dresser, etc. The urge to procrastinate will be decisive. You may find yourself getting strangely in shape when you take up a new hobby, like running (been there).

Fifth, Insanity: But there comes a time when you can procrastinate no more. You will write then, possessed by a spirit of desperate productivity the likes of which you may never otherwise know. You will find you can exist on nothing other than coffee for days on end, as if from some miraculous, biblical tale. Once the frenzied writing subsides and you sleep for the first time in weeks, re-writes and edits begin. Stay strong, and remove all possible weapons (knives, staplers, cats) from your home.

Sixth, Elation (again), Frustration, and Apathy: Then comes the time when you can write no more. You've fought the good fight. You've reached the end of your semester. Your project has emerged from the cocoon of your seminar class into the big wide world. Everything is now out of your hands. This can inspire a complex blend of emotions including, but not limited to: relief, ecstasy, pride, joy, fear, frustration, helplessness, lostness, separation anxiety, anger, confusion, apathy, and, perhaps, a new-found understanding of mortality.

Sounds familiar? Or are you in the middle of a stage right now? If you are, do not feel stressed. Almost all thesis writers will have gone through these problematic emotional stages. They will pass eventually, and you will achieve the final excellent outcome. But how? Dr Sonia Greenidge (2019) provides three tips for managing thesis writing stress: (a) break it down, (b) be specific and (c) free writing. Break it down refers to breaking the writing period into smaller periods instead of dedicating a whole day or more extended periods each day to write up. It can be 45 minutes' writing and followed by 15 minutes' break. Being specific refers to having a clear idea of what you will write and planning to write a specific paragraph with clear goals instead of general writing. Finally, free writing is a great stress release, in which you can simply write what you think and just keep going. Sometimes researchers find they can write whatever comes to their minds, which can be very useful. The main point in free writing is that you can find yourself in the writing flow and reduce the stress of not writing. You can always come back and tidy it up at a later point when your mind is refreshed.

Career pathways

Interestingly, not every research (mainly PhD) student has a career in the academic field. In January 2020, Paul Yachnin from a Canadian university reported his team's research on PhD graduates working non-academic jobs. According to his report, only 66% of the 1,500 PhD graduates (i.e. 990 graduates) are employed in higher education. However, it is common for these new PhD graduates to stay in university to start sessional teaching or adjunct teaching. In the US, it was reported more than 70% of the academic lecturers are sessional or adjunct, and in Canada, the rate is 50%. The employment rates are similar among other countries. They are not permanent positions, and some new PhD graduates have to teach in multiple universities to get by.

Yachnin (2020) comments that according to the Conference Board of Canada, 'the often isolated nature of PhD studies and the stigma that some students feel in pursuing a non-academic career can make networking especially difficult'. This can be why PhD graduates feel unsure about the most effective methods of pursuing non-academic positions. In Professor Yachnin's (2020) TRaCE project, 26% of PhD graduates are self-employed or work in a range of non-academic sectors.

We can reveal a 'shocking' truth in this chapter for you. Since the COVID pandemic, many universities are now working towards job cuts. For example, more than 30,000 jobs could be lost from universities in the United Kingdom, according to Consultancy London Economics (2020). In May 2020, Australian universities also reported a loss of more than 20,000 university jobs. Thus, the impact of COVID and the predominance of careers in sessional teaching have shaken many PhD graduates' faith in academia as a career option. Moreover, it is observed that many and more people want to leave academia either by choice or out of necessity. Some PhD graduates or early-career researchers are starting looking into careers in industry, government and other sectors.

Therefore, career pathways and deciding to leave or stay in academia can be stressful for many PhD graduates or during the final years of PhD candidature. While it is difficult, we recommend you take the last few months to reflect and rethink.

STUDENT EXAMPLE

Since her PhD, Christina has been a postdoctoral fellow, but she has already decided to leave academia. *'There are too many PhD graduates and too many postdocs, applying for too few full-time positions. I am not alone, and I know many other colleagues realise that we do not stand a chance ...'*

Make sure you are prepared to start an academic career as sessional teaching staff or seek employment outside academia. No matter what you choose, we recommend you look widely for career pathways within your significant areas. Broadening the career horizon should be a compulsory programme for PhD candidature during their final years so you can better understand how your PhD can lead along many kinds of career pathways instead of just one. We will demonstrate some energy building programmes in later chapters of this book to show what you can do to achieve your career goals.

Before we end this section, we would like to emphasise that research graduates are highly employable in other academia, industrial and professional worlds. The main career goals for a research graduate should be your potential and your abilities to learn quickly.

Mapping your journey to success

- You may encounter different stressors at the end of your studies.
- Stressors include the higher level of academic performance requirements and career pathways.
- For undergraduate students, you will be required to prepare for a big transition from university life to beyond university life.
- For returning or mature age students, you will look into the career goals.
- For international students, stressors will also include social and emotional stress when deciding to stay in the host country or return to your home country.
- For research students, you will be required to face challenges including developing your data analysis skills, completing your thesis writing and finally deciding what career pathways you will pursue.

Recommended activities

It is recommended you contact student services for contact details of career services in your university. If you are in your third year or the final year of your studies, please book an individual session with your career officer to discuss your future career opportunities.

PART
THREE

DEVELOP PERSONALISED WELLBEING STRATEGIES

7

Building physical energy

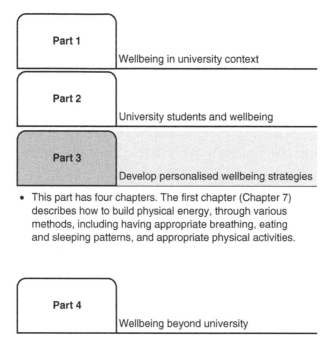

Figure 7.1   Chapter summary

There was a time when physical energy was related solely to athletic activities, used to discuss athletic muscle building for sports, which was the domain of the professional athlete or highly motivated person. We are here to assure you that physical energy is also vital for university students, regardless of your inclination for sport. Yet, many university students view university life as associated with academic work, library trips, laboratory experiments, public speaking opportunities, report writing, etc. By doing this, we risk seeing our time in university solely as an intellectual venture and neglect the physical self in preference for the intellectual. Yet many universities provide gyms for their students and staff to use.

Figure 7.2   An Australian university gymnasium

In gyms, students and staff can use the equipment and have the opportunity to attend classes organised by professional trainers. Many researchers, such as Heijen et al. (2016), have found that motor activities stimulate the brain-derived neurotrophin responsible for neural conversation, forming new synapses, long-term potentiation and brain neurogenesis (De Giorgio et al., 2018). Motor activities play a significant role in preventing metabolic, respiratory and cardiovascular diseases. In addition, they can support, increase and reactivate the cognitive processes useful for learning neurogenesis (De Giorgio et al., 2018). Therefore, with all the known benefits for our brain development and cognitive processes, doing exercise and keeping our physical levels up are vital to our study and work. However, we must always take into account that every one of us is different. We may have different living styles and physical habits. For example, some people are more active in the mornings, while others are more creative in the evenings or late nights. One of the authors of this book was known for many years for his late night working habits and subsequent 'I can't really think properly until 10 a.m.' activation mode to start his daily work! So, he changed his routine to get up at 6 a.m. When asked why, he responded, 'it gives me more time in the afternoon to walk the dog'. Therefore, our habits can change and alter owing to many factors.

Thus, with all these different styles and personal needs, when should we start physical activities, such as choosing to join a gym or scheduling time for regular physical activity? Some of us have always enjoyed athletics or were raised in families that valued such activities; hence the motivation may have come from early childhood. Moreover, some people have excellent time management skills and view physical activities, such as gym membership, as fitting within their schedule. Some of us may attend a gym or commence a physical routine as a new year resolution to start the year, but not all of us will fulfil the resolution. In the end, many gym memberships or physical exercise plans have been wasted. Data show more than half of gym members continue to pay for a service year after year, yet they never actually go to the gym. Della Vigna and Malmendier (2006) did a study about this 'paying not to go to the gym' and found most gym members only go to the gym 50 times per year, i.e. 4.17 times per month, compared to their anticipated 9–10 monthly visits to the gym.

Economist Thomas Schelling (1980) commented that we had two selves: the present self and the future self. Our present self will usually trick the future self into making good decisions or pre-commitment. Our present self is highly motivated to meet immediate desires most of the time. However, our future selves will work hard to achieve long-term goals.

Nevertheless, in this book, we are not focusing on saving money on gym memberships, nor will we share how to build athletic bodies in this chapter. Instead, we use this common issue to share with you that physical energy building is not about fast-tracking. We will need to commit our present self and future self to this long-term goal to achieve high levels of wellbeing in university life.

Consider the following scenarios:

- You found it difficult to focus during an early class; you had to drink multiple cups of coffee to stay concentrated on your studies. You wonder how your peers can remain active and fresh during their class activities.
- You have spent the last few nights catching up, completing a soon to be due assignment, and then found the next task is due just a few nights later! You feel tired and doubt whether you can complete the following assignment on time.
- You live a fair distance away from your campus, and you have to commute one to two hours to your campus by public transport, but you often find yourself falling asleep during the journey.

The above scenarios could be some examples of low physical energy. Without sufficient physical energy, you may find it challenging to concentrate on your studies or even to find the motivation to study. Therefore, we need to focus on how to build our physical energy and hone our physical muscles. Chapter 2 has shown you three areas, and this chapter will continue to discuss how to develop your physical energy and train yourselves to reach the best outcome. We will also share success stories, looking into your needs at different year levels.

Breathing patterns

As we have already shared with you in Chapter 2, breathing patterns can help self-regulation to relax and recover from stress and anxiety faster. Research also shows that therapeutic activities such as meditation can reduce anxiety, sharpen memory, treat depression, promote more restful sleep, and even improve heart health. Thus, extending exhalation is a source of energy when maintaining wellbeing in our lives. Maybe you have already learned that when you feel yourself getting angry at something or someone, you can breathe in and hold it for three seconds, then breathe out slowly. You notice you become a lot calmer after a few repetitions. This breathing pattern (particularly with a slower out-breath) has proven helpful as a stress or anger management technique. Sundram et al. (2014) studied the effectiveness of deep breathing exercises in a stress management training programme. They found the breathing exercises programme significantly improved participants' stress levels and can be used as a coping strategy to alleviate stress.

So what are 'normal' breathing patterns? According to LoMauro et al. (2022), breathing patterns refer to our respiratory rate, i.e. the frequency of breaths in a unit of time and the amount of air cycled during breathing. An average breathing pattern is 12 breaths per minute and 500 mL per breath. Moreover, our breath is a powerful tool to ease our stress and reduce anxiety. Some breathing exercises can make a big difference in our life. However, most people take shallow breaths, which can zap your energy.

We all know the saying 'take a deep breath', as a phrase to help relieve stress and frustration. It works as a form of meditation. By taking a deep breath, you can learn how to take bigger breaths into your belly.

WebMD shows us some common deep breathing techniques. They recommend that you match how long you breathe in with how long you breathe out during your deep breathing exercises. For example, count to five when breathing in through your nose and breath out through your nose to the count of five also. You can work up to breaths that last up to 10 counts or 2 minutes. The following is a technique recommended by WebMD (2022):

1. Get comfortable. You can lie on your back in bed or on the floor with a pillow under your head and knees. Or you can sit in a chair with your shoulders, head, and neck supported against the back of the chair.

2. Breathe in through your nose. Let your belly fill with air.
3. Breathe out through your nose.
4. Place one hand on your belly. Place the other hand on your chest.
5. As you breathe in, feel your belly rise. As you breathe out, feel your belly lower. The hand on your stomach should move more than the one that's on your chest.
6. Take three more full, deep breaths. Breathe fully into your belly as it rises and falls with your breath.

Another breathing technique was published in a 2018 article in the *Journal of Medical Professional Practice* titled 'How to perform the 4-7-8 breath to relieve unhealthy stress'. In this article, the author detailed how to do a 4-7-8 breathing technique, by making exhalation twice as long as inhalation:

Place the tip of your tongue against the tissue behind your front teeth. Exhale completely through your mouth, making a whoosh sound. Close your mouth, and inhale through your nose to a count of four. Hold your breath for a count of seven. Exhale slowly through your mouth to a count of eight.

Several of the students we talked to commented on the benefits of practising deep breathing in university life.

STUDENT
EXAMPLE

Anne is a third-year undergraduate student, and she relayed to us the strategies she uses to support moments of stress. Anne explained that she engaged in part-time work after university hours; she enjoyed her busy weekly schedules: studying and working, and with working payment, she found she was financially stable, could afford something she wanted to buy and enjoyed her time doing both study and work. However, when the examinations period approached, she noticed her timetables clashed constantly, and she found challenges in managing her time. Her employer helped by reducing working hours to spend more time preparing for her examinations. She also suggested she sought support from a university support officer for advice on how to work out 'transition' strategies between returning from work to quickly settling down to study. Anne explained that one suggestion was related to deep breathing. After learning some great breathing pattern skills, she could calm herself down and enable herself to concentrate on her studies. '*I found when I focused on my breathing I can help myself ignore other issues around me, particularly the distress from my work. So it works very well. It really helped with exams.*'

Anne sought a strategy to help her transition between her work and studying, and deep breathing strategies satisfied her needs. Joseph is another student who was advised to practise deep breathing.

STUDENT
EXAMPLE

Joseph is a research student undertaking a PhD degree in Educational Psychology. He discussed with us that he had found some concerns about his time management and felt he was always behind his schedule for milestones in his study. When his supervisors asked him to produce some work, he found it challenging to work as scheduled. Initially, he thought he had procrastination issues and sought help from a study skills professional development unit offered through his university to work out a strategy. Being productive can bring a high level of satisfaction and accomplishments. Therefore, when Joseph looked at what was causing his procrastination issues and what could help him develop moments of productivity, he said that one recommendation was practical deep breathing strategies. Initially, Joseph was reluctant to use it and thought it would add a high-stress level and delay his work even longer. However, after trying it for a few days, he could already find he is benefitting from this strategy, as it brings him calmness and made his mind clearer and more focused. *'When I am behind my schedule, I become reckless and find it difficult to focus on my work. All I am thinking about is being late for my work and worrying about the consequences. After I use the deep breathing strategy, I feel a lot more focused after 2 to 5 minutes of breathing and work on my strategies to complete my assigned tasks easier.'*

To sum up, learning how to use breathing patterns can help you quickly build your physical energy and lead you to succeed in your university studies.

Eating habits

As we discussed in Chapter 2, food can provide our bodies with energy, including our brains. Working in front of a computer can be energy-consuming. Thinking can consume 20% of the body's energy use. Therefore, it is not uncommon to feel hungry in the middle of completing an assignment. It is commonplace for university students to need to work later in the evening, especially after all day working on campus or other commitments. You will need to sit down with books to be read, assignments to be completed, and exams to be prepared for. Much of the time, these tasks require us to sit in front of a computer with not much physical movement. Sitting by itself only consumes 60–130 calories per hour (Healthline, 2021); we have observed some academics using standing desks to help burn more calories while working, rather than being seated. However, no matter whether you sit or stand during your studying time, you are not burning as many calories as you would during more rigorous physical activities, such as walking, running and jumping. However, even with the limited calorie expenditure standing or sitting while studying, our brain works very hard and burns many calories: typically 320 calories per day are consumed from thinking. Thus, after three to four hours of studying, we feel exhausted and hungry. Eating is necessary to supply energy for learning.

Muñoz-Rodríguez et al. (2021), in a study in Spain, stated a healthy diet improves the quality of life and helps prevent various diseases among the general population and university students alike. It is common for university students to experience nutritional disturbances due to the expected changes during their university life. In addition, as we discussed, university students may also experience both physical and social stress, lack of time, and changes in living arrangements. Therefore you may find it challenging to maintain healthy eating habits. Lack of physical activities and a poor diet contribute to university students having even worse eating habits. The following patterns are widespread: skipping meals, constant fast food consumption, and low fruit or nutrition consumption (Muñoz-Rodríguez et al., 2021).

Moreover, stressful university life can cause you to develop some dietary disorders, such as stress eating disorders. As we have discussed earlier, you may feel hungry during your studying, and, likely, you will fetch some food to satisfy your appetite or potentially comfort you when you feel stressed. In order to be able to work at the same time, you may choose some higher fat food or fast food. Sproesser et al. (2014) note that approximately 40–50% of the population consumes more food under stress conditions. This eating in response to stress is a type of maladaptive self-regulation. However, stress hyperphagia is only one element of eating behaviour in everyday life and only provides very limited insight into our knowledge of eating. Most of us react to the valence of stress situations by eating more. It happens more often when we are confronted with a negative situation and reverses when we are eating less in response to a favourable situation.

Di Renzo et al. (2020) studied dietary habits in Italy during the COVID pandemic. Under the lockdown restrictions caused by COVID, two significant influences on diet emerged: (a) staying home and stockpiling food and (b) staying home with limited outdoor or in-gym physical activities. Additionally, for those in educational settings, virtual classes replaced attending classrooms on campus, therefore restricting movement even further. As a result, our previous dietary habits were interrupted and driven by the logistical restrictions of lockdown conditions and the resultant boredom and stress caused, resulting in higher energy intake or more food consumption with limited burning of energy. In particular, the 'comfort foods' are richest in sugar and carbohydrates. Although they can encourage serotonin production to change our mood, they increase our risk of cardiovascular diseases, inflammation and other possibly severe complications.

During the 2020 pandemic			
85% of the adults changed eating or food preparation habits	**41%** of parents were snacking more	**24%** of women reported eating more food	**17%** of men reported eating more food

Figure 7.3   2020 Food and Health Survey (International Food Information Council Foundation. 2020)

Besides the stress caused by academic work, university students also experience stress caused by social networks. Pannicke et al. (2021) discussed how peer pressure could also influence your dietary habits. You will be asked to participate in various social networking activities during your university life, including social eating and drinking. Nevertheless, in Muñoz-Rodríguez et al.'s (2021) study, they found more than half of the participating university students said they had tried to follow a diet and wanted to be 'slim' to be beautiful. Moreover, almost three-quarters of the participants showed a lot of interest in increasing their knowledge about the relationship between diet and health and wanted to improve their dietary habits. Those students studying medical-related subjects expressed more interest in learning about diet and health relationships than the other students and were keen to adopt healthier dietary habits. We would recommend that we all try and achieve this goal!

Therefore, it is essential to follow a healthy diet, as it can impact our health, including modulating processes of inflammation and oxidative stress. A healthy diet is not simply a low-calorie diet; it should include proper nutrition from fruits and vegetables and monounsaturated fatty acids, such as fish, nuts and olive oil. Nutrition plays a critical role in contributing to our health and wellbeing. With proper nutrition, we can stay active, and improve healthy ageing. Thus, food choice acts importantly towards a healthy diet.

Overall, making healthy choices and developing reasonably good dietary habits will include a high level of self-regulation and require further training and work. We will discuss how to develop your self-regulation abilities in the following chapters while discussing social, mental and spiritual energy development. This section will focus on food knowledge and understanding what and when we should eat.

You may already know that we should only consume a certain amount of calories every day, dependent on factors such as your gender, age, height, etc. Food provides us with nutrition and energy for our bodies to function and our brain to use for work and study. Therefore, eating and having a healthy eating style is essential. Leyse-Wallace (2013) states,

> Nutrients at inadequate, excessive, or imbalanced levels may produce a variety of effects on the brain and central nervous system. These effects may range from preventable mental retardation to transient discomfort resulting from low blood glucose or caffeine cravings. Food insecurity can influence the quality of life or even the will to live. The will, beliefs, emotions, and decisions made by the mind and environmental influences such as culture and food availability ultimately result in our food and nutrient intake. The emotional influence of food on the experience of comfort and security begins in infancy and continues throughout life. (p. xxvi)

Thus, the question emerges: what should we eat and how much should we eat?

A certain amount of calories are needed for our daily physical and mental energy use. According to Sarah Klemm, in an article published on the Academy of Nutrition and Dietetics website (2019), the estimated calorie needs for women is between 1,600 and 2,200 per day, and the estimate for men is between 2,000 and 3,200 per day. However, she also pointed out that it could vary according to our needs and age. For example, pregnant women need more calories than women who are not. Another example is that active, mentally or physically, activities require more consumption of calories.

Some research shows that the less we consume, the longer life we will have (Willcox et al., 2004). However, some of us developed a misconception that under-consuming means a healthy lifestyle. Unfortunately, being underweight can also cause a lot of health problems. Therefore, as Sarah Klemm (2019) further commented, we should listen to our bodies:

- Weakness, shakiness and irritability may be signs of hunger for many people.
- Pacing yourself is an ideal way to assess fullness. For example, slowly eat half of your meal and then take a pause. Give your body a chance to begin to digest the food and think about how good it is to feel comfortably full and satisfied.

STUDENT EXAMPLE

Qing is an international student from an Asian country who was in the first semester of her postgraduate studies in Australia. She found adapting to the new lifestyle and cultural differences quite challenging. Therefore, she turned to stress eating. She found it initially did calm her

(Continued)

and gave her a level of comfort; however, she later noticed it did not help her fit into her new lifestyle. She stated to us that she eventually sought support from a nutritionist to gain insights into her eating behaviours as well as enquire about 'stress eating'. For many international students, coming to a new country to study includes understanding and getting used to changing food. In Qing's case, she noticed the differences and had issues with western and eastern food and found herself quickly indulging in 'sweet' and 'high calorie' food intake. Working with her nutritionist, Qing indicated that she was able to get a better sense of her calorie intake as well as understand the nutritional value of the food she was eating. Even though there are many differences between foods in her home country and Australia, she found it easier to adjust what she can eat and when she should eat. Qing also stated that she was encouraged to attend other outdoor physical activities to build her confidence levels in networking with her peers and continuing her academic work.

To sum up, learning how to develop healthy eating patterns can help you build your long-term physical energy.

Sleeping patterns

Interestingly, during the conversations we had with our students we found not many realised the importance of developing good sleep patterns. True, we all have our sleep rhythms. For example, some people work better in the morning, while others work late at night. Whilst your body may indicate to you 'the set best time to work', it is recommended by medical experts that we should go to sleep at a reasonable hour as an essential and productive step to a more energising morning start.

Sleep is not just part of our daily routine, it is an essential physiological process for humans (Lemma et al., 2012). Many university students often report poor sleep quality due to increased social activities and academic demands. Schlarb et al. (2017) found that more than 50% of university students do not have an appropriate level of sleep quality, and some also have an insomnia disorder. Sleep problems have a considerable impact on your daily life, and – of particular relevance for this book – your ability to focus on your academic tasks and examinations. Lund et al. (2010) also noted that university lifestyles create precipitating factors that enhance stress-related sleeping difficulties. They also commented that students might be more susceptible to hyperarousal related difficulties because of maturational changes in the neuroendocrine system.

As we said in previous chapters about living conditions, there is a chance that you will be sharing with a roommate, which often leads to a forced change of lifestyle. According to Schlarb et al. (2017), approximately 90% of university students have roommates, and 41% of them wake up at night owing to the disturbance caused by others. Lund et al. (2010) report that most undergraduate university students (aged 17–24 years old) spent 7.02 hours sleeping, with about one-third having more than eight or more hours of sleep per night. It was also noted in Lund et al.'s study that more than half of undergraduate university students go to bed after midnight (on weekdays) and get up around 8 a.m. (weekdays). Weekends are scheduled a lot later than weekdays, with most of the students going to bed around 1:45 a.m. and getting up times changing to 10 a.m. on weekends. Sleeping patterns also include staying up late (e.g. until 3 a.m.) at least once a week.

Moreover, owing to the extra social events, long work hours, the freedom of university schedules and the need for concentrated bursts of study, there is a tendency for university students to become 'night owls'. When we interviewed students for this book, they all indicated very different sleep routines and patterns, and it was also found that a lot of your sleeping and getting up times differ vastly. These inconsistencies in your sleep patterns can bring challenges and create particular circumstances that will result in sleep disturbance. Gaultney (2010) found that more than a quarter of all university students are at risk of sleep disorders. These disorders include insomnia and nightmares.

Sleep disorders obviously have a very bad influence on sleep quality. Sleep quality was strongly related to your daytime performance, including academic performance. Moreover, it was also associated with your health, mood and all-in-all wellbeing. For example, poor sleep quality has a negative impact on your mood. You may experience feelings of anger, confusion, depression, fatigue and inattention because of poor sleep quality. Sometimes, you may also find poor sleep quality is related to a physical illness. Or it might lead to an increased willingness to skip classes in order to catch up on sleep. Researchers have also found that poor quality sleepers are inclined to drink more alcohol. For example, Schlarb et al. (2017) found poor quality sleepers used alcohol to induce sleep twice as often as other students.

Unlike breathing and eating habits, you may feel less control over sleep patterns. For example, you try to change your lifestyle by going to bed earlier and rising earlier to kick start your day. However, your brain may remain active and keep you awake. Your plan and good intentions can be easily sabotaged! Moreover, psychological concerns such as stress, anxiety and depression can also contribute to your sleep disorder. Some of you may have already noticed the association between sleep and our mental health problems, and they do go hand in hand in terms of our wellbeing. Please refer to Chapters 4–6 to find information about student services in a university and how such services can help you manage your stress. Moreover, in the following chapters, we will also share how to build our mental, social and emotional and spiritual energies to manage our stress and maintain our wellbeing.

Furthermore, during our interviews with students and generally over our period of working in higher education, we have noticed that many university students have their own 'mechanism' to keep themselves awake and engaged during the daytime. One of the most frequently mentioned is a regular caffeine intake! Research shows that drinking coffee in the morning can have direct stimulant benefits on daytime alertness and performance, and have a limited negative impact on night time sleep (St. Hilaire & Lockley, 2015).

However, some students reported having a moderate intake of caffeine per day (e.g. more than three cups of coffee per day) or drinking coffee before bedtime. No doubt, caffeine intake can temporarily boost your energy to stay awake and focused. However, research has shown night time caffeine intake can contribute to a worse sleep disorder. For example, Mercader and Patel (2013), in a paper about caffeine intake, state that two to three cups of coffee taken at bedtime can disturb our sleep considerably, especially for middle-aged people. In 2004, studies conducted by Landolt et al. showed that caffeine could influence our sleep by interacting with our adenosine receptors. Therefore, consider when and how often you partake of caffeine drinks, and we don't recommend having a coffee just before bed!

Schlarb et al. (2017) found that some sleepers used alcohol to help induce sleep. Alam and McGinty (2017) state alcohol has the ability to induce sleep rapidly, and that's why it is often used as a method to reduce self-stress, anxiety and insomnia – in particular, consuming alcohol one to three hours before bed-time decreases sleep latency, increased time spent in nonrapid eye movement and increased slow-wave activity of the nonrapid eye movement during the first half of the night. However, it was found during the second half of the night, sleep patterns changed, with an increase in sleep stage transition, wakefulness and rapid eye movement. Without alcohol consumption, the sleeping promotion system is more active than the waking promotion system. Although it will take a bit longer for the sleep promotion system to work than alcohol consumption, once you fall asleep, the waking promotion system works slowly to wake you and gives you a long night's sleep. With alcohol consumption, the wake promotion system is more active than the sleeping promotion system. That's why you may wake up earlier than during non-alcohol consumption. It then leads to the debate: should we or can we consume alcohol before bed? We recommend not to. Even though alcohol consumption can induce sleep faster, it does not help sleep quality through the night. Moreover, when alcohol consumption becomes chronic, namely 'overconsumption', other health-related issues can be triggered.

Well then, if we are looking for a good night's sleep, what should we do? During our interviews with some of our students, we heard some helpful sleep tips that may contribute to a night of good sleep.

STUDENT EXAMPLE

Catriona is an undergraduate health student; however, she has completed another degree in business before. Now she is working to have a career change to become a midwife. One of the practical ways she shared with us was that her maintaining wellbeing is about her sleep patterns. *'Maybe because I am a health student, I am aware of the medical issues and pay attention to my physical health.'* Catriona commented: *'I normally go to bed at 11 p.m. This regular pattern helps me to sleep quite well.'* Catriona also talked about the quiet time before bed. *'I have a period of quiet time before bed and spend it on reading or other reflection activities. I also try really hard to limit screen time before bed. It helped me to maintain my health, wellbeing and fitness.'*

Going to bed at a regular time and not always changing your sleep pattern can contribute to falling asleep quickly and having a good night's sleep. When we occasionally have a hectic night working or studying, e.g. preparing for examinations, we should try to re-establish our regular sleep routine as soon as possible.

Physical activities

In this section, we will discuss exercise, including what kinds of exercises and how frequently we should do them. At the beginning of the chapter, we noted that almost all universities have gyms on their campuses; however, during our interviews with students for this book, only a few of the interviewees were actually using their university gym. All of the interviewed students had distinct exercise schedules and preferred other locations to do their exercises. Some used gyms close to their house, but the majority reflected that they preferred to exercise outdoors when possible. Sibley et al. (2013) studied the relationships between exercise motivation, regulations and fitness among university students. Interestingly, many researchers (e.g. Haskell et al., 2007) recommend that adults have at least 30 minutes of moderate physical activities at least five days a week. Not many young adults, including university students, are following this guideline. Some research shows only 10% of young adults are engaged in the recommended physical activity (Sibley et al., 2013).

Undertaking physical activities can provide participants with numerous health benefits, including decreased risk of coronary disease, stroke, diabetes, depression and decreased blood pressure and cholesterol. Additionally, other research has shown that physical activities positively impact our improved mental health and cognitive capacity. Many studies have demonstrated the effects of acute exercise between study sessions and their positive impact on university students' learning efficiency. For example, Lambourne and Tomporowski (2010) studied the effects on cognitive performance during and after physical exercises, such as cycling and treadmill running. Their results showed that cycling could enhance your performance during and after work-outs, and treadmill running only leads to a slight improvement after exercise. Ji et al. (2017) studied the effects of acute exercise on university students' cognitive performance in temperate and cold environments. They found acute moderate exercises have a positive impact on students' processing speed and working memory in temperate and cold climates. Other researchers (e.g. Latzman et al., 2010) found acute exercise can also influence male university students' cognitive flexibility. In other words, exercise, in whatever format you choose to do it, will be beneficial for your health and your studies!

With regard to the other benefits of participating in physical activities, Guo et al. (2020) studied seven kinds of exercise interventions for university students suffering from depression. They found that tai chi is the most efficacious intervention, followed by yoga, with dance being the third most effective programme to alleviate depressive symptoms. Other activities such as running, volleyball, basketball and badminton were also found to be helpful, all coming in fourth place. Another example of the value of exercise was related to us by Bill.

STUDENT EXAMPLE

Bill is a mature age student and has almost finished his teaching degree. He had an IT degree before and was a technician, before deciding to make a career change. When we were discussing his focus management strategies, he mentioned he goes surfing regularly during the week (if not daily). *'Surfing calmed me and helped me focus on what I need to do'*, Bill told us. *'I would feel not at ease if I hadn't surfed on the day.'* When asked whether he would like to become a professional surfer, Bill laughed, *'No, I surf because I find it relaxes me, but I consider it as a significant part of my daily life and would like to continue doing it.'* Bill also shared the story with us that once he had been stuck on ideas for an assessment task, he went for a surf, had a bolt of inspiration whilst surfing and ended up getting a good grade for his assessment task!

Of course, not every university student will consider surfing as their regular physical activity to improve learning performance – surfing is a challenging activity, which may not be appealing to everyone. Moreover, it also requires access to the ocean and expensive surfing equipment. Therefore, choose physical activities that suit your location, lifestyle and budget. The two authors of this book like to walk. The main criteria are just to participate in physical activities that help you to maintain your health and wellbeing. When we interviewed other students for this book, we learned about some of the other physical activities that they like to participate in.

STUDENT EXAMPLE

When we interviewed Catriona about her physical activities, she introduced her methods of the triangle of health, wellbeing and fitness strategies she used for her physical activities. '*As studying to become a midwife can be a bit stressful, I found engaging in exercises is very help-ful to reduce my stress. I went on a boot camp and running after doing my essay, and it really helped to calm myself down.*' She also added, '*friendship can contribute to physical activities. When doing physical activities, I find it boring and hard to continue without someone to share the moment with. However, when I do it with a friend, I find it much more fun and continue. For example, I walk my dog with my friends at least 4 to 5 times a week. During the walk, we discuss our life issues while at the same time walking a few miles easily.*'

Catriona's comments highlight how important it can be to make physical activity a social time. Think whether this approach could work for you too.

We also interviewed students who do indeed use university gyms to participate in physical activities.

STUDENT EXAMPLE

When asked why she came to the university gym, Melanie commented, '*it is convenient for me, as I attend campus classes at least four days a week. The gym also gives us students a great discount on my membership, and it saves me a lot compared to joining another gym. By the way, the discount rates also apply to the tutorials from personal trainers. I found it very attractive.*' Melanie also added other benefits of using the university gym: '*I also attend group classes, such as pilates and yoga classes. I've met some really cool people outside of my own study area.*'

From Melanie's story, we can see university gyms provide their students with a good facility for structured physical activities, such as the provision of phys-ical equipment, weekly physical classes and individual personal trainers. The gym can provide some students with opportunities to undertake structured physical activities and a chance to network with people from your university but not necessarily working within your discipline. Nevertheless, people may find all kinds of activities attractive, and they can take personal time to do moderate physical activities with their friends. For example, walking (dogs) with friends and cycling around where you live is a very common physical activity among university students.

In summary, in this chapter, we have introduced how to build our physical energy to maintain our wellbeing. A high level of physical energy can help us feel alive and energetic for our learning activities and improve our academic performance. It can help us develop a healthy lifestyle throughout university life and beyond university. We have looked into breathing, eating, sleeping and physical activities with some successful examples. The examples have demonstrated university students' varied strategies to help build fitness, extend focus time, and manage stress from examinations and time management.

Mapping your journey to success

- It is essential to build your physical energy for a successful university life and to maintain your wellbeing throughout and beyond university.
- Building physical energy includes developing breathing, eating and sleeping patterns, and appropriate physical activities.
- Building physical energy can be developed together with other areas of energy, such as mental, social and emotional and spiritual.
- You can build physical energy according to your own needs, and there is no set pattern for everyone to follow.

Recommended activities

After reading this chapter, please reflect on your living habits and styles, including your understanding of breathing, eating and sleeping patterns, and physical activities. Please review all the physical areas and complete the relevant sections of Appendix B.

8

Building emotional energy

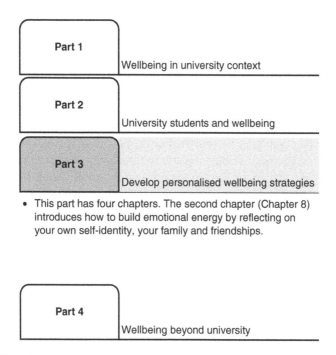

Figure 8.1   Chapter summary

As we discussed in Chapter 2, people's emotions can be divided into two kinds: *positive* and *negative*. Positive emotions include enjoyment, challenge, adventure and opportunity, while negative ones include fear, frustration, anger and sadness. Therefore, this chapter will show you how to have more positive emotions and reduce negative emotions. To build emotional energy, we will first need to understand people's feelings.

Many of us use social media platforms, such as Facebook, Twitter, Instagram, etc., and a very popular function of using these media platforms are 'emojis'. During the last few years, emojis have been developed into including many faces to present our emotions. Using emojis can be very helpful to provide emotional cues in our conversation. For example, you can use to represent happiness; to show your sadness or unhappiness. Other emojis include excitement, depression, fear and many different emotional feelings. We are all very familiar with the use of emojis, however are we familiar with the meaning of the emojis? In our daily reflection and check-in, we should ask ourselves if we need help building emotional energy. MacCann et al. (2020) discussed students' social and emotional skills developed by schools and universities, such as emotional intelligence (EI), and how EI can increase students' academic performance. Many other studies (e.g. Martins et al., 2010; O'Boyle et al., 2011) have found emotionally intelligent people perform better in their jobs and have better health and wellbeing.

Moreover, EI has become an essential skill for university students to develop for their wellbeing and future workplace success. When we look into how to build EI skills, we firstly need to understand what emotional and social competence is. Bar-on (2006) has shown five domains of emotional and social competence: interpersonal competence, intrapersonal competence, stress management, adaptability and general mood.

Consider the following two scenarios:

- You have been preparing for your final examinations for the last few weeks. You are confident that you have studied the critical content knowledge to pass the examinations. However, you do not like the atmosphere of examinations. Moreover, you have a sense of fear to sit *any* examinations. It is not because you are not prepared. You just do not enjoy the examination context.
- You noticed you have a group task to complete in your studies, and your lecturers have assigned you to a group of other students who you don't know. You are anxious about what your group work will look like and how you can contribute to this group.

The above scenarios are some examples of how context can impact your emotional energy. Without sufficient emotional energy, you may find it challenging to work and perform well in your university life. This chapter, then, will show you how to build your emotional muscles.

Social and emotional development

Before we discuss how we build emotional energy, it is important to comprehend how we develop our social and emotional senses over the course of our life journey. Every human starts to develop social and emotional capacities from infancy.

Our first social and emotional activities probably come from parent–infant communication. One of the greatest psychologists, Freud, pointed out two critical drives for social and emotional development: self-preservation and procreation. Our social and emotional development is closely related to our physical, language and cognitive development.

Another psychologist, Erik Erikson, built his theory about the development of the ego and fundamental trust relationship during the infancy period. Interestingly, he described the development of a sense of trust as 'an essential trustfulness of others as well as a fundamental sense of one's trustworthiness' (Erikson, 1968, p. 96). Trust can help us develop our sense of ego and 'find' ourselves a sense of identity, of being ourselves and someone other people can trust as well. Young children who do not develop a sense of trust at a young age will have low social and emotional energy in adulthood. Yet, regardless of our early childhood experiences, developing social and emotional energy is always a worthwhile venture.

One of the critical aspects of social and emotional developments during early childhood is self-awareness. Although we have developed our self-concept and a sense of identity since birth, we build our reflection and self-awareness through the experiences we encounter as we age. We start to understand ourselves and have more self-regulation, self-concept and personal identity. Do you remember the first time you looked at yourself in a mirror? When you saw yourself for the first time in the mirror as a child, you were studying yourself. You looked at your own eyes, nose, mouth, hair and body shape. It may be the first time you understood your eye colour and tried to relate to who you look like, i.e. your parents. These reflection stages are considered the 'gold' standard for identifying the emergence of objective awareness of yourself in the younger years. This visual self-recognition also leaves a lot of questions about yourself and your appearance, especially as you age and start to compare yourself to others. When you move into middle childhood and later adolescence, you will have a heightened awareness of self-concept and self-esteem. Simple reflection or self-awareness will turn to self-evaluation. It is very common to have changes in our self-concept and self-esteem.

During adolescence, we transition from childhood to adulthood. We integrate the various stages and develop our complete egos or adult identifications, which can be seen in such models as ecological theory (Bronfenbrenner, 1977). The adult identifications include self and gender identity and some knowledge of one's intellectual and physical skills. Due to physical development during adolescence, we learn and understand sociocultural factors associated with health behaviour and gender differences. Moreover, adolescent social relations are considered through the concept of peer groups. The peer group is important to our social relations. Peer crowds provide adolescents with a social model in behaviour, attitudes, values among friendships, partnerships and overall interpersonal or peer relationships (Prinstein & La Greca, 2002).

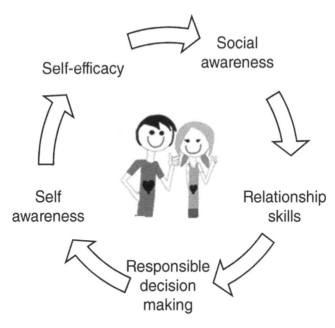

Figure 8.2   Social model of adolescents

In summary, we develop our social and emotional capacities throughout our life, starting from birth. Starting from bonding with our parents and family, we develop our self-awareness, self-efficacy, social skills and social networking strategies and skills. However, we also have different social and emotional capabilities because we all grow up along different life paths. Therefore, when you are at university, it is counterproductive to compare yourself to others in terms of how you deal with particular situations. We can learn from how others carry themselves, but it will serve no purpose to critique or criticise your own or others' social and emotional behaviours.

Friendships and loneliness

As has been mentioned several times in this book already, during your university studies you will encounter many people and some of these will go on to become your future colleagues and friends. It is important to consider the important role friends can play in your life. Among your friends, who do you think you can turn to when you are in trouble or need support? Even though we start to become more independent and less conforming as we grow from a child into an adult, we will always have friendships, as a basic human emotion is the desire to be accepted by other people or peers. Many of us value honesty and commitment within our friendships and strengthening and consolidating these relationships are important.

Other than family relationships or intimate relationships, probably no other human relationship is more valuable in our life than friendship. We find friendship embedded within our histories and stories, such as the famous *Winnie-the-Pooh* stories by A. A. Milne. The eponymous teddy bear Pooh has many an adventure with his friends, Piglet, Eeyore, Kanga, Roo and Tigger. Piglet, in particular, is Pooh's best friend. They help and support each other during happy as well as sad moments in their lives. Some famous quotes on friendship come from the A. A. Milne tales (1956): 'promise me you will always remember: you're braver than you believe and stronger than you seem and smarter than you think' or 'a friend is one of the nicest things you can have and one of the best things you can be'. Such sayings and stories find their way into our childhoods and help shape the way we think about the people close to us.

The term 'friendship' has changed through the ages. Earlier, it meant a voluntary and chosen bond available to free man, different from the terminologies of 'kin' or 'love'. Later, it referred to intimacy, respect, mutual help, shared activity and confrontation (Volpato & Contarello, 1999). We are certain that you have your own personal definition of friendship, which will guide many of the decisions you make in relation to how you deal with people.

STUDENT
EXAMPLE

Felicity was an international student and a self-proclaimed 'extrovert'. In her home country, Felicity enjoyed studying with her friends and also liked to have social gatherings during the weekend or holidays. Therefore, when Felicity came to Australia to study, she started to look for new friends after settling into her study routines: '*I really wanted to do well in my studies, but I also wanted to meet as many new people as I could. I love interacting with different kinds of people.*' She began living in Australia in student accommodation (Unilodge) organised by the university. In the student accommodation, Felicity had her own room, but she shared the kitchen and a bathroom with five other students. She liked the communal lounge area in the accommodation housing, where she stated that she would meet with her housemates and they could share topics of interest. Many of the students who lived in the university student accommodation were also international students from various countries. For Felicity, the first friend she made was also another international student. Felicity explained that it was helpful to gain trust in another international student as they could empathise with one another, and share their common interests and challenges, as they had similar social identities. Felicity explained that she and her friend were very different in terms of their chosen areas of study as well as their ethnic and cultural backgrounds. Yet, she explained, that as long as we can understand the group boundaries of different interests, ethnicities and cultures, we can make the best use of them and have successful interpersonal relationships.

Zografova (2019) wrote about the nature of group identity among intergroup members, including different ethnic groups. She studied the conditions for positive contact among the members. She concluded that identity is not a stable construct but discursive based upon how individuals and collectives distinguish themselves in their relations with other individuals or groups of people.

Social identity

Looking at how we make friends in university, one of the critical steps we need to examine is understanding our social identity. Bliuc et al.'s (2011) research focused on university students' social identity and how variations within identity impact approaches to learning. They notably defined social identity as 'the aspects of a person's sense of self that depend upon their identification with social categories or groups' (p. 418). Interestingly, Bliuc et al. (2011) found our individual self-image derives from the social groups we perceive ourselves belonging to. Identity is connected with our personal values and emotional significance. Undoubtedly, our identity can shape our lives and is meaningful to us. Our social identity also determines our reflections on our sense of belonging to social categories or groups. For example, we have observed that mature age students will often be drawn to one another, based on common life experiences and states of belonging. It is because humans have developed a social conformity after many thousands of years of evolution, and we feel safe in and obliged to stay with the social group. Other reasons lie in the dichotomy of a perceived 'us versus them' mentality. The terminology of group boundaries has been studied. Many studies have found that if the group boundaries are not clear and contacts between groups are weak, conflicts between social groups rise. We make choices every day, and we have our unique ways of acting or responding to many simple or complex situations. These daily choices and reactions are influenced by the social categories and groups to which we belong.

The social life in the first year of university plays an important role in helping university students form their identity. Erikson (1968) stated that during university life, students can establish a sound understanding of identity formation, in which they experience different values and roles, a perceived sense of personal wholeness and continuity. G. R. Adams et al. (2006) studied 351 first-year university students' psychosocial maturity and identity formation and investigated the impact of their family and university relationship environments on the students' identity formation process. The next section discusses what identity formation is and why it is useful to understand it.

University students' identify formation

To form your identity as a university student, you will explore a range of identity options and alternatives and start the process of developing your commitment to a set of values, goals and convictions. This process can be active or passive, and you might be influenced by your peers and family to adopt similar beliefs and social values. During this process, you start your emotional development and commitment as a university student. Finally, once your commitment has stabilised, you will have a definable sense of self and a sense of commitment and responsibility. Then you have achieved your identity status. Once your identity status is complete, you will find you have high self-regulation and have assisted in your cognitive development, ego development, moral development and epistemic development (Moshman & Ebooks Corporation, 2015).

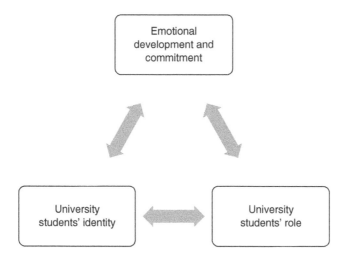

Figure 8.3   University students' identity formation

Identity formation is not a quick or easy process. It also involves using social-cognitive strategies. It involves self-relevant information processing, making our own decisions, and then constructing our sense of identity. G. R. Adams et al. (2006) have discussed three identity processing styles: diffuse-avoidant, normative, and finally informational styles, to cope with personal problems, make decisions, process self-relevant information and construct a sense of identity (p. 83):

> A diffuse-avoidant style is characterized by procrastination and an active avoidance of decision making, commitment formation, and identity negotiation.

A normative identity style involves passively adopting and following goals, standards, and expectations held and endorsed by significant others.

An informational style of dealing with identity issues and decisional situations is characterized by actively seeking out, processing, and evaluating self-relevant information.

During our time working in higher education, we have come across the following cases which reflect differing ways students react to group work:

- Terry considers himself a very approachable and easy-going person. Terry seldom raises his ideas in group discussion, whether the debate is choosing a place to have coffee or assigning tasks in academic work. Terry would usually prefer to work with a decision made by the whole group instead of having any conflicting or different opinions with others.
- Julia is usually considered a very quiet member of her group. She sometimes raises her opinions to her group and expects feedback from others. She feels she belongs if her voice is listened to, and her views are considered. However, if others do not agree with her opinion, she would quickly withdraw her opinion and stay with the group's decision.
- Robyn's friends view her as a strong character who always likes to share her opinion and initiates debate to consider differences amongst the group members' ideas. She is not dominant over the other group members; however, she is not afraid of speaking up for herself or her ideas. Although some members of Robyn's group view her as the leader of this team, she considers that all the decisions that have been made have been based upon a democratic process.

If we look into these three cases studies, we can find Terry, Julia and Robyn have different identity styles. To be more specific, Terry has a diffuse-avoidant style, Julia has a normative style and, finally, Robyn has an informational technique. Terry always wants to avoid being involved in making a decision and has 'full commitment' to his group's decision making. Meanwhile, a normative identity style consists of adopting and following a group's goals, standards and expectations, particularly when most others endorse them. Julia can be considered a typical example of this identity style, as although she has her own opinions, she follows the majority's decision when a conflict happens. An informational style is an active seeking out, processing and information evaluation. Robyn likes to share her opinions but will also follow up with others if she has different views and evaluate each other's opinions. Identity formation processing styles do not determine your social and emotional commitment in university life, nor influence your student identity. However, they may be related to your future identity formation after graduation from university and may influence your future professional planning and career life. For example, it was found that an informational style is positively related with future achievements.

Working in higher education, we understand the value of getting students to connect and work collaboratively in order to form connections. An example from our own practice is an activity we do which highlights the importance of collaboration. We do this with first-year students, asking them to participate in a 'survival game', with the purpose of helping these students to understand the importance of collaboration and group work. This survival game provides a scenario, either in freezing cold weather or a boiling desert condition. Participants are then given a list of items they could use to survive in an extreme situation. They have to rank the items from the most important to the least important against survival needs. All the participants are required first to work out the ranking themselves (without discussion with others). Then they are asked to participate in a group discussion and rank the items again as a group given a timeline of 20 minutes. Each group consists of 10 students. During this group discussion, they are given space to express themselves freely. At the end of the 20 minutes, they determine the group's ranking. Finally, we provide them with the list given by survival experts, and they can compare and discuss.

The survival game is not about testing whether the university students have excellent survival skills or not, rather, the participating students are asked to work in groups to collaborate and make joint decisions. We use this game as an activity in the first tutorial among first-year students. Besides the participating students, we also invite two other students (also from the first year) to observe each group of students. The two observers have to identify and note who the ice-breaker(s), humour-maker(s), peace-maker(s), or quiet participant(s) are. At the end of the activity, all participants are asked to answer the following reflective questions:

- How understood and listened to did you feel in the group?
- How much influence do you feel you had on the group score?
- How responsible and committed do you feel to the decisions that were made?
- How satisfied are you with your group's cooperation performance?
- How would you assess your learning about group work issues in this workshop?

Most participants enjoy this activity and reflect on their behaviours during the activity. We do not identify the participants' identity styles in the survival game activity. However, we do ask the students to think about their identity processing styles based upon their behaviours during the activity. Students are encouraged to think about when the group make decisions and how the decision processes are made. Interestingly, students are also asked to identify their identity styles by reviewing their problem and information processing strategies. Most participants have had a stable self-concept and a strong sense of purpose to express themselves, and have had a certain degree of tolerance. They often use some consensus or voting to work out the rankings for some particular items. It is a very interesting activity to conduct among first-year students, and we believe it has helped participants to reflect on their social identity formation.

Friendship forming

We have discussed identity formation in the course of your emotional development and emotional energy building. Now we will move to a discussion of friendship formation. Most university students start to make acquaintances and sometimes friends during their first year of study. Making friends is the process of social integration and embeddedness in a social network. Klaiber et al. (2018) have noted that the quality and quantity of new friendships made by first-year students significantly affect their emotional and academic adjustment to university life. We are all different, some of us might be introverts, others extroverts, and some are a mixture of both! For extrovert people, you enjoy being around others, and in fact, you may have what some deem to be 'human intelligence'. Psychologist Gardner (1983) established a theory which incorporated multiple intelligences, one of which is human intelligence. People with human intelligence reach complex cognitive feats and have high levels of motivation and self-awareness. However, in our experience, not every extroverted person has human intelligence. A lot of introverted people have very high human intelligence as well. Instead of expressing this in an extroverted manner and having an abundance of friends or acquaintances, they may just choose a few people to become close friends with. There is no formula for your friendship formation, and there are no set rules for friendship forming either. You will become aware of the personality types you feel comfortable with in the higher education setting. These people may challenge you intellectually and provide motivation during your time at university.

For most university students, their social network is formed through understanding their social identity. This social integration is a powerful predictor of morality, though, and it can impact your academic performance and wellbeing. If your friends pay a lot of attention to academic achievement, there is a good probability that you will too. Indeed, if your close friends often go to the gym to do physical exercise, you will follow them to the gym too. Selfhout and his colleagues (2007) studied the role of similarity in music preferences in the formation and discontinuation of friendships. Their results showed that if you enjoy similar music to other people, you may well become friends. The reasons behind this are pretty simple: you can share your opinions and enjoy conversations about a topic you are all interested in. Your social identity can form within this friendship. Similarly, there is a reason that you chose the course you did: so you already have a great starting point when meeting new people. From there, other similarities (and differences) will emerge through the collaborative process of studying in higher education.

During COVID, many university students experienced loneliness, a negative subjective experience (Labrague et al., 2021). This loneliness was caused not least by a lack of social relations and interactions. As lecturers, we heard multiple stories from students sharing such feelings, and in many cases, the one to two hour Zoom workshop was one of their main opportunities for social interaction during the pandemic. Much research has shown many young people, including university students, experienced a greater prevalence of loneliness during the pandemic. Instead of going to campuses to attend classes or participate in workshops, the classes had been changed to an emergency online learning mode. Rather than studying in libraries or having face-to-face group discussions, students' studying schedule had to be organised and accommodated within their living space. Students may have been living in shared accommodation before lockdown, with acceptable interactions with flatmates. However, relationships with flatmates may have changed during the COVID period, for example more concern with each other's hygiene habits than before. Therefore, when we go through extreme circumstances such as lockdowns, we need to ensure we find ways to maintain our social interactions and have realistic expectations of each other. Even during 'normal' times, being a university student can have moments of loneliness and feelings of isolation, especially when studying for higher degrees such as a doctorate. Thus, it is important to work on how to help yourselves in this challenging period by making use of your friends and developing your wellbeing and exploring your emotional energy needs. Maxi shared her experience of being well integrated in her social network during COVID and maintaining her wellbeing by creating a *book club* with her friends.

STUDENT
EXAMPLE

Maxi, a third-year undergraduate student, has been studying remotely during the COVID period for almost two years. She had a year of face-to-face learning in her first year of university study and made some friends early on in her degree. However, when the COVID pandemic hit, Maxi was forced to study online. She could see her university peers in the online learning platform (e.g. Zoom) and complete her assessment at home: '*Even when I saw my peers and friends in Zoom meetings and breakout rooms, it was not the same as the actual real classroom learning.*' When asked how she managed to remain socially integrated, she told us, '*My friends and I really enjoyed reading. We developed a book club for ourselves. We set up a schedule to read together online. The books were not always academic or related to our study, they could be novels, thrillers, newspapers, or any social media papers we are interested in.*' She explained the benefits of being in this book club: '*I found it really helps to maintain my wellbeing, particularly during stressful times. We shared our thoughts, laughed together on some funny topics and discussed any topics we found interesting from the books.*' She also mentioned that crucial to keeping the club going was that she and her friends made sure it was scheduled and that they were regularly involved in it: '*That's what interests can do for you. They keep you engaged and continue participating in this activity.*'

Maxi shares with us a really wonderful example of what can be done to network with your study friends and have realistic expectations of each other. Whilst you share the common goal of attaining your degree, it is wise (and fruitful) to share other experiences and bond over topics of interests that might be outside of your study area.

Attaining and using social support

Much research has studied how social support (e.g. Li et al., 2018) can improve your positive psychological state, like the positive impact on your sense of well-being. The surrounding social context also has a significant influence on your opinions and behaviours. Social support provides you with a sense of security and helps you address many challenges. The more substantial the social support networks around you, the more benefit you will gain from that social support. It may help you to achieve your academic goals and be more socially integrated into the university academic environment.

Now we will show you some steps to making good friends during your time at university. The Students' Union at a UK university (2021) provides 10 tips:

1. Join online groups for freshers (online resources to support first-year students)
2. Sign up for clubs and societies
3. Say hi to your neighbours (if you are living in university accommodation)
4. Attend faculty activities
5. Try freshers' activities out of your comfort zone
6. Strike up a random conversation
7. Hang out in communal spaces
8. Keep yourself open
9. Invite people to do things
10. Remember, everyone is in the same boat

These 10 ways may be beneficial in helping you make friends. However, it may be different for each of us. As we have already shown you in the previous section of this chapter, you will need to understand yourself before choosing how you want to make new friends. Some of the students we interviewed shared their success stories in making friends at university.

STUDENT
EXAMPLE

Joe told us about the start to his undergraduate studies at university. He was very familiar with the city and university he attends, as he was born in the city and had heard about the university and really wanted to go there. When he was in his Year 12, he stated that he participated in an open day campus tour of his future university. Joe was very excited to receive his offer just before Christmas and started his journey in February.

Joe was an active student, and he used to attend clubs in secondary school, including an environmental awareness club and a sports (hockey) club. He talked about the importance of participating in the Orientation Week of his first year, usually held the week before the semester starts. In Orientation Week, Joe attended informal workshops with his peers. He stated that he was aware that one of his school acquaintances was attending the same campus and doing the same course as him. So Joe reached out to his high school peer and they planned to attend all the Orientation activities together. *'The first day is daunting and stressful, especially if you are among a group of strangers and do not know anyone. Coming from high school, where you sort of know everyone, it was a bit strange, but kinda good to get a fresh start. I was lucky as I had one person I knew from the same school attending the same course as me ... I think it helped us both. I knew he was in the same boat as me and was very happy to be involved in the activities I suggested to attend together. We then went on to meet some really cool people who we shared classes with later.'*

We think that Joe showed great initiative in reaching out to his high school friend, and it appears he was successful in having a good start to his university life and had a great Orientation Week. Joe, now in his second year, went on to say that he still sees his high school friend regularly during workshops, but that they both now have a wide network of friends from within their course.

STUDENT
EXAMPLE

Tracy is a postgraduate student; when we interviewed her, it was her first year of postgraduate studying in university. Although Tracy already has a degree, it was done nearly six years ago. She has been working full-time after graduating from her first degree and decided to return to university to undertake a postgraduate degree for further career development. Tracy chose to do her postgraduate degree part-time, as she is still working full-time. Tracy has a hectic schedule and can only attend evening classes. The university she attends has accommodated its postgraduate students' needs by starting classes at 5 or 6 p.m. When Tracy has evening classes, she always leaves her work half an hour early to attend to her studying. Tracy is in a relationship, so she will go home after she finishes classes.

Tracy stated that she could not make herself available to attend Orientation Week activities, but ensured that she watched all the recorded videos by the university to get familiar with the academic requirements. However, Tracy still felt a little different when she attended her first class. Unlike her memories of her first undergraduate degree, where she was studying with hundreds of other students in her degree, she found herself in a much smaller postgraduate class. *'I found I was one of the 15 students in my class, and instead of attending a large lecture, we attended this small group of students in one tutorial room.'* Tracy also noticed her classmates were from different age groups and came from different backgrounds as well. *'It*

(Continued)

145

was very, very different from my first degree; I found people who are undertaking postgraduate courses can come from such different walks of life! But we all came here to study for similar purposes. When I first went to my class, it was a kind of awkward, though I soon found people with similar backgrounds to me, plus we had similar lifestyles and basic interests with each other.' Tracy continued, *'It was great to know other people in the group and we shared Facebook IDs and stuff like that.'*

When asked what other benefits she has found while making friends in her university life, Tracy said, *'Having a friend is very helpful. Once, I was busy with my work and could not make the evening's class. I was a bit concerned; I didn't want to miss any important information to complete the subject. However, when I texted my friend, she was kind to take notes for me in the class. We often share our notes, so I was grateful that she could attend the class and I could still have the important parts shared by her. I am very grateful to have a good friend, and it has been a great experience in my postgraduate degree.'*

The close friends that Tracy has developed in her postgraduate degree also formed a study group on Facebook. According to Tracy, the group is growing more prominent with others doing the same course. On this Facebook group, Tracy and her friends share ideas on completing assignments and discussing problematic academic concepts and assessment tasks. Interestingly, beyond normal etiquette rules, Tracy stated that they had very specific rules about the Facebook page and that its purpose was for the discussion of course content and not for criticising staff or other students within the course. Which sounds like a very reasonable strategy to keep the group on task and support each other's learning.

STUDENT
EXAMPLE

James started his PhD journey almost a year ago. He had achieved his first milestone successfully, and when we interviewed him, he was well onto his journey of PhD research. PhD candidature can be a very lonely experience, as even with the growing number of students doing a PhD in higher education, actually doing the PhD generally involves doing individual research (even within teams). Every PhD study is different, and all research students are completing their projects. Moreover, research students meet their research supervisors individually.

James said, *'I am working with nine other PhD students in a large, shared office. Once we walk into the office, we will be very quiet. The other students are either reading, writing, or reflecting in the office. We cannot talk aloud in the office. An office is an honoured place for us, and we respect other PhD students.'* James continued, *'Friday afternoon is different, though. We can bring food to share with each other in the office. We can share the stages of our research. Although ten of us are sharing this office, almost all of us are in different stages of our research. For example, Winny [pseudonym] is close to completing her research.*

I saw her quite a lot during my candidature. She has written most of her thesis and has been having a lot of meetings with her supervisors. Finley [pseudonym] is similar to me. She just started her PhD. She is busy with her preparation for her first milestone. Not all students come to study in the office, and I haven't met two of them yet. I heard they are working and only studying part-time. I enjoy working in my office, as I can concentrate on my reading when I know others are doing the same.'

When asked to describe what emotional support he has received, James said, '*I enjoyed the workshops organised by the faculty research office. Those workshops include writing, research methodologies and methods, fieldwork, data analysis and wellbeing. I liked the wellbeing programme, as we can share our thoughts about many things that happened in our research. For example, in the last wellbeing workshop, one of the researchers used some theory to discuss why we should look after our wellbeing and the impact we shall experience. Most importantly, I made some friends during these workshops, during the subgroup discussion in the workshops. Although they are from different faculties than mine, we started our PhD at a similar time, and we could share many similar topics, and we could also compete with each other to make positive progress in our research.'*

Universities hold a prominent place in society and can be a perfect place to be around like-minded people and make friends. Making friends may not happen immediately; it may not occur on the first day or first week of your university life, but you will have many opportunities to make friends. Friendship can help you form your social identity and achieve your academic goals. Positive social support can help us develop our emotional energy. For example, James mentioned his research peers competing with one another, which helped him focus on his progression in his studies, and which serves as both external and internal motivation for his studies.

Utilising family support

This final section discusses how to maximise family support to build your emotional energy. Family support includes drawing from economic status, educational levels and the family structure (Yu et al., 2015). Family structure builds unique family emotional bonds for everyone. For example, if you were born into a family of three or more children, they will have different family cohesion from others born in a family of one or two children. For example, much previous research has shown the position of being a middle child and how they bond with their siblings and their parents. Moreover, people who grow up in a single-parent family may also have different emotional intimacy and emotional intelligence owing to the close relationship to a primary caregiver.

For many of us, we have gained insight into the value of education from our families. In addition, we grow and learn from our parents and families since birth. The role of parents, family rules and family ideals towards education becomes apparent and instilled. Ultimately, there is a wealth of research that suggests the family environment is considered an essential factor in children's mental health and wellbeing, which of course is the springboard to successful beginnings in education. Whilst we appreciate that no two families are *equal*, in every sense of the word, understanding the level of support your family can provide will go a long way to your university success.

Similar to other forms of social support, such as friendship, family support can play a vital role in university students' emotional energy building. We have also heard many reports of the importance of family, especially during the COVID pandemic period. The following example is from Nancy, who returned to live with her parents and study online at home at the onset of the pandemic.

STUDENT
EXAMPLE

Nancy is a second-year undergraduate student and she shared her social integration and wellbeing strategies. *'When I had to move back to my parents, I felt a bit relieved. I moved to the university city and shared with two other girls in a city apartment. I worked as an assistant in a retail store, but the store had to close owing to COVID. I could not work, which put a bit of financial pressure on me. Luckily, I have very kind parents, and they let me move back in. Although I am looking forward to moving out again, I felt safe and lucky that during that period of time, I do not need to stress about financial issues and could continue studying online.'*

Experiences in the family are among the most important contributions to our wellbeing (Vandeleur et al., 2009). Skills learnt during our time living in the home environment give us interpersonal skills and help us develop our social bonds with other people. Aloia and Strutzenberg (2020) explored the influence of family cohesion and relational maintenance strategies on stress in first-semester college students. They suggest that family cohesion boosts university students' internal capacities to acclimatise stress. The academic, social and emotional benefits of family cohesion can certainly reduce low stress levels among university students, particularly during the first semester of the transition period.

STUDENT
EXAMPLE

Jenny is a second-year postgraduate student teacher, and she shared her family support and wellbeing strategies with us. Jenny was a mature aged woman and a mother of two. Although she has to do many family chores, she also enjoys studying at the university. '*As a mature age student, my university life is quite busy. In the morning, I normally drop off my older children at school, the youngest child at childcare, and then I can attend university studying. My husband has to travel a lot for his work, but luckily my sister lives close by. If I am too busy with my work, my sister will also help me care for my children. I am so grateful. My sister is ten years younger, and she has already completed her university and now is a primary school teacher. She likes my children and always has a good time with them. Other than help with looking after children, I sometimes also seek academic help from her. For example, my sister is really good at essay writing and shares tips with me on academic writing. Plus, as a teacher already, she discusses lesson plans I have created and gives me feedback. With her assistance, I have gained a lot of confidence and with only very little stress while taking my studies. She is not just my sister, she's also my best friend!*'

Jenny's story is an excellent example of the role of family support in successful performance at university. Whilst not many of us will be lucky enough to have a sibling already working in the career pathway we have chosen, Jenny's story highlights that we can seek family support in many ways. By having support when needed, be it financial, emotional or even 'freeing' of our own time, family can provide a multitude of support factors. Therefore, if you are in a position to have family support, consider ways you can tap into this wonderful resource to support your studies. Just as importantly, ensure you invite and thank your family when you do graduate, as they will have shared your educational journey!

In summary, in this chapter, we introduced how to build our emotional energy to maintain our wellbeing. Positive emotional energy helps us acknowledge happiness in our own lives and provides us with the resources to conquer challenges and support our peers. This process requires us to choose our friends wisely and be involved in positive social networking. Although we cannot determine our families, we can work *with* social family support. Through reflection, consider your own life and how any, or all, of these strategies can be integrated within your studying journey and help to form your identity within your university life.

Mapping your journey to success

- It is essential to build your emotional energy for successful university life and maintain your wellbeing throughout and beyond university.
- Building emotional energy for a successful university life includes understanding ourselves, developing strong self-awareness, and building vital social networking.
- Building emotional energy can be done by finding our social identity and identity forming.
- Families can be essential in building positive emotional energy that can be a lifelong resource for us.

Recommended activities

After reading this chapter, please reflect on your social identity, identity forming and self-awareness. You may also reflect on your friendship and family situation. Finally please review all the emotional areas and complete the relevant sections of Appendix B.

9

Building mental energy

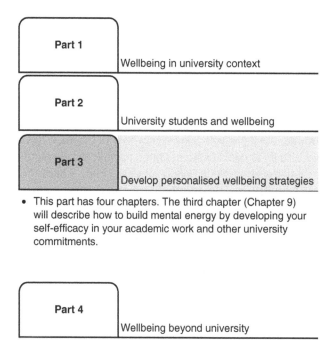

Figure 9.1 Chapter summary

We discussed 'mental muscles' in Chapter 2 and how mental muscles can help us concentrate on building energy internally and externally. They refer to our competencies related to self-efficacy, self-awareness and self-development. When we discuss mental energy, we cannot view it in isolation. Instead, it needs to be built together with our physical and social and emotional energies.

There are many benefits to having strong mental muscles, as they provide us with realistic optimal mental energy, effective time management and creativity.

University students represent a unique population, and their wellbeing and mental health are influenced by the dynamic transitional period of independence, particularly among school leavers. It may be the first time for school leavers to live away from home and venture beyond the relative safety of the home environment. For all people, regardless of experience, the commencement of university provides a unique challenge (and opportunities) and requires a stimulating period of academic adjustment. This transition period of independence involves rapid and interrelated changes in body, mind and social relationships. We have discussed in Chapters 7 and 8 how to manage the transition in terms of our physical health and in our social relationships. This chapter now shows you how to develop your mind and enhance your mental status during your university life. As Stallman's (2010) research shows, university students are five times more likely to be diagnosed with a mental health issue – which points to the fact that you need to take proactive choices about your own mental health.

Consider the following two scenarios:

- You have always been a high achiever and want to try your best and perform at a high level. However, sometimes you feel relentlessly pressured by this demand of the idea of being a 'perfectionist' and forever worry about the influence of your current academic performance on your future employment. You have a reputation for being very good at studying, but it hits you with anxiety. Your peers respect your need to be perfect, but they also try to avoid being assigned to work with you in groups.
- You are a new university student. During your secondary school time you were always considered to be a 'high level' student. However, when you began university study, you noticed most of your peers were also successful in their work. This sudden competition surprises you and sometimes brings you frustration. Even when you spend long hours, and intense commitment, you do not always achieve the results you want; your feeling of personal exhaustion made your efforts counterproductive.

The above scenarios could be examples of you going through some mental issues, and you may have lost appropriate focus and realistic optimism. As Loehr and Schwartz (2005, p. 94) described in their book:

> Mental capacity is derived from a balance between expanding and recovering energy. The capacity to stay appropriately focused and realistically optimistic depends on intermittently changing mental channels to rest and rejuvenate.

Without sufficient mental energy, you may find it challenging to work and perform well in your university life. This chapter, then, will show you how to develop these qualities to build your mental muscles.

Self-efficacy

Ten years ago, a group of researchers (Richardson et al., 2012) carried out research to measure the influences of a range of 50 factors on university students' GPA (grade point average). These factors include personality traits (e.g. introvert or extrovert), motivational factors, self-regulatory learning strategies, learning approaches and psychosocial contextual influences. A psychological construct, self-efficacy has been found to be the most vital factor with regard to university academic performance.

So what is self-efficacy, and why does it have such a strong power over our learning performance and outcome? Bandura (1977) defined self-efficacy as a person's perception that they have the skill and capacity to undertake a particular action or task. Self-efficacy sometimes works together with other psychological constructs such as self-esteem and self-concept. To simplify the definition, self-efficacy is your belief in your capacity and motivation and behaviour in your studying. It is about the influence of your beliefs and expectations on your achievement of goals and managing your behaviour, emotions and motivations. It has a substantial psychological impact on whether you can solve a problem, complete a task, and achieve your goal. It helps you persist in reaching those milestones.

STUDENT EXAMPLE

Yue was a mature international student who wanted to study to become an early childhood teacher. She had been working in a childcare centre, and her passion towards care for children had given her a good reputation among her children's parents and her colleagues within childcare centres. Although Yue could practise her work, she sought support for academic help. *'I am mature age, and I want to be an early childhood teacher. I enjoy being around children, and I think I will be a good teacher. However, I did have issues with my academic work, and I was worried that I did not have the ability to pass the assignments. I had attended universities a long time ago in my home country and had not been involved in academic writing since then.'*

Whilst she noticed that she needed academic support, such as reading and writing at a university level, she had excellent practice-informed ideas about being a good early childhood teacher. Her long working experience in the discipline had given her a tremendous practical background to understand educational theories. Therefore, Yue set up regular meetings with her lecturers, not just to help her academic work, but also to check her self-belief to complete her university work. Yue told us that she noticed after the meetings with her lecturers, she felt confident in her abilities to do well in completing her assessment tasks. This belief supported her to have a high level of self-efficacy in becoming a great early childhood teacher and feel confident in her ability to do well in her degree. Yue stated that whilst she never considered herself to be exceptionally skilled at academic writing, she developed the capacity and confidence to do her best work. Her strong self-efficacy helped her develop her motivation and willingness to persist in completing her degree.

Do you want to know if your self-efficacy is high or low? Try to answer the following questions:

- Do you always stick to your goals and try to reach them, even when something unexpected happens?
- Are you able to stay calm to cope with unforeseen issues?
- When you are confronted with a complex problem, do you usually try to work to solve the problem or avoid getting profoundly involved and give up?
- When you face challenges, do you view them as a learning opportunity to learn new skills or something to be avoided?

If you answered yes to all these questions, your self-efficacy is quite strong. If your answers are no to all of them, your belief in your abilities might be quite low. As we just showed you, self-efficacy is potent energy for successful university life. We would like to help you build your self-efficacy in your own talents and skills.

Firstly, we will show you what self-efficacy is and how it can influence your beliefs in your abilities. Other than Richardson and her colleagues, many other researchers have pointed to the importance of understanding our self-efficacy and have conducted studies in this area. In Bandura's book (1997), self-efficacy theory has four primary sources (see Figure 9.2) of efficacy belief: performance accomplishments, vicarious experiences, social persuasion and physiological reactions. That is, self-efficacy has a significant impact on our performance. Moreover, actual performance experiences of success and failure also energise our self-efficacy development. For example, you will feel more motivated and have stronger beliefs if you experience success, but experiencing failure leads to a decrease in your efficacy expectations. It is the psychological impact of your performance experience. However, we also want to emphasise that occasional experiences of failure do not diminish self-efficacy. For example, you will typically complete two to three assessments for one subject. You will feel low efficacy if you do not do well in your first assessment. However, it should not stop you from honing your abilities to continue onto the second or the third assessment and achieve better overall outcomes in your subject. When lecturers design assessment tasks, best practice recommends that the first assessment should support future assessment tasks. Therefore, learn from feedback in the first assessment and use it to support your ongoing tasks.

Often, people who have high levels of self-efficacy have the following attributes. They tend to view challenges as something to achieve rather than something to fear. Instead of feeling discouraged by failure, they will see it as an opportunity to learn quickly, grow, and recover from a loss. They like to be active and take a more involved role in activities to reach their goals. In our teaching experience in higher education settings, we have seen many students who fit these descriptors and generally these types of students will have sustained success over the

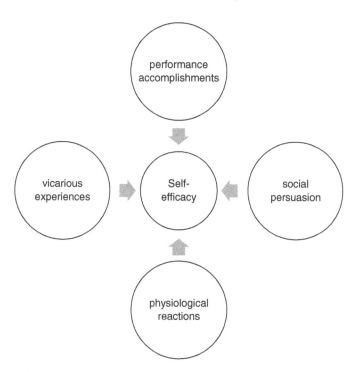

Figure 9.2   Self-efficacy and its influential factors

duration of their studies. The four primary sources of self-efficacy will now be described in more detail, beginning with performance accomplishments.

Performance accomplishments

Within a university academic context, self-efficacy is, then, conceptualised as academic self-efficacy, in which people make judgements about their ability to attain educational goals successfully. In fact, the relationship between self-efficacy and various learning environments has been studied by many researchers, including prior-to-school, formal schooling and higher education students (Honicke & Broadbent, 2016). No matter what educational settings self-efficacy is studied in, it is found that academic self-efficacy positively correlates with academic perfor-mance. The importance of self-efficacy in academic performance is that it can motivate self-regulated learning. Self-regulated learning is often punctuated by examination results and GPAs, it also involves contextualised social, motivational and cognitive factors. Some academics, such as Alhadabi and Karpinski (2020) and Talsma et al. (2021), developed a framework to extensively study a variety of complex data modelling and mediation techniques.

Talsma and her colleagues, for example, studied first-year university students' learning beliefs and their academic performance outcomes during the COVID pandemic. COVID-related changes on their capacity to perform and potential consequences for self-efficacy and academic performance were focused on. University could only provide limited access to libraries and face-to-face support because of the closure of campuses. Some students also found it challenging to concentrate on work because the at-home study environment can be full of noise and distractions. In addition, university students had to study online, which required almost everyone to be fully equipped with the tools to function successfully. These factors can impact performance outcomes because of a lack of self-efficacy, confidence, and motivation to pursue emergency remote learning. Students may lack the time management and technology skills to engage effectively with the learning materials. This research confirmed the importance of understanding the relationship between learning performance and university students' self-efficacy.

STUDENT EXAMPLE

Hui was an international PhD student. Hui started her international studies in Australia as a master's student. She then pursued her research as a PhD student. Hui was a great student back in her home country academically. She received many awards for achieving outstanding academic outcomes and was a scholarship recipient. Hui has since developed a strong self-efficacy about her belief to be able to study and chose to come to Australia to establish her professional work further.

However, when she attended her first class in her master's degree, she shared with us a moment of self-doubt. *'When I picked up all the books and materials I had to read from the bookstore, I was so overwhelmed by the volume. On top of that, I also learned I would not attend examinations at the end of the semester. Instead, I would need to complete almost 100,000 words assessments across all the subjects during the year. When I picked up the reading materials, I also noticed I felt shocked and lost confidence in whether I could finish the piles of books and achieve a high standard I used to have. Then I walked into the classroom and attended the workshop [for the] first time with my peers. My confidence got even lower because I found myself mute and could not contribute much in the class. Other people seemed great at expressing themselves in the workshops, discussing the topics, and learning from each other. I think my self-esteem dropped to the lowest level of my academic life.'* Hui laughed and continued: *'The first three months of my studying in Australia was difficult, and I was in survival mode. I knew I needed to seek help from others.'*

Universities offer academic support to help students develop their academic reading and writing capacities. *'I went to the academic teaching and learning unit offered by the university, and they showed me a timetable for academic workshops they offered and also the name of [an] academic for me to work with. Since then, I have made myself attend academic*

workshops. I followed the advice and suggestions from the academic learning advisor on prac-
tising my reading and writing skills to do my reading and writing more effectively and efficiently.
I received two Credits and two Distinctions for my first semester's subjects. My belief in my own
work returned, and I continued the hard work. By the end of the second semester, I received
three Distinctions and one High Distinction!'

Your performance accomplishments have also been shown to be the most potent source of efficacy belief. That is, if you achieve successful performance in your studies, you will also have a high level of self-efficacy – but this does not happen without putting in the hard work and energy to achieve your goals.

Vicarious experiences

As we can see from Hui's story, we learn from other experts' knowledge, and sometimes we draw from other people's experiences. Our vicarious experiences are developed based on observing other people's successful or unsuccessful experiences. Vicarious experience is also a potent source of self-efficacy. This is because we can learn from vicarious experience efficiently, rather than purely relying on trial and error for experience. For example, when we were children, we may have observed other people riding a bicycle. We may have watched and observed a parent or friend ride, had training wheels at first or were given tips of how to ride a bicycle without falling off. Ultimately though, we still need to ride the bicycle ourselves, but the observation, support and tips support a quick transition to learning how to ride a bike for young children. It is a very efficient way of learning. Instead of immediately jumping on a bike, constantly falling off and getting hurt, we learned from other people's experiences and understood the best support to help us.

These others from whose experience we learn might be experts, experienced people or peers. According to Bandura (1997), we develop our self-efficacy when we observe the successful performance of others, and at the same time, our self-efficacy decreases when we see others fail. However, the impact from these other people can be different, and your context of learning makes a differ-ence in the effects of vicarious experience. For example, we have observed students who learn very quickly from watching others' unsuccessful attempts and learning what works and what does not – turning this learning into success. Furthermore, we will increase our self-efficacy when we successfully observe experts or our lecturers modelling and demonstrating 'what works'. The reasons behind this are that you, as university students, have the confidence not to repeat errors, which can be transferred to your increased confidence in studying and practice.

On the other hand, when you are engaged in competition, observing peers' success can lead to an initial drop in self-efficacy if you do not as well, but can also serve as a motivational tool to support your self-efficacy to achieve higher results. You will be frequently communicating with both your teachers and classmates in your university life. Therefore, social and information sharing with teachers and peers can facilitate student resilience and adaptation.

Chan (2015) did research on vicarious experience among nursing students' learning journey. When nursing students acquire new clinical skills, they may not have been exposed to them before. For example, nursing students can perform an operation on models as practice, not actual patients, before starting their professional experience. When the nursing lecturers frame the vicarious experience of a medical incident in which the model commits errors, the nursing students' self-efficacy in performing clinical procedures is crucial. Chan's study found that providing instructions with positive and negative examples helped the nursing students enhance their self-efficacy. It was found to be cost-effective and efficient in training nursing students. Moreover, nursing lecturers keep track of any incidents involving nurses and nursing students. These track records can be used to provide instructions to students on how to avoid similar errors.

El-Abd and Chaaban (2021) studied the relationship between early childhood pre-service teachers' self-efficacy and their vicarious experience in classroom management. For early childhood teachers, it is essential to develop strong self-belief about their ability to manage children's behaviours, to minimise the distractions caused and help manage their children's learning process. The stronger the teachers' self-belief, the easier it is to manage their classrooms. This self-belief referred to the extent to which a teacher believes teachers can teach under whatever context, including the most challenging teaching context (El-Abd & Chaaban, 2021). Moreover, it is an essential factor related to student achievement motivation and classroom misbehaviour. Although teacher educators or academics have been found to influence student teachers' efficacy during the teacher training period, the peer learning experience has also been found helpful in student teachers' self-efficacy development. First-year undergraduate student Malcolm highlighted this to us in the example below:

STUDENT
EXAMPLE

Malcolm is a first-year undergraduate student. Like many other first-year students, he has joined a Facebook page formed by previous students enrolled in the course. There is a section on the Facebook page with a collection of tips offered by earlier students on how to maximise your time during your degree to ensure you are ready for success from year 1 of the degree. Malcolm explained that the social media site, run by the students, included practical information such as key contact people and services, but also the types of academic behaviours to model for sustained success. '*I found this section saved me a lot of time, and showed me a side of university life that I wasn't really aware of. It was so useful for me as a first-year student, plus there were so many people who really cared about not only their study, but also their future careers, it was really inspiring.*'

Malcolm also stated that he joined his university's student society and again explained that the value of having this organised by students offered many professional development opportunities. '*Our Student Society was useful in giving me opportunities to learn from other people. I didn't have to do too much, but it was great to get involved and see how the more experienced students dealt with organisational issues. I think it will help as I get closer to my own graduation.*'

Social persuasion and self-efficacy

Social persuasion is an intentional social influence on individuals to adopt an idea and conduct some action. For example, if you have a friend who performs well in their university life, there is a high chance you will also be influenced by your friend to believe you have the ability. It is particularly true if your friend is similar to you. Your parents can influence your belief as well. Suppose you grow up in a family that values and supports education. In that case, there is an excellent opportunity to develop your efficacy belief that you also have the capacities to do well or even better. If you are not in that situation, part of your drive will need to be from an internal motivation or through other social networks. That is, the social and emotional energy you have created can be used in developing your self-efficacy. Your peers' complimentary comments can help serve as cues concerning your capabilities. There are two persuasion routes (the central and peripheral routes) to describe your peers' comments. For example, your peers think you are a good essay writer, this is validated as you score well on essay style tasks. However, the peripheral route is usually superficial with the emotional involvement of your peers (Petty & Cacioppo, 1986). Moreover, if you are not motivated, you will rely more on the peripheral cues, such as a 'well done' email from your peers, to gain self-confidence. On the other hand, if you are highly motivated and can process the information, you will likely choose the central route to persuasion to build your self-efficacy.

In the last section, we discussed the value of 'observation' in the evaluation of vicarious experiences. It has been noted that observation also has a role with regard to social persuasion (Nob, 2021). The message source in social persuasion can come from peers, parents, families, academic lecturers, and all of these can contribute to your development of self-efficacy during your studies. Nob's innovative research separated these messages or the sources of persuasion by looking into the 'source credibility' of the peripheral cues. What is source credibility?

It refers to the trustworthiness of the source. In going through the Facebook page, Malcolm trusted and benefited from the credibility of the sources. As he knew the Facebook page was created by current and former students, the page held more validation in his eyes. Do you have a favourite website that you go to for tips on hobbies you are interested in (e.g. we use IMDb when deciding if we want to watch a movie or not)? This is an example of your willingness to receive persuasion from what you consider to be a highly credible source.

Most university students are supported to shape their ideas and judgement on discriminating persuasive messages according to the quality of the source – those that are more credible (e.g. references from peer-reviewed academic journals, academic lecture notes and lecturers' comments) and the less credible ones (e.g. a YouTube, generalist websites or a peer's comments). As you might imagine, it has been found that social persuasion from high credibility sources has higher self-efficacy than low credibility sources (Nob, 2021). Below we share some common examples of the social persuasion you might receive and how to make the best use of it to develop your self-efficacy.

STUDENT EXAMPLE

Riley had only just started her master's degree two months ago when we interviewed her, hence she is a first-year postgraduate student. One of her first assessment tasks was to work in groups to complete an investigating project, including a presentation, and writing a final report based upon their investigation. Riley indicated that her prior experience supported this process: '*I have been working full time since I graduated with my first degree, but that was quite a few years ago now. While working, I have been collaborating with other colleagues all the time, so doing group work is not strange to me. I enjoy group work actually, and usually find two heads are better than one! I will admit though sometimes group work can be difficult because we have to assign different roles to complete the task and sometimes this is challenging to bring it all together within different schedules and lives, but it sure does make the task easier when you are on the page and support each other.*'

Riley continued: '*When I was working full-time I found group projects helped me to develop many skills and high self-beliefs. In the workplace, "success" usually depended on an achieved outcome, something to work towards; there was usually a proper structure to the project design. I enjoy working in a collaborative group project because I can share my skills with my peers, and at the same time, I can learn new skills as well. I found the same thinking worked at university too. For example, in that first assessment task, when we broke the complex tasks into parts and steps, we learnt each other's expertise areas. I took on the "group leader" as I had strong planning and time management skills based on my prior work experience. The other member took on the "editor role" as they had more recent academic experience than I did and made sure the entire assessment came together. Throughout the process we worked on individual sections, giving and receiving feedback from each other. The sort of feedback can be the most difficult … and fun part of [a] successful group. Sometimes those challenging discussions are so fruitful. While challenging each other, we researched through different sources and found effective ways to express our own voices and perspectives. In the end, we produced a meaningful assessment through teamwork and collaboration to achieve our group goals.'*

Riley's case shows an excellent example of group work. However, as we all know, sometimes teamwork does not go as smoothly as we would like! When this occurs, how to assess your individual competence fairly across all group members is challenging. Much of your work is currently evaluated based upon the whole team's work outcome. However, even when a group receives an excellent mark, this does not mean all members have completed the group work evenly. Sometimes, working with other peers, who have different levels of competence to yours, can be stressful. This then requires the use of self and peer assessment in terms of teamwork. Riley's example shows that many students value using these techniques positively, as self and peer assessment can foster your learning by developing your critical thinking skills, self-regulation and problem skills (Planas-Lladó et al., 2021).

But how to evaluate teamwork? One widely used scale is the Comprehensive Assessment of Team Member Effectiveness (CATME) (Ohland et al., 2012). This tool has been used to assess how students contribute to teamwork and the ways they work with each other. Other peer evaluation methods have also been developed to analyse team members' contributions once the group activity is completed, with the notion being that the students who have done a significant and outstanding job in the activity should be rewarded with a higher mark – but obviously this will depend on your subject's lecturer.

STUDENT
EXAMPLE

Belinda is a third-year undergraduate student who has a very different view towards group work than Riley. *'To be honest, I don't favour group work. Instead of working in groups, I prefer to work independently. I find there is a lot of extra time and effort required for group work and I don't have much time to spare! It's really difficult to assign tasks equally too, and I find I end up having to be the leader of the group and have to do most of the work to make sure the group work is a good quality … In my opinion, group work should also be assessed by group members, making realistic calls on who contributed to the quality of the work, but I've actually never seen this done well.'*

Belinda raises some fair points about group work, and to evaluate and assess others' work, you must have strong communication skills. This requires you to listen, observe and provide constructive feedback to others. The factor of social persuasion has been considered an essential contributor to building our self-efficacy in group work. The evaluation feedback you offer is critical to helping your group members work collaboratively on tasks. However, negative feedback or competitive comments will cause some group members to lose self-esteem and contribute as little as they can. Therefore, understand that you will have positive and negative experiences when you engage in group work at a university level. Not all people have the same goals and dedication to their studies. We recommend that establishing strong communication between members from a very early stage is really important and having clear expectations of each other will support successful completion of tasks.

Physiological reactions

Why we respond to social persuasion differently relates to our physiological reactions. Each of us exhibits different psychophysiological responses to stimuli based upon our explicit and implicit evaluation of the information and the source it came from (Cornick & Blascovich, 2017). During the learning process, individuals with increased self-awareness should perceive increased demands more favourably compared to others with lower self-awareness. Evaluating situational needs and personal resources is related to physiological reactions. If we have more significant resources to complete a task, we will exhibit positive physiological responses; on the contrary, if we do not have enough resources, our physiological reactions will be negative. Moreover, if we feel challenged or threatened, our physiological responses will include physical responses such as higher heart rates and sweating. Therefore, we produce physiological reactions when we are overly challenged during our academic performance journey.

STUDENT EXAMPLE

Therese is a fourth-year undergraduate student. She has almost finished her degree, and she shared her thoughts on undergraduate students' reactions to negative feedback in group work.

'Yes, almost everyone has gone through group work, and sometimes the lecturers will group us randomly. This means we could end up with someone we did not know much before. Sometimes, it was a great experience as it forced us to get to know other people and develop ... new friendship. However, sometimes we can be grouped with other students you know you will have issues with ... Some of these people could be a bit ... critical and tricky to work with.' Therese laughed and continued, *'They appear to get stressed really quickly and insist to be the*

"leader" of the team and like the project to be conducted "their way". Well ... it could be stressful for an easy-going person like me. The comments that came from them could be quite negative and daunting and stressful to be honest! They made you doubt your work and your abilities to complete the task.

'My strategy to work with these people is pretty straightforward. I look at myself first, think about the things I am good at and share this with the group. I let my group members know my strengths and what I can contribute within the scheduled time to get the task done. I also make sure we make a chart of tasks so we can be clear about who does what, then ... get on with it!

Therese actually has a very realistic and considered way of dealing with group work. She takes the physiological reaction of stress, her peers' and her own, and uses practical internal strategies to consider how she can get the task done. If, like Therese, you can develop similar strategies to deal with stressful situations during your university studies, you will find you lessen your own physiological reactions immensely, which will ultimately be good for your own health.

In the above sections, we have discussed the four components of developing our self-efficacy, including performance accomplishments, vicarious experiences, social persuasion and physiological reactions. We have also suggested some strategies in helping you understand the interactive relationship between the four components and self-efficacy.

Developing self-improvement skills

We discussed the importance of self-efficacy in developing our mental energy in the previous sections of the chapter. Along with understanding our self-efficacy and relationships with peers, academic and other source information, we will discuss and demonstrate how to develop our self-improvement skills during university studying.

As Kanwal Ameen (2013) found in her case study on personality development and communication skills, self-development refers to developing individual characteristics such as their behaviour, attitude, mindset, and way of perceiving things and seeing the world.

Self-improvement skills include the following critical abilities: problem solving, decision making, mental skills and creative thinking. By working on these essential skills, you will enhance your self-improvement skills. Problem solving includes logical structure, understanding the meaning of the language expression, making a judgement and determining what to view and use. Decision making utilises analytical skills to understand meaning and situations to assess the pros and cons of potential outcomes. In addition, you also consider the consequences of actions. Mental abilities include cognitive behaviour, improved memory and analytical capabilities. Creative thinking has a high level of flexibility, enhancing potential and bringing originality.

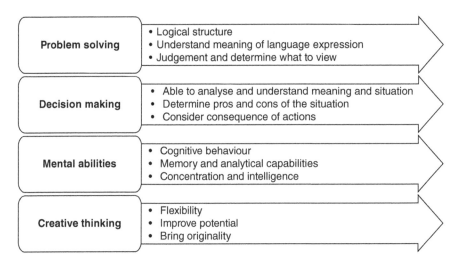

Figure 9.3   Four areas of self-improvement skills

We will now outline three primary areas in which self-improvement can support the building of mental energy: (a) communication and thinking skills, (b) mental ability and (c) creative thinking and mental models.

Communication and thinking skills

We have learned that communication and thinking skills are crucial for success-ful performance in individual and group work in our daily activities in university (Mahdy & Zaghloul, 2020). Therefore, it is necessary to ensure all university students are equipped with powerful mental energy and the right tools to acquire communication and thinking skills as they progress through their aca-demic journey. Communication and thinking skills are essential in developing your self-efficacy and consequently your judgement regarding your belief and capabilities to perform academically.

Communication and thinking skills are inseparable. Communication provides you opportunities to share and evaluate concepts and ideas. Thinking abilities allow you to focus on your mental activities to analyse information using logic and reason in a critical manner. Therefore, developing communication and think-ing skills helps you establish your confidence in your capabilities and performance and increases your self-efficacy.

When we discuss mental energy, we refer to the soft skills other than academic working skills; you will need these skills to speak publicly and tactfully, manage your team and present your work. They include effective communication, problem solving, logical thinking skills, listening skills and readiness to change and a sense of flexibility. In addition, thinking skills can help you differentiate what is right and wrong, have better relationships with others and develop your creativity and imagination to achieve personal and interpersonal goals.

STUDENT EXAMPLE

David is an international student currently in his second-year postgraduate degree. When asked to share his problem-solving strategies, he said: *'As an international student, I need to develop a sign of powerful courage to speak publicly and express freely about my opinion. English is not my native language, so I have had to rely on my thinking skills to express myself in group discussion … Yes, I consider myself a quiet contributor, but my peers respected me because I often came up with great ideas in group discussions … I listen carefully and try to summarise their ideas together while I was listening. Sometimes I have to take a note to record the important ideas I found from the conversation. It gave me a good chance to reflect and find a better way … if there is any.'*

David raises a wonderful point about thinking skills, which is to be an expert listener. There are times when we are 'waiting to speak' and may not actually take the time to listen properly. But as David suggests, learning how to listen carefully and then turn that into a productive outcome (for David this was a summary of the group's discussion) allowed him to share high level communication skills. Therefore, if you are not a 'vocal' person, using David's strategy to listen wisely will still allow you to contribute with your peers in a way that will certainly help their and your own academic development. With effective communication and thinking skills, you are equipped to analyse what other people, including your peers and academics, are saying and understand the correct meaning of the context of their discussion, in turn, impacting better decision making. In addition, you have the skills to properly analyse the situation by considering all the pros and cons to make the final decision.

Mental ability

Mental ability or intelligence refers to the skills that enable people to accomplish their daily activities (Mahdy & Zaghloul, 2020). Mental capability can be developed in combination with communication and thinking skills. One's mental ability includes such characteristics as the ability for critical thinking and the capacity for purposeful, self-regulatory judgement resulting in interpretation, analysis, evaluation and inference of events. It also involves higher-order cognitive skills in the activities of university students, such as their academic performance and the ability to cope with life events (Liu et al., 2021). University students with high mental ability will promote self-learning and have high degrees of success in training (Burkolter & Kluge, 2012). Our mental ability is a strong predictor of performance and correlates with our cognitive behaviours, motivation and intellectual abilities. Moreover, our mental ability is related to our personality traits as well.

STUDENT
EXAMPLE

Wayne just started his postgraduate degree. Considering himself to have reasonable high mental ability, he commented, '*I hadn't really thought about my mental abilities! But I guess from a young age I noticed that I did have high intelligence in particular areas, such as spatial orientation. Something I was drawn to with my first degree and I have been working in civil engineering for the last few years and now coming back to do a Master of Architecture, as I am really passionate and interested in speculating about the future of our urban environments … I guess another "intelligence" is the ability to sit and work for long periods by myself and maintain that "focus", to read deeply and widely and think about the implications of my studies for working towards my goals.*'

Wayne touches upon differing kinds of mental abilities in his description. Firstly, the ability for critical thinking, as he suggests, about urban environments. As authors of this book, we must admit that when we enter an urban environment, our first thoughts don't turn to architectural engineering, yet the way Wayne's mind works, clearly he does! Therefore acknowledging what motivates and stimulates you to think critically about a topic will help determine pathways of study and specialist areas of learning. Secondly, Wayne also spoke of the ability to focus for long periods of time. If you have not studied for some time or are not used to prolonged periods of intense study, make sure you work your way up to this goal. It may mean that you need to build in special routines or allocated times for study, but finding a way to have specific focus time will support your mental functioning.

Creative thinking and mental models

More so than in the school sector, university students must develop strong creative thinking skills during their studying journey. Your lecturers will tend to provide you with the knowledge, but the application and explanation of that knowledge is usually dependent on your own creativity thought processes. This is particularly important to research students who are attempting to discover new knowledge, such as master's or doctorate candidates. Studies (e.g. Barrett et al., 2013) have indicated that mental models represent a particular form of knowledge that contributes to performance on creative problem-solving tasks. Thus, for research students, to fill the gap in human knowledge via innovative research requires creative thinking and problem-solving skills.

Creative thinking plays a significant role in contributing to problem solving. Barrett et al. (2013) said there are two kinds of mechanisms in creative problem solving: firstly, inducing adjustments in ideas to improve their workability, and secondly, influencing people's basic understanding of the problem. Our understanding of problems is the first step to creative thinking, no matter which kind. Framing the problem, employing the concepts and then conceptualising the required actions are also closely related to developing our creative thinking skills. Creative thinking is correlated with our mental abilities and mental models to understand the complexity of a problem.

STUDENT EXAMPLE

Brooke is a second-year research student in the field of engineering. During her first milestone stage, she learned to work on her research questions and solve them by using various research methods. *'After a year of studying, I realised the importance of being a research student: it is not just completing a series of assessments to be marked or attending workshops. The important part of being a research student is understanding our research areas in-depth and finding out a gap in human knowledge that we can answer or fill in after our research journey. During the first year, I had to use my creative thinking skills in relation to developing my research questions and evaluate the research problems for quality, originality and elegance.*

'I have found some useful creative thinking strategies. Firstly, I found the use of mind maps useful. It helped me organise my thoughts and existing knowledge about the areas of my study. Using mind maps also helped me brainstorm my ideas for future practice and share my ideas clearly with my supervisors. Other strategies included developing self-confidence and challenging myself to experiment with ideas about thinking.'

As can be seen in the above example from Brooke, in order to stimulate her creative thinking, she used the strategy of mind maps. She was then able to share these ideas with her supervisors in order to support her thinking processes. When we need to create something new, we need to think about what processes stimulate our thinking – therefore find strategies that work for you.

In summary, in this chapter, we have discussed how to build our mental energy to maintain our wellbeing. Vital mental energy building equips us with firm beliefs about our abilities in relation to academic performance and develops new skills for a future career. This process is related to our physical energy and emotional energy. With high mental energy, we can have high problem-solving and thinking skills. In addition, it also helps us with proper decision making and coming up with creative thinking and problem-solving strategies.

Mapping your journey to success

- It is essential to build your mental energy for successful university life and to maintain your wellbeing throughout and beyond university.
- Developing mental energy also means working on your self-efficacy levels.
- Mental energy production can help you stick to your goals and help you reach the results you desire.
- Mental energy helps us to stay calm when working with challenging issues.
- Most importantly, developing mental energy provides opportunities to learn new skills, such as problem solving and creative thinking skills.

Recommended activities

Please reflect on your self-efficacy levels and look into how to improve your self-skills through the four areas: problem solving, decision making, mental skills and creative thinking. Finally, please complete the relevant sections of Appendix B.

10

Building spiritual energy and setting your goals

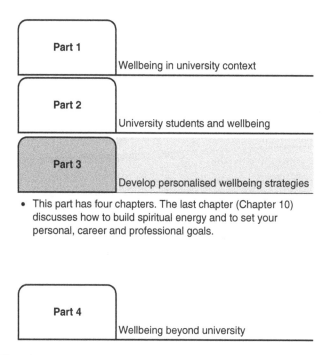

Figure 10.1   Chapter summary

We introduced spiritual energy in Chapter 2, and described how it comes from a connection to deeply held values and a purpose beyond ourselves, as it supports us with passion, commitment, integrity and honesty. Developing your spiritual energy can be seen as a devotion to your purpose, the discovery of which will serve as a foundation for future goals and achievement. It is a rich source of renewal, emotionally and spiritually, and it can undoubtedly provide a profound source of meaning and deep satisfaction.

Most university students, particularly school leavers, are still making sense of their goals, including their personal goals, academic goals and professional goals. You have set certain goals by choosing the particular discipline you are studying; doing a degree can take three to seven years to complete. Some of you may even change your discipline area during your studies. Developing spiritual energy is a long-term commitment, not just necessary in the first semester or the first year of your degree. It could be beyond university life. Spiritual energy is the most powerful energy in developing our resilience; it is the power source for our motivation, perseverance and direction.

Consider the following scenarios:

- You started your degree over a year ago, and this is the first time you have a placement in your profession. After two months of working in the profession, you wonder if this is the career you will envision yourself doing after your graduation.
- Since childhood, you were asked to follow your parents' pathway. To help you achieve what you will become, your family help you set your academic and professional goals. Now you are close to graduation. You are unsure what you would like to do after your studies are finished. Do you still have the same goals as facilitated by your family?
- Because of a change in circumstance, you have had to change your career pathway. It might be for practical reasons, with life and family commitments, you are too busy and often you have to work and be away from your family temporarily, which you are not comfortable with. But you are unsure if it is worth studying again.

This chapter will discuss the meaning of our study and career pathways. We will then also work on setting your goals and planning, including academic goals, personal goals and professional goals. Before we do that, we will again emphasise the development and growth of our energy. The strength of our energy is powered spiritually, mentally, emotionally and physically (see Figure 10.2).

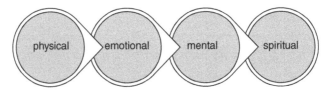

Figure 10.2   Strength of energy

The power of the human spirit is known for its complexities within human development, as its characteristics lie in the complex pattern of the interactions of cognitive abstraction, symbolic language, and self- and interpersonal awareness

(Cupit, 2007). To understand spiritual energy, one way to consider these compo-nent elements is to analyse how they interrelate, which can be considered through dynamic systems theory.

Dynamic systems theory studies a human's development behaviours. During periods of development, each of us starts to understand ourselves as having a meaning or purpose for being. This may come when considering our roles within long-term rela-tionships, general living requirements, ethical moments, and religion contemplation. Thus, our spiritual energy comes from various components, and it can persist despite component change and self-organised behaviours. It helps us know our-selves by name and separate from others and remain ourselves despite change. With spiritual energy, we create a situation around ourselves that makes us someone we want to be, and these creations are genuinely unique to ourselves. For example, you may be studying the same discipline as your classmates, yet your unique rea-sons and motivation for being there are all your own. The compelling sources and energy that drive you are derived from your deeply held values and a purpose beyond self-interest. It creates a destination for us and promotes our desire to invest energy in a particular activity or goal. We are undoubtedly becoming fully engaged when we care and feel what we are doing really matters to us.

While it is difficult to measure our spiritual energy, we would like you to read the following questions and score yourselves on a scale from 1, the lowest, to 10, the highest.

- How excited are you getting up to go to university and work in the morning?
- How much do you enjoy studying and look forward to becoming an expert in your disciplinary field after graduation?
- Are your university studies guided by a deeply held set of values, such as kindness, honesty, authenticity, or respect?
- How confident do you feel that you have the ability and willingness to contribute to your chosen field of work?

If you answer higher than 9 for each of the questions, it suggests that you have developed a powerful sense of purpose and meaning to what you are studying. On the contrary, if your answers are lower than 7 for each of these questions, it shows you are going through some unsteady motions of developing your spiri-tual energy. Keep in mind that your evolution within your career will ebb and flow, so developing a consistent approach to your spiritual energy will support consistent levels of academic production. Constantly, we ask ourselves the meaning of our lives and are questioned in what we are doing and by new chal-lenging responsibilities. There are, however, many levels of spiritual development through physical, emotional and mental development.

Unfortunately, the journey of university studying can be bumpy for most of us. Sometimes, the challenges even push us to the brink of giving up, being 'overwhelmed' by the volume of work involved. We call upon our potential and persistence and create our work's meaning. We celebrate and treasure our every accomplishment, but the sense of accomplishment does not just end with a celebration. Many of us are not satisfied with being ordinary in our studies or work, and we want to be better and the best we can possibly be. This process of being better causes a reality wherein we feel too busy to search for a deeper purpose. We walk through our daily life and meet our obligations without reaching for something more meaningful.

Dewey (1933) described 'reflection' or 'reflective thinking' as 'active, persistent, and careful consideration of any belief or supposed form of knowledge in light of grounds that support it and future conclusions to which it tends' (p. 7). Geng et al. (2019) also state that reflective practice can provide essential insights into how personal beliefs and life experiences act as a lens or filter for framing and understanding experience. Reflective thinking does not mean that you are simply writing down what you have done in the past or what you would like to do in the future. Instead, it is related to your understanding of what you did and what would be significant.

So what is reflective thinking? It is not a complicated process; however, it does require a certain level of in-depth critical thinking and reflection.

Firstly, reflective thinking requires us to keep a journal of our experience, and then it will be used as a basis to think about and make sense of what we have written. For example, while in class, you have recorded your lecture notes while your lecturers are delivering content details. The notes can be used to review the content yourself after the class, especially when you cannot remember the exact content, but these provide you with a chance to recall the content and truly understand it. It is a representative example we use commonly to achieve a productive learning outcome while studying. However, reflective thinking does not just refer to reviewing, it also includes critical thinking.

According to the Foundation of Critical Thinking (2021):

> Critical thinking is the intellectually disciplined process of actively and skilfully conceptualising, applying, analysing, synthesising, and evaluating information gathered from, or generated by, observation, experience, reflection, reasoning, or communication, as a guide to belief and action. Its exemplary form is based on universal intellectual values that transcend subject matter divisions: clarity, accuracy, precision, consistency, relevance, sound evidence, good reasons, depth, breadth, and fairness.

Critical thinking can provide us with a more in-depth understanding and clearer picture of what we are learning and help us make sense of the learning content and then add it to our meaning-making process.

STUDENT
EXAMPLE

Carmen was an international student who came to Australia to study as a primary school teacher. Carmen's home country was Timor Leste. In her final year of learning, she was asked to write a reflection essay about her understanding of a critical issue in education. Carmen shared a very in-depth reflection about her knowledge of the differences in teaching Attention Deficit Hyperactivity Disorder (ADHD) students between Timor and Australia to promote ADHD students' rights to live and get a good education:

'I used to think that students with special needs did not have to go to school.... In Timor, not only are children with ADHD not diagnosed, but also they do not get the necessary medication. It is sad to know that all children who have disabilities cannot go to school and get access to education......

After doing the observation during my placement in Australia, of this much I am sure, that students who are not diagnosed with ADHD can show the same types of behaviour as the ADHD students.'

Carmen's reflection is a combination of her expectation and her lived experience. Initially, Carmen did not know how to teach ADHD students, but after her placement and degree, she has developed a thorough understanding and knowledge about how to teach these students. Carmen's reflection has also changed her career pathways. Now she is an outstanding teacher in her home country and a devoted researcher, advocating how to teach ADHD students.

Similarly, many university students have used reflective thinking to set their academic, personal and professional goals. In the following sections, we will discuss using reflective thinking and spiritual energy to build goals.

Setting goals can help you reach the objectives you seek. Kissam (2021) says, 'goals, just like many other tools, are one of the compasses that students can use to take that next step in life confidently, no matter the circumstance. Setting attainable benchmarks is a great way to stay on track while working toward a larger target.' According to Price-Mitchell (2018), setting goals can boost academic performance and increase your self-confidence, motivation levels and autonomy to do things independently.

Set your academic goals

Firstly, we will discuss how to set your academic goals. We will show you what academic goals are, the differences among your academic goals, and finally, how to set realistic academic goals.

Understand academic goals

Many of us interchangeably discuss academic goals and professional/career goals. In fact, they are closely related, and they often go hand-in-hand. The obvious reasons behind this include the fact that our chosen career pathway is closely related to the level and type of education and training we have chosen. For example, if you want to be a mechanical engineer, you will need to study for a degree in engineering. That said, our academic goals are typically set and completed within a timeline, from three years to 10 years; however our career and professional goals can take longer, often articulated with short- and long-term goals as well as broad objectives.

Typically, academic goals have different levels, depending on the work skills required by the future job. For example, if you want to be a tradesperson, such as a welder, electrician, or auto mechanic, you will have vocational skills training, which is not a lengthy formal education.

Many comprehensive universities have vocational skills training, associate's degrees, bachelor's degrees and research degrees. Many universities use associate degrees or vocational skills as degree pathways to do higher education degrees. An associate degree is usually a one- or two-year degree in which students can earn a degree in a field that allows for higher levels of professional options and can be used as a steppingstone or bridging pathway to a bachelor's (three or four years) educational degree. A bachelor's degree comprises full- or part-time studies in a university, and it is the first step in the ladder of formal higher education. It usually includes general skills studies with a concentrated focus on a dedicated work requirement. A bachelor's degree can pursue a broader range of academic disciplines. A master's degree is the next level up from a bachelor's degree and requires a student to complete an additional year or two of formal higher education. A master's degree has a focused professional and highly specialised line of work or high level business management roles. Some master's degrees include research work, including presentation of research projects. Finally, a doctorate is usually the pinnacle of higher education. It requires three years or more of education to complete a dissertation and in-depth research project presentation. A doctorate degree is an essential requirement for university academic employment.

Now we have shown you the levels of academic degrees in universities, you may have a clear understanding about the degrees available. Depending on the area and discipline in which you would like to work in the future, you will set different academic goals.

Differences among academic goals

No matter what degree you would like to achieve, there are differences between common academic goals and specific related academic goals. This section will tap into their differences to better understand academic goals. The specific academic goals usually include the following areas.

Firstly, course completion is a common academic goal. For all students the completion of a degree is a significant achievement. For some students, there may have been significant challenges during the completion of your degree, which can in turn make completion that more rewarding. For example, one of the authors of this book completed a PhD whilst caring for two young children which made the final result even more fulfilling. Whether you complete the course within a standard full-time timetable or an extended part-time schedule, course completion for academic achievement is an important goal.

Secondly, achieving a certain level of grade point average is another common academic goal. Grade point average (GPA) reflects what you, as a student, have earned in the academic degree. GPA can qualify students for financial scholarship grants and certainly be used for future job employment. In addition, GPA is also an essential factor in determining whether a student can enter certain specific disciplines or be admitted into another studying programme, such as a master's or research degree.

Finally, another common academic goal is the completion of a research project. It is particularly important for research students or postgraduate degree students to pursue specialised professions and work with experts in the field of interest. It can help graduates find other career pathways such as research assistant, laboratory assistant or directors in an academic field, instead of professional disciplinary areas.

Indeed, common academic goals apply to every university student. There are, however, some other academic goals, viewed more specifically for some students.

These students are first completing a degree by using the standard time schedules or a fast-track schedule. Depending on your career pathways, family and financial commitment or community needs, you may choose to complete your degree within the standard schedule or complete it during a shortened timeline. For example, the state of Victoria, Australia, needs thousands of qualified three-year kindergarten teachers to be employed by the end of 2029 when the three-year kindergarten project starts. These changes need a high level of collaboration between universities and governments to provide a fast-track schedule for potential early childhood educators to complete the degree in a short period of time. For some graduates, taking this opportunity to be offered a scholarship and complete a degree before starting their employment is an academic goal.

Secondly, academic goals vary if you aim to achieve different outcomes for your family and careers. We have seen many students make a career change within five years after they graduate in their first degree or even in the middle of their studying. This is very common, and factors influencing decisions can come from family changes. Once we met a student who had to transfer to another area because she had to move to another city with her family. The university in the new city did not have the course she was currently studying. Other examples include the first few semesters' experiences you have had so far. For instance, we have another student currently studying to be a secondary school teacher. However, after conducting her first placement and professional experience as a pre-service secondary school teacher, she decided that she was not suited for teaching in secondary school. Instead, she wanted to transfer to be a primary school teacher, as, after the placement, she realised she enjoyed working with younger students. Your experience during practical experience can be a major contributing factor to your academic goals and direction. Other factors can include a basic interest change also. It is not very common, but some university students change their career interests after a year or a few months of studying. It happens more often in research degrees. Some university students entered the research journey without realising quite what was entailed within the research journey and potentially the levels of independent work and commitment required. Rigler et al. (2017) report that the attrition rates in doctorate candidatures are as much as 50% for face-to-face research programmes and 50–70% for online programmes. These high attrition rates do not represent the lack of training or confidence of doctorate candidates, but might include factors such as candidate socialisation and support systems, candidate preparedness, and financial considerations.

It is absolutely fine to set your own academic goals, as in the end, it is your academic journey, and you are aware of what energy you can put into the work and how much time you can commit to your studying. In the next section, we will show you how to use your spiritual energy to set realistic academic goals.

How to set realistic academic goals

For many undergraduate school leavers, coming from a high school context to a university environment can be challenging. It will mainly rely on you to work out your schedule, finance and career pathways. This can be exciting but also daunting in face of the realities. Not many school leavers clearly understand how many hours a subject can take you per week or per semester, and not many of you know how long it will take you to write an essay, prepare for exams, or do group work. It takes time and experience to understand your energy, strength and weakness.

When we are setting our goals, the first important task is to know who we are, who we would like to become and, most importantly, what difficulties will influence our actions and outcomes. You may also think about what you will accomplish short-term and long-term and what skills you will learn and master. Other than that, you will be aware that your goals need to be aligned with your personality, lifestyle and values/spirituality.

Universities offer their students assistance in setting realistic academic goals. We will now consider an article by Burka (2003), who highlights student experiences during an English class when enrolled at the University of Texas to consider how impactful students' goals are on success. In the article Burka (2003: 92) states, 'the University of Texas has more going for it today than ever before: unregulated tuition, unfettered diversity, smart students, winning sports teams, first-class cultural facilities, academic programs with buzz, and finally, an administration with realistic goals. So why isn't it living up to its potential? Good question.' Although this story is about UT's inability to achieve greatness in the way they expected, there were a number of identified barriers to students' success: lack of money, lack of self-satisfaction and lack of values and aims from the students. Burka attended a class for an hour and a quarter and found that the 37 students only listened and took notes, but they did not ask many questions. Burka pondered that it could have been problematic content that prompted the lack of questions (the class was about the poet Walt Whitman, who was the first poet to break free of rhyming). The lecturer helped the students feel the power of the idea of democracy. Burka also mentioned that 37 students in a class is very small compared to the average class in a large lecture hall. When interviewing the lecturer they stated,

> Students came into the class anticipating it would be boring and tough. They had had bad experiences with English in high school. They thought they wouldn't enjoy the reading, and they didn't like subjective grading. If the university didn't require it, ninety-five per cent wouldn't take it. My challenge was to convert them to the idea that reading literature can be enormously fun and challenging in a good way. (p. 92)

As in Burka's visit to the University of Texas, many universities require their first-year students to participate in lectures or seminars on introductory subjects in relation to their degree with an emphasis on unpacking preconceived notions about what they need to learn. Students are asked to fulfil an essay requirement demonstrating their understanding or a certain level of discussion and reflection. You are invited to answer some questions, analyse and argue for your opinions and statement. This is the first part of undergraduate studies, which helps to develop your spiritual energy.

Steps in setting your academic goals

Setting realistic academic goals also means creating meaningful goals. Ultimately it is an individual process, one that requires you to dwell on your own inner thoughts and values. It is related to your own personality, motivation and even personal or career goals. In this section, we refer to the SMART goals system:

- Specific
- Measurable
- Achievable
- Relevant
- Time-bound

Look at the following two goals:

One: I will attend all my classes and study for at least three hours a day after university to achieve a 4.0 GPA or higher by the end of next semester.

Two: I will attend my classes and study one and half hours to two hours a day at night after family commitments. I will achieve a 3.5 GPA by the end of next semester, then aim at a 4.0 GPA by the end of the semester after next.

Taking the two goals into comparison, we can find both goals are worked out well, although they are set slightly differently. Compared to the first goal, the second goal also aims at a 4.0 GPA and attending all the classes. Both goals are unique, with specific hours and measurable GPA goals. They, however, have slight differences, including achievable goals, such as reaching a 4.0 GPA in different timelines. The first goal is set for one semester. In contrast, the second goal is set for two semesters. The goal maker of the second goal also has family commitments, which could be relevant to that student, while the first goal maker can commit to three hours per day. No matter what goals you set, you should always look to the SMART criteria and make realistic goals.

STUDENT EXAMPLE

Bill was a fourth-year undergraduate student when we talked with him about his spiritual energy building and setting his academic goals.

'*I had my first degree in technologies, but after working as an IT specialist in the field for a while, I quickly realised that it was not a career pathway I wanted, it just didn't motivate me. I changed my career pathway and decided I wanted to be a teacher. It made me have to rethink a lot of my goals and how I wanted to achieve them.*'

Bill continues, '*When I got back to study I had to develop strategies to support me to be successful in my studies. In order to achieve a realistic academic goal, I set smaller goals, such as daily, weekly, and monthly goals, as well as the final goals for the year or a few years. I make them clear by writing them up and putting them next to where I can see them every day. I found it useful by reminding myself what goals I am aiming to achieve. It was not easy to get back into study, but having goals really helped.'*

Bill also spoke about how he maintained his spiritual energy whilst studying: *'I was always really into surfing, I find it to be a great meditation activity, I set the goal to go surfing multiple times a week to clear my head. During surfing, I could relax and concentrate more about my health and future. After my surf each time, I found myself more focused on my studying. As I was changing my academic goals during my career change I really needed to balance my move back into study. So having an outlet like surfing really helped so much.'*

Not every student will go through an experience like Bill's. However, his expertise provides us with a great example of how to set realistic academic goals and build spiritual energy through physical, emotional and mental energy. While the onus is on you to set your academic goals, we would like to share how you can plan those goals with the help of others.

Set academic goals with support from universities

We have shown you the many facilities offered by universities in previous chapters. As we discussed, universities also provide relevant support to help you set your academic goals by building your spiritual energy. This section will show you some practical activities or workshops you could consider participating in or attending at your own institution, if they are offered, and we also suggest some strategies shared by other successful students.

Almost every university has a teaching and learning unit which specialises in providing academic support to students and staff. For example, in a UK university a community of practice website offers LinkedIn Learning for all of its staff and students. On this website, you can access a varied range of video tutorials to help all currently enrolled students develop their learning goals. In addition, its Arena Centre holds regular events to support teaching, workshops and seminars to support and share best teaching and learning strategies.

STUDENT EXAMPLE

Catherine is a fourth-year undergraduate student who has been using academic skills support offered by her university. When asked what support she found most useful, Catherine said, *'My friends went to workshops on referencing, examination preparation, group work and oral presentation and found them useful; but I found the workshops that showed me how to think critically and ask critical questions to be the most useful.'*

(Continued)

She continued, '*The workshops helped me to develop the habit of asking questions about my studies ... especially the theoretical bits. This helped me go further into considering many perspectives, weighing my thoughts and finding an answer. I find it really useful to apply critical thinking to issues in certain contexts ... just always ask questions! I was lucky, I also had great lecturers who told me, "Do not stop asking questions!" So, I feel encouraged to keep reflecting and to be critical about what I am learning and to question what I read.'*

Support from universities can also help you practise reading, note-taking and writing during your academic studies. This is not just referring to copying information into the assignments. For example, many university assignments require you to read and write critically. Like Catherine, you can take notes to show connections between ideas and critically analyse your sources. Instead of copying, you can reflect on your own values and experiences and consider how they influence your own understanding of what you believe to be logical and reasonable. It can involve thinking and learning about policies and cultural and religious influences. Again, asking questions (and being confident to do so) is an effective way to think critically and explore connections between ideas. The critical analysis skills you develop in consultation with academic advisors can expand your thinking habits over time to become more aware of your discipline area's essential concepts and debates.

STUDENT EXAMPLE

Catherine went on to discuss a service provided by her university that supported her ability to think critically. '*When I was finding that my mind was not focused and I couldn't think as clearly as I wanted, I participated in meditation workshops. My university offered a lunchtime drop-in meditation session a few times a week. I found it really helped me regain my focus and think more clearly. Then, I could really focus on my studies again.'*

Utilising all of the facilities offered by your university, such as Catherine did, can help you maintain a sense of energy that can allow you to focus more effectively on your studies, especially during times of stress or when you feel not at your best.

Set your personal goals

The focus so far has been on academic goal setting and how to set realistic academic goals and that goals should be set with the characteristics of differing end goals in mind. Now we will go on to discuss some of the areas relating to personal attributes that support realistic personal goal setting.

Researching on personal goals

Unlike academic goals, personal goals are what you want to achieve for yourself in life, which can include family goals, business goals and lifestyle goals. This is related to achievement in life and goals set towards achieving them. It is again self-motivated and keeps you in a positive mood. Your personal goals can be short-term or long-term goals, depending on whether the goals can provide you with long-term direction and short-term motivation.

Some examples of personal goals include:

- New Year's resolutions

Many people use New Year's resolutions to continue (or begin) good practices, accomplish a personal goal and improve basic lifestyles at the start of a new year.

- Attending a gym every week

In Chapter 6, we have advocated that health is wealth, and regular exercise a week can reduce your risk of heart disease, obesity, diabetes, high blood pressure and depression. Setting a personal goal to attend a gym every week can help you maintain your health and wellbeing.

- Keeping a daily journal and stress management

Stress, whilst at times unavoidable, can have a negative impact on our health and lifestyle. Keeping a daily journal can be a helpful, therapeutic activity, and an easy way to track thoughts, ideas and release stress, which supports stress management.

- Volunteering in community engagement activities in a charity or non-profit organisation

It can be fun and meaningful to devote your time and energy to help those in need and to have an opportunity to meet new people, learn new skills and boost your résumé. Volunteer work can create meaningful community engagement opportunities and give us a sense of our community's needs.

- Being more organised!

Organisation means better management in the fields of time management and task management. Better time management can help you spend your time and day with clear aims and priorities. You can then organise your tasks based upon the priority task list you are working on to work effectively and enjoy your leisure time.

All these personal goals come from our background or our individual facets. These personal factors include our self-beliefs and cognitive skills and operationalised self-efficacy and adaptability (Burns et al., 2018). Chapter 9 showed you the critical role self-efficacy plays in mental energy building. In building self-efficacy, self factors can be considered within the personal factor domain. Bandura (1991) found self-factors represent the essential transitional steps between the primarily cognitive processes of self-factors to the active behavioural factors.

Different lives and different goals

Self-factors underpin self strategies, and they provide a strong foundation for self-beliefs, forethought, monitoring and management that guide and inform our goal setting. As discussed in previous chapters, students who have high self-efficacy can self-regulate in challenging the face of change, novelty and uncertainty to achieve their goals. Therefore, in this section, we will be looking into the self-factors such as age, gender, culture, as well as other factors that influence your studying journey.

We have provided 'lived experience' strategies throughout the book from successful university students and graduates. Their personal experiences are real and helpful. These stories come from the students who have different lived experience and differing backgrounds. Although they are all successful students, and the strategies can be applied to other students who have similar experiences, it is clear that some strategies can be better applied to certain students, dependent on social factors. For example, international students' strategies may be more beneficial among international students owing to their unique lived experience of moving from one cultural setting to another. To help set your personal goals, we will discuss the following factors (independent factors) and their impact on your personal goals.

Age

University students consist of school leavers and mature age students. We have discussed the possible stressors according to your age. For example, school leavers are on their way to completing their teenage period, and their life experiences mainly come from school settings. At the same time, mature age students have had life experience and work experience. Age differences can determine your ways of thinking, mindfulness and life needs. For example, mature students may already have families, elderly parents and young children to take care of. Mature age students' lives may have more 'moving components' than school leavers, and personal goals may differ. Regardless, both age groups will still have academic goals, however your personal goals may differ, which can impact on how you approach your studies. Therefore give consideration to how your current age impacts how you approach your university studies.

Gender

Gender is also another self-factor that may influence your personal goals. A few years ago, we researched gender stress in some particular professions and presented related papers at an international conference on diversity. In the same session with two other presenters, it was interesting to find some socially acknowledged gender-biased professions. For example, in education and nursing fields, females are the dominant gender, and males are more common in science and engineering.

Gender differences do not simply reflect on our physical appearance. They reflect on the ways of our lives. For example, Cocchiara and Bell (2009) found that women, in particular, are exposed to the following stressors: multiple roles, lack of career progress, and discrimination and stereotyping. Women also report higher stress levels relating to career achievement. On the other hand, research conducted in relation to male stress (Gyllensten & Palmer, 2005) acknowledged that men also experience gender-specific stressors. In particular, men are more concerned about their level of control at work and their achievement-oriented behaviour.

This difference causes many stresses and responses among male and female university students. A number of studies reviewed the gender differences in stress and found women tended to report higher levels than men, based on their exposure and response to stressors less likely encountered by men (Jick & Mitz, 1985; Nelson & Quick, 1985). The 2014 *Stress in America* survey consistently found that women report higher stress levels than men and are more likely to report physical and emotional symptoms associated with their stress (American Psychological Association, 2015). The stressors come from the role played by gender. Nelson and Burke's (2002) study examined the relationship between gender, work and health. Their framework included individual differences for gender, family dynamics and gender, and gendered intervention strategies for managing stress. Although there have been dramatic changes in family dynamics, women are still, in the main, responsible for domestic chores. At the same time, men are still considered the family's income earners. Furthermore, for example, women are more likely to take on family-related roles in their work life, such as nursing and teaching.

The stress response theory, developed by Horowitz (1976), has been used to understand how different genders react to stress: fight-or-flight in men or tend-and-befriend in women (Horowitz, 2001). While men report lower stress levels and are less likely to report anxiety symptoms, they are less likely to relieve or manage their stress effectively. They also tend to respond in a more immediate, reactive fashion. For example, Bird and Harris (1990) found that adolescent girls rely more heavily on their support networks when stressed, while adolescent boys typically engage in activities that involve aggression and physical release.

Therefore, women tend to be more socialised for interpersonal interaction and provide more social support to others (Brody, 1985; Eagly, 1987). In contrast, men do not use emotional display as much as women (Brody, 1985; Grossman & Wood, 1993). Consequently, women are more engaged in emotional regulation and focus more on feelings, while men regulate their emotions to a lesser extent (Kruml & Geddes, 2000). However, it was also noted that men could feel a greater sense of achievement when engaged in their work (Simpson & Stroh, 2004). It is important to note that whilst these historical research studies reflect gendered discourses, they do not necessarily reflect individuals. Rather, understand that your gender may impact your studies, but you are not confined by your gender. Be aware of how gender may impact your studies and use strategies that have been suggested in this book to support your spiritual energy to persevere and attain your academic and personal goals.

Cultural background

Globalised, multicultural and intercultural friendships exist in universities as a diverse community (Vaccarino et al., 2021). In this intercultural friendship, people from different cultures develop understandings towards and of each other, consequently promoting a healthy environment for diversity. Thus, developing intercultural friendships provides all university students with many benefits and advantages which may influence their personal goals. This is particularly true for international students who study abroad and need to build their social and emotional energy. Many studies have found that working with domestic students can be beneficial for international students' academic performance and sociocultural adaption (Vaccarino et al., 2021).

The factors which have been identified as influencers in developing intercultural friendship include an awareness of cultural differences, personality, communicative competence, proximity to host countries and frequency of contact, and support from universities (Liu et al., 2019). It is essential to point out that cultural differences and individuals' moral identities are closely related (Jia et al., 2019). It is known that coming to a shared understanding of the word 'culture' is a challenging process (Vaccarino et al., 2021), as 'culture' may have different meanings to different people. Coming to a shared understanding can make it difficult for intercultural friendship to develop. Cultural differences can be a barrier for international students to make friends with domestic students – even more so than individual differences (Zhou et al., 2008). Among cultural differences, the most frequently mentioned were cultural-emotional connectedness, which Volet and Ang (2012, p. 25) describe as, 'The students' perceptions of feeling more comfortable, thinking along the same wavelength, and sharing a similar communication style and sense of humour when interacting with peers from the same cultural background.'

As we know, communication with others who have similar cultural backgrounds can be relatively easy as we generally understand each other's communication cues and have a deep and complete understanding of the social context. Thus, this level of cultural-emotional connectedness enables us to maintain a sense of identity or moral identity within our social context. One of the critical aspects to developing this cultural-emotional connectedness is language. The lack of a common language can be a barrier that may prevent people from interacting and forming relationships. Therefore, language differences are related to the breadth and depth of discussion necessary for developing an intercultural relationship (Vaccarino et al., 2021). Many domestic students do not understand or communicate with international students because they do not speak the same language and are 'unable to utilise ground techniques to create common grounds for shared meaning' (God & Zhang, 2019, p. 320). The lack of interactions can negatively impact on international students' social development. Thus, one of the personal goals for international students could be to constantly work towards improving their language level to support high level communication with domestic students and thus to support social and emotional energy development. Also, it is a wonderful opportunity for domestic students to reach out to international students and demonstrate patience, kindness and the potential to expand your own networks and perspectives.

Socioeconomic background

University students come from different socioeconomic backgrounds; however, it is known that students from low socioeconomic backgrounds face more challenges with regard to retention and success than other students (Sadowski et al., 2018). Students' socioeconomic backgrounds are closely related to their preparedness for university, access to support and course/programme difficulties.

In research conducted by Karimshah et al. (2013), where over 1,000 undergraduate students participated in an online study, the authors identified that 'while most students experienced a combination of financial, relationship, mental and physical health stress, students from low SES backgrounds experienced more stressors as well as higher levels of stress' (p. 5). A large project, 'Effective teaching and support of students from low socioeconomic status backgrounds:

Resources for Australian higher education', was conducted. Practical advice for teachers and higher education policymakers/leaders, including resourcing and supporting low SES student teachers, has been proposed (Devlin, 2013). So, if you are a student from a low SES background, certainly you may face challenges beyond those of other students, and it is crucial you are aware of the resources available to support you in your studies. Find support from your government, look for scholarship opportunities and reach out to see what additional resources can be attained through your university. Ensure you set SMART goals that maintain high standards of yourself in terms of both academic and personal goals.

Set your personal goals with university support

When we talk about our personal goals, we also need to be 'realistic' in terms of understanding our backgrounds. For example, if you are a new international student, your first personal goal may not be to embed yourself in local customs and behaviours. You may need to start working on your language skills and building your intercultural friendships. Another example, if you are feeling run down and tired owing to a lack of physical energy, it is important to focus on developing good physical strength before you build your mental energy. As discussed before, ultimately your spiritual energy will be founded upon and draw from your physical, emotional and mental energy.

Thus, setting realistic personal goals for yourself is essential, as university campuses are a mix of various students from different, unique backgrounds. In relation to supporting university students' wellbeing, much research has found that social interactions are crucial for maintaining your physical, mental and social wellbeing (e.g. Ateca-Amestoy et al., 2013; Vowels et al., 2022). Thus, in relation to supporting university students, universities foster interaction opportunities. For example, many subjects have provided their students with intercultural skills to become globally minded. Your wellbeing can be positively influenced by engaging with diverse peers.

STUDENT EXAMPLE

As a second-year postgraduate student, Eve received the following support: *'This entire Master's has been a complex roller-coaster; there are two academics who have inspired me by being brilliant in their field, as well as being an amazing support for us students. They have been outstanding lecturers and have made their units enjoyable, relevant and accessible. I am not alone in feeling gratitude toward them. Many of my peers hold the same sentiments. I am currently listening to their recordings, and their manner, tone and profound knowledge of teaching definitely supported my learning.'*

Like Eve, the support for enhancing student success identified by students (Sadowski et al., 2018) includes consistency and transparency of delivery and a dedicated academic advisor and increased peer connections. So, it is important when you get an opportunity to give formal feedback about teaching staff, that you take the time to recognise the elements they do well and areas they can improve upon. They will be grateful for constructive feedback that will improve their own pedagogical practices. Universities will have student services departments, which we discussed in Chapter 4. You may also make use of these services in building your personal goals.

Set your professional goals

Finally, this chapter will discuss how to set your professional goals, as this is strongly related to your building of spiritual energy. We have discussed the differences between personal goals and academic goals and career or professional goals earlier in this chapter and learned career goals have been used to build your understanding of the meaning of your work.

Setting measurable professional goals will help you realise your success in your work, and they are related closely to your qualifications, degree(s) and other academic requirements or achievement. They are also tied into your academic and personal goals.

Connect professional goals with academic goals

When you are working on your goals, including academic and personal goals, you may also think beyond your academic goals in university and establish your professional and career goals. As we know, the final aim of why you are attending a university is often to get into your desired career. Thus, connecting your professional goals with your academic goals can provide you with a clear path to the future you want.

One such example is that of leadership. Leadership experience is vital in any professional career you go into. Thus, setting a goal to gain a leadership position and having leadership experience within a professional student club or organisation is beneficial to your future professional goal. By connecting them properly, you go beyond the generic goal of just attending an organisation. Instead, you are gaining experience for your future career.

Other goals include building strong connections in a mentorship programme. Being involved in a mentorship programme can help you learn from other people in your field. You can connect with professionals who can support your growth and development. This can build your skills, social network and strengths, and enhance your résumé.

Alex is finishing her postgraduate degree. As a mature age student, she had worked in the same profession she is studying in before she decided to attend further study in her postgraduate degree to further her career pathways.

'I wanted to continue my studies and felt I was at a stage of my career where I needed new challenges. I chose to focus on doctoral study, and my goal is to become an academic working in a university one day. I have developed a positive relationship with my potential PhD supervisors. I know I will need their support or approval to be admitted to my PhD. I have been sending my work to Dr. ... and we have been polishing my proposal to submit my application. I found it very helpful to get an understanding of what a PhD candidature looks like academically. Dr. ... also introduced me to the other current PhD students, and it broadens my view about academia.'

As we can see from Alex, she has definite goals beyond her current job role and has set a goal of attaining a doctoral qualification as well as moving into academia. Alex sees her current work and study as being pathways to a future career, which certainly shows growth and alignment within professional and academic goals.

Another very common goal you can set is to work in an internship within your chosen field. It is a great way to get your foot in the door in the career or the organisation in which you are dreaming of working. Furthermore, if you carefully connect your academic work with professional goals, you may consider volunteering or being an intern in the final year or years of your degree. In our experience, we have seen many of our graduates get jobs quickly by using this approach.

Connect professional goals with personal goals

We have discussed personal goals in an earlier section of this chapter. We have learned that individual goals are connected with our own selves and can be related to our health, happiness, social life and general wellbeing. Unlike personal goals, professional goals are related to what achievements you would like to accomplish with your education and career. Professional goals also have a significant impact on your personal life.

Planning for goals

If you are planning for goal setting, the most challenging part is timing because it is something you cannot control, and sometimes things will not happen exactly on time or in the way you first envisioned. Therefore, when we plan for goals, we will set short-term goals and long-term goals. We can set goals according to a schedule and build our goals around time-related factors.

Short-term goals should be easily measured and help you move along to the next short-term goal, while long-term goals can help with viewing a long-term impact on your academic, personal and professional goals. For example, suppose you want to get promoted to a certain level in your professional career (as a long-term professional goal). In that case, you can plan for setting deadlines for completing a degree (short-term academic goal) and what personal goals you need to develop to help achieve them (short-term and long-term personal goals). By separating the goals from timelines, you can avoid a lot of disappointment or setting any unrealistic expectations in your goals. Furthermore, it will help you to identify what support you will need to achieve the short- and consequently long-term goals.

Other than timelines, we recommend you set your goals according to your own needs, not based on social media or other people's goals. Societal pressure can make you feel you need to complete something by a certain age or more, but everyone is different, and there is no right or wrong timeline, rather what suits your personal context. Focus on yourselves to achieve milestones based upon your own needs and life and consider what supports you need along the way. Having said that, by all means use positive examples from your own contexts or even social media to inspire you to strive for your very best – but remember, your best is what you are looking for, not someone else's!

Goals and spiritual energy building

We have dedicated an extensive part of this chapter on setting goals, and the reasons behind them are a basis for building our spiritual energy. Even though plans can be short- or long-term, big or small, we use them to understand our context and situation and develop energy to achieve the goals. More specifically, setting goals can provide energy to reach them, an internal drive that allows us to achieve the best version of ourselves. It is very important to celebrate short-term goals and share these accomplishments with friends and family, but always keep in mind there is a bigger picture that will help you strive for the long-term outcomes.

We discuss the measurement of goals, which can help us to determine how to use spiritual energy. It is suggested we put our goals somewhere visible. It may provide you with a certain level of motivation to achieve your goals. In terms of the relationship between goals and motivation, many researchers have conducted studies on this. For example, Dik et al.'s (2008) study aims to 'present initial psychometric evidence for a novel approach to assessing goals and motivation for individuals engaged in the career decision-making and planning

189

process' (p. 24). One of the theories Dik et al. (2008) used is Social Cognitive Career Theory. It helps university students to exercise agency through the interaction of their self-efficacy beliefs (see Chapter 9), outcome expectations and personal goals related to their career decision making and planning processes. Therefore, spiritual energy relies on your mental energy and confidence in your ability to perform a task and the ability to determine outcomes of successful performance. In addition, spiritual energy building also works with your personal goals, as it helps you in your intention to engage in the task and generate the goals. Thus, spiritual energy links your goal-directed behaviour with high levels of self-efficacy. These behaviours result in some valued outcomes. The Social Cognitive Career Theory processes the development of our interests and motivations, our career and personal goals, and finally, our academic performance. It allows you to emphasise your self-efficacy and outcome expectations for specific tasks, which supports goal achievement. Figure 10.3 shows the process of spiritual energy building.

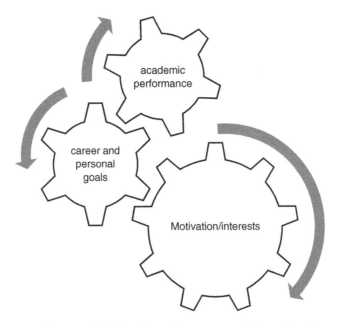

Figure 10.3   Spiritual energy building based upon Social Cognitive Career Theory

Although each individual will have different motivations, interests and personal and career goals (depending on your unique concept), your spiritual energy is linked with learning constructs. It is reflected in your perception of how well your energy can contribute to establishing a successful career and personal life.

Many researchers (e.g. Duffy, 2006) have studied the role of spirituality in spiritual energy development, and they have found mechanisms linked with the career development process. Spiritual energy has been applied to life domains and goals and is behind the motivation to integrate work with one's overall sense of purpose. Spiritual energy helps provide meaningfulness in your life and helps orient values and goals which support shaping learning constructs and is a compelling source of energy towards career development.

STUDENT EXAMPLE

Lynn is close to being a qualified speech pathologist. *'I actually have a bachelor's degree in education, but after doing placements it was so obvious the number of children with speech delays and [I] was amazed that speech therapy could influence young children so much. After one year of teaching I knew I wanted to be a specialised speech therapist to help young children. So, I didn't really change my goals, rather found a specific focus where I know I can make a difference.'*

Lynn's example shows a strong integration of motivation, self-efficacy and continuing performance in her chosen field. What she shared with us demonstrated that once you find an avenue for your passion, your spiritual energy will manifest into clear decision making about where your goals will lie.

Mapping your journey to success

- Your spiritual energy can be developed with the other energies – your physical, social and emotional, and finally, mental energy.
- Understanding spiritual energy means understanding personal, academic and professional goals.
- Motivation and interest play an essential part in building your spiritual energy.
- Social Cognitive Career Theory can be used to understand how to build learning constructs using spiritual energy.

Recommended activities

This chapter is the final chapter of Part 3 of the book. Although this chapter focuses on developing spiritual energy, it also covers setting goals including career, personal and professional goals. Please complete the relevant sections in Appendix B.

WELLBEING BEYOND UNIVERSITY

11

Wellbeing beyond university

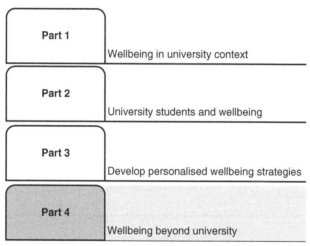

Part 1 — Wellbeing in university context

Part 2 — University students and wellbeing

Part 3 — Develop personalised wellbeing strategies

Part 4 — Wellbeing beyond university

- This is the only chapter in this section and the final chapter of this book. It discusses the issues and strategies in maintaining wellbeing after your university studies.

Figure 11.1   Chapter summary

We celebrate your success at university, and your degree is conferred on graduation day, and leaving university means another transition, from an academic world to society. Baxter-Wright and Davies (2019) published an article based on the results from a City Mental Health Alliance survey on university students' mental wellbeing after leaving university. The research shows 49% of students' mental wellbeing declined, and post-university mental health issues are very common. Therefore, when you complete your studies at university, your journey of wellbeing is not finished with your degree. It will carry on beyond university.

Baxter-Wright and Davies' (2019) research found a few common issues that may influence your wellbeing after university, including financial pressure, adulthood, and just the feeling of the 'unknown'. The transition from being recognised by lecturers and your circle of friends to a completely different world can be daunting.

STUDENT
EXAMPLE

Grace completed her PhD approximately five years ago, and she has been working in the higher education context for over three years. When asked about her wellbeing strategies after university, she commented, '*I was very proud to have achieved what I'd set out to achieve. I graduated feeling well prepared in many aspects of life, in particular, ready to walk into the academic world working in a university. I had worked in my university as a sessional tutor during my PhD candidature. I gained a lot of invaluable life experience, such as tutoring in workshops and tutorials and marking and consulting with students. I thought it would be easier for me to find a university lecturer position. However, after submitting over twenty applications to various universities, I only received one interview opportunity, it was a stark reminder of how competitive university positions are to win. I was prepared for my academic skills, but looking back, I felt less prepared for dealing with the disappointment associated with finding work and managing my mental health over that period. I found myself restless while waiting for the outcomes of applications. At the time, I didn't use university career support, as I thought they were only for undergraduate students. In hindsight, that was a mistake. Now, after a couple of years, I realise I should have used the university supports more effectively, as it not only helps with building your résumé but also assists in working on your professional career aspirations after university. I now have my own PhD students and getting prepared for life after your studies is something we focus upon.*'

Grace's example is common, especially for those studying research degrees. It is easy to get so lost in your research that you forget to ask yourself, 'what comes next?' Until graduation, university students face a reasonably well laid out progression path. For example, you use the education system as a guide and look ahead to the next step. There are course rules and programme schedules for you to follow. These rules and plans are structured, and the learning constructs have been set out for you to get prepared for your university life. However, you may still feel unprepared or underprepared for life after university.

Macaskill (2013) published a research paper that identified the peak period for mental health problems was before 24 years of age. With most school leavers graduating from university before 24, this finding suggests that post university graduates' mental health is truly worthy of attention. Therefore, in this chapter, we will show you how to look after your mental health and wellbeing beyond university with the current support services from the university and how to use the energy built from the last chapter to help your wellbeing during your career.

Strengthen the connection within university learning communities

Although after graduation you may feel university life was 'just another' period of your life, many graduates find it helpful to strengthen the connection within university learning communities. Every university offers an alumni page, and all graduates can register and keep connected.

Many research papers have discussed the excellent practice of alumni groups. For example, Skari (2014) addressed college alumni and knowledge sharing. She drew in her research on Social Exchange Theory, in which social interaction and relationships are investigated. Social Exchange Theory helps us to understand how people strengthen relationships within organisations with a desire to act with integrity. This theory frames 'giving' as a two-way process, and it is also used to 'acknowledge the relationship between alumnus and alma mater as a reason for giving' (p. 26). Alumni can motivate the excellent intention deed for graduates. They give positive feelings towards the graduates' alma mater and their design to be part of the learning community and help with the need for the institution to achieve their desires.

Yes, it is true, alumni are often contacted in the hopes they will make donations to support the work of the university. However, the maintenance of the relationship between the university and its alumni allows this continued giving behaviour. Many universities use alumni services to keep their alumni connected and engaged. Services include cultivation and community building through events and publications. Some universities also offer alumni mentorship for graduates based upon their student experience and connections, as a further form of giving. A mentorship programme is beneficial for both alumni and current students in universities, as it helps develop a community of practice. Therefore, investigate what alumni services you can become a part of and stay connected with your university, post your studies.

Support from university to prepare for your future career

All universities provide career support for their students and graduates. For example, the University of Melbourne offers career support and employment advice services to students and alumni. These include career resources videos, career insights and alumni mentoring.

Career resource videos provide students and alumni with practical resources to help through the career development journey. These helpful videos include tips for networking online, career confusion, and how to conduct an informational interview with a professional. Career insights provide skills and strategies from other fellow alumni and academic experts for you to become a career leader. The alumni to alumni mentoring offers graduates helpful career advice.

STUDENT EXAMPLE

Ray has just graduated with a degree in accounting and shared with us his views having just freshly graduated and moving into the work sector. *'My university was great at providing career support to its students, including me, and continues to offer outstanding alumni services for graduates. Although I felt as though I had gained all of the technical skills I would need for my future career within my coursework, I was still nervous about navigating my career path. Some parts of graduate life made me feel a strong sense of transition, and sometimes it made me think regression from my work. I know this feeling of leaving university is temporary, and the feeling of isolation and helplessness is natural when I think about my future career and how competitive it is to find work. Which is one reason I decided to move back to my hometown, which is a bit smaller but gave me an opportunity to get a job.*

'After three months of graduation, I have still been in constant contact with my university friends; we support each other in ways that we can and it's great to have networks that we know will help as we move through our careers. I moved back to a regional place to begin my work, so, yes, the emotional energy I had from my colleagues or class friends supported me through finding myself and confidence and standing with a sense of independence.' When asked about the alumni services offered by his university, Ray replied, *'The university website for alumni does provide a certain level of preparation for our "next stage", and self-awareness to make critical decisions. So I would say it's been really helpful, not just for me, but I know my friends are also members.'*

The above example sheds light on the fact that there is not necessarily a 'one-size-fits-all' upon which to base your transition out of university life. Rather, use available resources (such as alumni services) to support you in finding your pathway. In the next section, we will show you how to develop a lifelong strategic plan to achieve and maintain your wellbeing, and consider the resources that could be available to support you in your journey.

We can't recommend enough that you join the university alumni group when you graduate. The benefits that university alumni bring include keeping you updated about any new information and help build your career.

For example, Australian Catholic University graduates can join an online platform (ACU Alumni Connect), where you can share advice wherever you are in the world to explore, connect and have access to broader opportunities.

In particular, the opportunities include continuing library access and ACU career development and employability services. This support includes an online portal for job opportunities, appointment bookings and events, access to jobs, internships, career advice and reviews. In addition, a step-by-step process is provided for you to build professional and competitive job application documents.

Internship

Hunt and Scott (2020) proposed a reliable way of estimating the impact of internship, particularly with regard to prevalence, quality and motivation at six months after graduation. You may have heard about internships during your university life, and it has prompted debate in university sectors. Some people think it can promote higher employability to compete for 'graduate-level' jobs, while others believe the unpaid internship confers class advantages in accessing certain resources. Silva et al. (2018) have found that university work placements can improve employability and labour market outcomes. In the UK, the 'sandwich' placements, including paid and unpaid internships, have been shown to have positive results on academic grades and increase the chances of finding a job. Internships can offer different experiences, including emotional experience in the work sector, the nature of feedback whilst 'on the job' and the ability to build quality relationships which may extend beyond the internship, all of which can impact your professional identity. Successful internships can enable, guide and support you in strengthening your sense of self and competence, thereby harnessing your inner strength, and developing a subsequent professional identity to pursue worthwhile, autonomous and transformative outcomes within the internships and future workforce opportunities.

Planning energy building and exercises beyond university

In the last four chapters, we showed you energy building for wellbeing in the following areas: physical energy, social and emotional energy, mental energy and spiritual energy. Although we have discussed them separately, we have shown you that they are linked closely and should always be exercised together (see Figure 11.2).

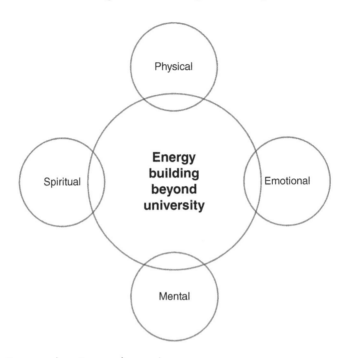

Figure 11.2   Energy planning and exercises

When you graduate from university and start working, you must ensure you maintain your wellbeing and consequently your energy building techniques. Although there are many different needs and demands from work beyond university life, the same techniques can still be applied to look after your wellbeing. Therefore, energy planning and exercises will need to be developed and worked on throughout your university life and beyond.

Long-term hard work will also impact your wellbeing during your career pathways. Many researchers have studied how to 'recover' from work demands, noting these demands can impact our effort and personal resources, which may cause exhaustion, lack of energy and stress. Typically, we need to rebuild our energy after work.

The Effort-Recovery Model (ER model) (Meijman & Mulder, 1998) emphasises that energy rebuilding needs to be done away from work and requires self-focus. Therefore, family and home environments are considered default recovery areas. You should spend your evenings, weekends, or holidays recovering from stress and relaxing. The ER model was used to demonstrate the dynamic interaction between work and family. Sufficient recovery from workload effects that build up at work is crucial to protect your daily wellbeing. The ER model posits effort and resource use in your stress systems, and negative load can trigger high fatigue levels and have a negative effect. Only when your psychophysiological systems are activated can the negative load reactions not be harmful to your wellbeing. This process is called 'recovery', and insufficient recovery will lead to stress and anxiety (van Hooff et al., 2018). Your daily recovery can be related to your off-job experience and psychophysiological recovery systems. According to Self-determination Theory, the three psychological needs are autonomy, competence and relatedness. These needs are essential to maintain wellbeing. Van Hooff and Geurts (2014) have found that off-job time can contribute to your recovery at the end of the day, and Mojza et al. (2011) discussed the relationship between off-job time and recovery the following day.

Other than these theories and models which pertain to the reasons behind our work-related stress, the Conservation of Resources (COR) Theory has been much mentioned in the literature and refers to managing our resources to maintain our wellbeing. The COR Theory is 'based upon the supposition that people strive to retain, protect, and build resources and that what is threatening to them is the potential or actual loss of these valued resources' (Hobfoll, 1989, p. 513). In the COR model, resources are the things that one values, specifically objects, states and conditions (Halbesleben et al., 2014). More recently, Bardoel et al. (2021) posited that COR Theory is a valuable tool for understanding resilience. Resilience as a concept is relevant to many individuals to maintain their wellbeing. COR has been used to understand various circumstances in analysing stress and burnout (Holmgreen et al., 2017). In COR Theory, various kinds of resilience have been proposed. 'Strategic resilience' involves positive actions in response to adversity, which are resource-enhancing, and 'acceptance resilience' involves positive actions in response to adversity, which are resource-preserving. The COR Theory can help you conceptualise how to use various resources to complete work by using time management skills, cognitive attention, physical energy while at the same time avoiding stress (S. Kim et al., 2017). Kim et al. (2017) further discussed that we have to replenish these resources during breaks. However, taking breaks can be difficult.

STUDENT EXAMPLE

Another former student, Si, who is now the assistant director of a childcare centre, discussed her own replenishment of resources strategies: *'Initially, I worked and used all my energy after graduation as the qualified teacher in the kindergarten room. Last year, I was promoted to the assistant director role, which I must admit I was really pleased about. I worked really hard to get that position. However, I found my life is busier than before, and I have been working non-stop during my personal time, I felt my work/life balance was out of control. Also, I found the longer and more continuous hours I worked, the less efficient and less effective I became.*

(Continued)

It also impacted my sleep too as I was thinking about all of the additional work I needed to do. I had been thinking about work during eating, walking, driving and even sleeping! Only until I finally noticed my sleeping patterns had been disturbed did I realise I needed to make some changes to "live my life".

'I did some reading about the importance of sleep and how to promote better life habits. Since then, I started to work on how to find a better balance to my work and life balance and rebuild my energy. I set up my schedule like this:

1. *Go to bed early and wake up early.*
2. *Go to sleep and wake up at the same times consistently.*
3. *Drink plenty of water every day.*
4. *Go and have a walk for at least half an hour daily … if not more!*
5. *Eat a balanced and healthy diet … but I still love chocolate!*

'I have been using this simple schedule for over six months now, which has really helped build my energy. I find I am more focused now during work and have become more efficient and I don't need to spend as many hours on my work anymore. I must admit, the changes took a while to get going, but I'm so glad I made those changes.'

Si's example shows how she is making good use of her resources to have adequate breaks cognitively, and it has positive effects on her work and life balance. Si's case is also a long-term example – remember change can take time.

Kai also described a more unusual method to take short-term cognitive breaks.

STUDENT
EXAMPLE

Kai is an international research student in his second year of research candidature. He explained to us how to enhance his concentration skills:

'I found when I spent more than a couple of hours on one task, like reading an academic book, I would feel tired and couldn't concentrate. I would then take a break for an hour or two but would find it so hard to get back into my work and I would always leave work to the last minute. A friend of mine actually showed me an effective method to have a mental break by doing juggling for a few minutes between tasks! I know it sounds strange, but I find it really works! Initially, I could only juggle two balls, and I found that I had to concentrate on the balls when I was juggling. If I were absent-minded, I would have missed catching them. Now I'm actually really good at juggling three balls. It is a great quick physical brain break which allows me to have a break from academic work but still keeps me focussed.'

Jett and George (2003) found that if the break lasts too long, it can reduce activation and promote procrastination, making us lose available time and, as importantly, disengage from the task. Thus, Kai's two to five minutes' juggling method allows him to take a quick cognitive break and detach from his work. He then finds more energy through this momentary recovery (S. Kim et al., 2017). The break can be used as a beneficial interruption leading to positive outcomes. Research, such as the studies by Halbesleben et al. (2014) and Bardoel et al. (2021), has shown breaks can enhance cognitive stimulation, job satisfaction, emotional wellbeing, work performance levels and creative output.

The above two examples have shown us the importance of the COR Theory to manage your wellbeing. We will now demonstrate how to manage your work and life balance and wellbeing by using the energy building theory.

Planning to achieve wellbeing

Sonnentag and Fritz (2007) developed *The Recovery Experience Questionnaire*, which discussed five recovery strategies: psychological detachment, relaxation, mastery experiences, control during leisure time and community experiences. Other researchers also have found the strategies to be excellent recovery methods.

Being physically away from work can be important for recovery. However, it may not be enough. You may still think about work while away from it. For example, you may still check emails and receive job-related phone calls from home and be occupied by engaging in job-related activities during holiday time. Or, you could lie awake at night thinking about all of the tasks you need to do for work the following day or week. When you are still thinking about job-related issues, your psychological systems are continuously challenged, and full recovery cannot occur (Sonnentag & Fritz, 2007). Therefore, it becomes imperative to become psychologically detached from work and not be occupied by work-related duties, going beyond pure physical absence from the workplace. Ensure that you also have clear work duties and keep a clear distinction between work time and your personal recovery time. During the COVID pandemic many people began working from home and this caused the home to become many people's new 'office'. However, as the pandemic conditions ease, it is vital to reclaim your home as a place where you make careful delineation between work and rest. It may take some time, but ensure you carve out time in your day that does not involve work or thinking about work. We have been showing you different ways of building your different energies in the previous chapters and it is clear that they can all be used to help achieve and maintain your wellbeing. In Chapters 7–10, we discussed each energy type individually; in this section, we will show you how to bring and build your energies together. For example, we will show you how to use physical energy to build social and emotional, mental and spiritual energies. In the previous chapter, we interviewed a university student, Ben, who enjoys surfing to develop his physical energy. When we asked him the reason behind it, he emphasised that surfing helped to clear his mind and that he could concentrate after his physical exercise. Studies show exercise can positively impact chemicals in the brain to improve your mood.

Basso and Suzuki (2017) studied the impact of exercise on people's moods, such as depression and anger management. It was suggested a 30-minute daily exercise routine might be effective for improving mood and controlling depression. It has been proven that one of the benefits of exercise is that it stimulates the release of cortisol, which helps your memory and alertness systems. However, leisure activities, including social and emotional activities and mental activities, are also a relaxation process. Relaxation can be connected with the four areas of muscles and meditation.

STUDENT EXAMPLE

Bea is a third year undergraduate student, and she also shared her resources replenishment strategies: *'Definitely ... I have attended some workshops run by the university about balancing life and work. I chose walking ... I enjoy walking after working, no matter how late it is. I have a dog, and that's a good excuse to get out of the house and have exercise with the dog. Sometimes I also like to call a close-by colleague for a walk together; she has a dog too. There is a reserve park not far from our houses, so we usually take a light walk in this beautiful natural environment while talking to each other. Since university, we have been friends, but we make sure we don't talk about work, rather we talk about life and have a good laugh. Plus, the dogs love it!*
    'Most of the time, if I walk by myself, I like to listen to podcasts or audiobooks of my favourite novels. They did help me with detaching from my work and help me to relax.'

Various relaxation activities can be chosen, to relax either body or mind; and these activities might need little or no physical or cognitive effort, which increases positive impact. And most importantly, don't feel guilty when you are not working! Your body needs to disengage from work, so prioritise that time and know it holds value and will ultimately make you more productive. We know personally that during your university studies you will constantly feel that you need to be 'doing' something, assessments, readings and so on. This feeling often follows you post your academic studies and into the workforce. You feel like you need to be constantly 'doing'; yet your body will not be able to sustain this level of energy. Therefore, how you plan your strategies will depend on your own needs and the individual ways you find to achieve and manage your wellbeing. Choose activities that motivate you and you find enjoyable. There is no 'right or wrong' activities, it's all about what works for you. Going back to previous chapters in this book will help you identify where you need to build your different physical, social and emotional, mental and spiritual energies.

Mapping your journey to success

- It is essential to map your journey throughout your university life and beyond university.
- Success does not simply refer to a successful career. It can be a lifelong learning journey.
- Energy building is dynamic – taking physical, social and emotional, mental and spiritual forms.
- Universities also provide tremendous and valuable support and resources for their graduates. Ensure you join the alumni group and make use of the resources it provides.

Recommended reading and activities

In August 2017, Rochaun Meadows-Fernandez published an article in *The Washington Post*, entitled 'There's such a thing as post-graduation depression. I know: I had it'. At the end of the article, Rochaun stated that 'I knew that to shake my feelings of sadness, I had to make some significant life decisions'. We recommend you stay connected with your university after your graduation by registering with the university alumni. Also please continue practising the energy building strategies and find the best strategy to suit you.

References

Abouzeid, E., Fouad, S., Wasfy, N., Alkhadragy, R., Hefny, M., & Kamal, D. (2021). Influence of personality traits and learning styles on undergraduate medical students' academic achievement. *Advances in Medical Education and Practice, 12,* 769–777.

ACU Strengthening Clinic and Gymnasium (n.d.). https://bigcitydesign.com.au/projects/australian-catholic-university-2/

Adams, G. R., Berzonsky, M. D., & Keating, L. (2006). Psychosocial resources in first-year university students: The role of identity processes and social relationships. *Journal of Youth and Adolescence, 35*(1), 78–88. https://doi.org/10.1007/s10964-005-9019-0

Adams, K. M., Hester, P. T., Bradley, J. M., Meyers, T. J., & Keating, C. B. (2014). Systems theory as the foundation for understanding systems. *Systems Engineering, 17*(1), 112–123. https://doi.org/10.1002/sys.21255

Aderibigbe, S., Antiado, D., & Sta Anna, A. (2015). Issues in peer mentoring for undergraduate students in a private university in the United Arab Emirates. *International Journal of Evidence Based Coaching and Mentoring, 13*(2), 64–80.

Akos, P., & James, S. (2020). Are course withdrawals a useful student success strategy? *NACADA Journal, 40*(1), 80–93. https://doi.org/10.12930/NACADA-18-34

Alam, M. N., & McGinty, D. (2017). Acute effects of alcohol on sleep are mediated by components of homeostatic sleep regulatory system: An Editorial Highlight for 'Lesions of the basal forebrain cholinergic neurons attenuates sleepiness and adenosine after alcohol consumption' on page 710. *Journal of Neurochemistry, 142*(5), 620–623. https://doi.org/10.1111/jnc.14100

Alfredsson Olsson, E., & Heikkinen, S. (2019). 'I will never quit dancing'. The emotional experiences of social dancing among older persons. *Journal of Aging Studies, 51,* 100786–100786. https://doi.org/10.1016/j.jaging.2019.100786

Alhadabi, A., & Karpinski, A. C. (2020). Grit, self-efficacy, achievement orientation goals, and academic performance in university students. *International Journal of Adolescence and Youth, 25*(1), 519–535. https://doi.org/10.1080/02673843.2019.1679202

Aloia, L., & Strutzenberg, C. (2020). The influence of family cohesion and relational maintenance strategies on stress in first semester college students. *Communication Quarterly*, 68(4), 457–471. https://doi.org/10.1080/01463373. 2020.1821735

Ameen, K. (2013). The need and impact of learning 'Personality Development & Communication Skills' in LIS education: A case study. *Malaysian Journal of Library & Information Science*, 18(1), 15–25.

American Cancer Society (2016, September 2). *Lessons from the Olympics help Shannon Miller through ovarian cancer treatment*. www.cancer.org/latest-news/lessons-from-the-olympics-help-shannon-miller-through-ovarian-can cer-treatment.html

American Psychological Association (2015). *Stress in America*. www.apa.org/ news/press/releases/stress/2014/stress-report.pdf

Anwer, S., Manzar, M. D., Alghadir, A. H., Salahuddin, M., & Hanneed, U. A. (2020). Psychometric analysis of the Perceived Stress Scale among healthy university students. *Neuropsychiatric Disease and Treatment*, 16, 2389–2396. https://doi.org/10.2147/NDT.S268582

Arslan, G., Allen, K-A., & Ryan, T. (2020). Exploring the impacts of school belonging on youth wellbeing and mental health among Turkish adolescents. *Child Indicators Research*, 13(5), 1619–1635. https://doi.org/10.1007/s12187-020-09721-z

Ary, D., Jacobs, L., & Sorensen, C. (2010). *Introduction to research in education* (8th ed.). Cengage.

Ateca-Amestoy, V., Aguilar, A. C., & Moro-Egido, A. I. (2013). Social interactions and life satisfaction: Evidence from Latin America. *Journal of Happiness Studies*, 15(3), 527–554. https://doi.org/10.1007/s10902-013-9434-y

Australian Association of Mathematics Teachers (n.d.). https://aamt.edu.au/

Australian Bureau of Statistics (2021). www.abs.gov.au/

Australian Catholic University (n.d.). Support from Academic Skills Unit. www. acu.edu.au/student-life/student-services/academic-skills-development/aca demic-skills-unit

Australian Medical Association (n.d.). *Ethics committees in health care institutions*. www.ama-assn.org/delivering-care/ethics/ethics-committees-health-care-institutions

Australian Psychological Society (2015). *Stress & wellbeing: How Australians are coping with life*. https://Psychology.Org.Au/Getmedia/Ae32e645-A4f0-4f7c-B3ce-Dfd83237c281/Stress-Wellbeing-Survey.Pdf

Australian Qualifications Framework (2015). Volume of learning. www.asqa.gov. au/rtos/users-guide-standards-rtos-2015/chapter-4-training-and-assessment/ clauses-11-14-and-22-implementing-monitoring-and-evaluating-training-and-assessment-strategies-and-practices#what-clauses-1-1-to-1-4-and-2-2-mean-for-your-rto

Australian Teacher Education Association (n.d.). https://atea.edu.au/

Bandura, A. (1977). *Social learning theory*. Prentice-Hall.

Bandura, A. (1991). Social cognitive theory of self-regulation. *Organisational Behavior and Human Decision Processes, 50*, 248–287. http://dx.doi.org/10.1016/0749-5978(91)90022-L

Bandura, A. (1997). Self-efficacy: The exercise of control. W. H. Freeman.

Bardoel, A. E., Drago, R., Duchek, S., Raetze, S., Kirkman, B. L. & Maynard, M. T. (2021). Acceptance and strategic resilience: An application of Conservation of Resources Theory. *Group & Organization Management, 46*(4), 657–691. https://doi.org/10.1177/10596011211022488

Barker, S. B., Schubert, C. M., Barker, R. T., Kuo, S. I-C., Kendler, K. S., & Dick, D. M. (2020). The relationship between pet ownership, social support, and internalizing symptoms in students from the first to fourth year of college. *Applied Developmental Science, 24*(3), 279–293. https://doi.org/10.1080/10888691.2018.1476148

Bar-On, R. (2006). The Bar-On model of emotional-social intelligence (ESI). *Psicothema, 18*, 13–25.

Barrett, J., Peterson, D. R., Hester, K. S., Robledo, I. C., Day, E. A., Hougen, D. P., & Mumford, M. D. (2013). Thinking about applications: Effects on mental models and creative problem-solving. *Creativity Research Journal, 25*(2), 199–212. https://doi.org/10.1080/10400419.2013.783758

Basso, J., & Suzuki, W. A. (2017). The effects of acute exercise on mood, cognition, neurophysiology, and neurochemical pathways: A review. *Brain Plasticity, 2*(2), 127–152. https://doi.org/10.3233/BPL-160040

Batt, A., Williams, B., Brydges, M., Leyenaar, M., & Tavares, W. (2021). New ways of seeing: Supplementing existing competency framework development guidelines with systems thinking. *Advances in Health Sciences Education: Theory and Practice, 26*(4), 1355–1371. https://doi.org/10.1007/s10459-021-10054-x

Baxter-Wright, D., & Davies, M. (2019). *Why is no one talking about post-university depression?* www.cosmopolitan.com/uk/worklife/campus/a22575047/post-university-depression/

Bean, J. P. (1982). Student attrition, intentions, and confidence: Interaction effects in a path model. *Research in Higher Education, 17*(4), 291–320. https://doi.org/10.1007/BF00977899

Belludi, N. (2008). *Use the STAR technique to ace your behavioural interview*. www.rightattitudes.com/2008/07/15/star-technique-answer-interview-questions/

Bendezú, B., Calhoun, C. D., Patterson, M. W., Findley, A., Rudolph, K. D., Hastings, P., Nock, M. K., & Prinstein, M. J. (2021). Adolescent girls' stress responses as prospective predictors of self-injurious thoughts and behaviors: A person-centered, multilevel study. *Development and Psychopathology.* Advance online publication. https://doi.org/10.1017/S0954579420002229

Berman, A., Bevan, J. L., & Sparks, L. (2020). Readiness to visit university counseling centers: Social support, stigma, and communication efficacy. *Journal of Student Affairs Research and Practice*, *57*(3), 282–295. https://doi.org/10.108 0/19496591.2019.1648272

Bird, G. W., & Harris, R. L. (1990). A comparison of role strain and coping strategies by gender and family structure among early adolescents. *The Journal of Early Adolescence*, *10*(2), 141–158.

Bliuc, A-M., Ellis, R. A., Goodyear, P., & Hendres, D. M. (2011). Understanding student learning in context: Relationships between university students' social identity, approaches to learning, and academic performance. *European Journal of Psychology of Education*, *26*(3), 417–433. https://doi.org/10.1007/ s10212-011-0065-6

Bonneville-Roussy, A., Evans, P., Verner-Filion, J., Vallerand, R. J., & Bouffard, T. (2017, January). Motivation and coping with the stress of assessment: Gender differences in outcomes for university students. *Contemporary Educational Psychology*, *48*, 28–42. https://doi.org/10.1016/j.cedpsych.2016.08.003

Boud, D., Cohen, R., & Sampson, J. (1999). Peer learning and assessment. *Assessment and Evaluation in Higher Education*, *24*(4), 413–426. https://doi. org/10.1080/0260293990240405

Boud, D., Cohen, R., & Sampson, J. (2001). Peer learning in higher education: Learning from and with each other. Kogan Page.

Boud, D., Cohen, R., & Sampson, J. (2014). Peer learning in higher education: Learning from and with each other. Routledge.

Boulding, K. (1956). General systems theory: The skeleton of science. *Management Science*, *2*(3),197–208.

Bowers-Campbell, J. (2008). Cyber 'pokes': Motivational antidote for developmental college readers. *Journal of College Reading and Learning*, *39*(1), 74–87.

Brody, L. (1985). Gender differences in emotional development: A review of theories and research. *Journal of Personality*, *53*(2), 102–149.

Bronfenbrenner, U. (1977). Toward an experimental ecology of human development. *The American Psychologist*, *32*(7),513–531. https://doi.org/10.1037/0003-066X.32.7.513

Brunsden, V., Davies, M., Shevlin, M., & Bracken, M. (2000). Why do HE students drop out? A test of Tinto's model. *Journal of Further and Higher Education*, *24*(3), 301–310. https://doi.org/10.1080/030987700750022244

Bryce, E. (2019, November 10). How many calories can the brain burn by thinking? *LiveScience*. www.livescience.com/burn-calories-brain.html

Burka, P. (2003). Greatness visible. *Texas Monthly*, *31*(10), 92–92.

Burkolter, D., & Kluge, A. (2012). Process control and risky decision-making: Moderation by general mental ability and need for cognition. *Ergonomics*, *55*(11), 1285–1297. https://doi.org/10.1080/00140139.2012.709279

Burns, E., Martin, A. J., & Collie, R. J. (2018, April). Adaptability, personal best (PB) goals setting, and gains in students' academic outcomes: A longitudinal examination from a social cognitive perspective. *Contemporary Educational Psychology, 53*, 57–72. https://doi.org/10.1016/j.cedpsych.2018.02.001

Chan, J. (2015). Using medical incidents to teach: Effects of vicarious experience on nursing students' self-efficacy in performing urinary catheterization. *The Journal of Nursing Education, 54*(2), 80–86. https://doi.org/10.3928/01484834-20150120-01

Cocchiara, F. K., & Bell, M. P. (2009). Gender and work stress: Unique stressors, unique responses. In C. J. Cooper, J. C. Quick, & M. J. Schabracq (Eds.), *International handbook of work and health psychology* (pp. 106–146). Wiley.

Coertjens, C., Brahm,T., Trautwein, C., & Lindblom-Ylänne, S. (2017). Students' transition into higher education from an international perspective. *Higher Education, 73*(3), 357–369. https://doi.org/10.1007/s10734-016-0092-y

Cohen, S., & Janicki-Deverts, D. (2012). Who's stressed? Distributions of psychological stress in the United States in probability samples from 1983, 2006, and 2009. *Journal of Applied Social Psychology, 42*(6), 1320–1334. https://doi.org/10.1111/j.1559-1816.2012.00900.x

Cohen, S., Janicki-Deverts, D., & Miller, G. E. (2007). Psychological stress and disease. *JAMA : The Journal of the American Medical Association, 298*(14), 1685–1687. https://doi.org/10.1001/jama.298.14.1685

Cohen, S., Kamarck, T., & Mermelstein, R. (1983). A global measure of perceived stress. *Journal of Health and Social Behavior, 24*(4), 385–396.

Cohen, S., & Williamson, G. (1988). Perceived stress in a probability sample of the United States. In S. Spacapam & S. Oskamp (Eds.), The social psychology of health: Claremont symposium on applied psychology (pp. 31–67). Sage.

Consultancy London Economics (2020, April). *Impact of the Covid-19 pandemic on university finances.* https://londoneconomics.co.uk/blog/publication/impact-of-the-covid-19-pandemic-on-university-finances-april-2020/

Corcoran, R., & O'Flaherty, J. (2017). Longitudinal tracking of academic progress during teacher preparation. *British Journal of Educational Psychology, 87*(4), 664–682. https://doi.org/10.1111/bjep.12171

Cornick, J., & Blascovich, J. (2017). Physiological responses to virtual exergame feedback for individuals with different levels of exercise self-efficacy. *The International Journal of Virtual Reality, 17*(1), 32–53. https://doi.org/10.20870/IJVR.2017.17.1.2886

Cox, P. L., Schmitt, E. D., Bobrowski, P. E., & Graham, G. (2005). Enhancing the first-year experience of business student: Student retention and academic success. *Journal of Behavioral and Applied Management, 7*, 40–68.

Creswell, J. W., & Poth, C. N. (2018). Qualitative inquiry and research design: Choosing among five approaches (4th ed.). Sage.

Cupit, G. (2007). The marriage of science and spirit: Dynamic systems theory and the development of spirituality. *International Journal of Children's Spirituality, 12*(2), 105–116. https://doi.org/10.1080/13644360701467402

D'Agostini, M., Claes, N., Franssen, M., von Leupoldt, A., & Van Diest, I. (2022). Learn to breathe, breathe to learn? No evidence for effects of slow deep breathing at a 0.1 Hz frequency on reversal learning. *International Journal of Psychophysiology, 174*, 92–107. https://doi.org/10.1016/j.ijpsycho.2022.01.008

Dao-Tran, T-H., Anderson, D., & Seib, C. (2017). The Vietnamese version of the Perceived Stress Scale (PSS-10): Translation equivalence and psychometric properties among older women. *BMC Psychiatry, 17*(1), 53–53. https://doi.org/10.1186/s12888-017-1221-6

Darabi, M., Macaskill, A., & Reidy, L. (2017). A qualitative study of the UK academic role: Positive features, negative aspects and associated stressors in a mainly teaching-focused university. *Journal of Further and Higher Education, 41*(4), 566–580. https://doi.org/10.1080/0309877X.2016.1159287

Deeley, S., Fischbacher-Smith, M., Karadzhov, D., & Koristashevskaya, E. (2019). Exploring the 'wicked' problem of student dissatisfaction with assessment and feedback in higher education. *Higher Education Pedagogies, 4*(1), 385–405. https://doi.org/10.1080/23752696.2019.1644659

De Giorgio, A., Kuvačić, G., Milić, M., & Padulo, J. (2018). The brain and movement: How physical activity affects the brain. *Montenegrin Journal of Sports Science and Medicine, 7*(2), 63–68. https://doi.org/10.26773/mjssm.180910

Della Vigna, S., & Malmendier, U. (2006). Paying not to go to the gym. *The American Economic Review, 96*(3), 694–719. https://doi.org/10.1257/aer.96.3.694

Devlin, M. (2013). Bridging sociocultural incongruity: Conceptualising the success of students from low socioeconomic status backgrounds in Australian higher education. *Studies in Higher Education, 38*(6), 939–949.

Dewey, J. (1933). How we think: A restatement of the relation of reflective thinking to the educative process. Boston, MA: D.C. Heath & Co Publishers.

Dik, B., Sargent, A. M., & Steger, M. F. (2008). Career development strivings: Assessing goals and motivation in career decision-making and planning. *Journal of Career Development, 35*(1), 23–41. https://doi.org/10.1177/0894845308317934

Di Renzo, L., Gualtieri, P., Pivari, F., Soldati, L., Attina, A., Cinelli, G., Leggeri, C., Caparello, G., Barrea, L., Scerbo, F., Esposito, E., & De Lorenzo, A. (2020). Eating habits and lifestyle changes during COVID-19 lockdown: An Italian survey. *Journal of Translational Medicine, 18*(1), 229–229. https://doi.org/10.1186/s12967-020-02399-5

Dodd, R., Dadaczynski, K., Okan, O., McCaffery, K. J., & Pickles, K. (2021). Psychological wellbeing and academic experience of university students in

Australia during COVID-19. *International Journal of Environmental Research and Public Health, 18*(3), 866. https://doi.org/10.3390/ijerph18030866

Doggrell, S., & Schaffer, S. (2016). Reduced withdrawal and failure rates of accelerated nursing students enrolled in pharmacology is associated with a supportive intervention. *BMC Medical Education, 16*(1), 40–40. https://doi.org/10.1186/s12909-016-0570-z

Douglas, J., Douglas, A., McClelland, R. J., & Davies, J. (2015). Understanding student satisfaction and dissatisfaction: An interpretive study in the UK higher education context. *Studies in Higher Education, 40*(2), 329–349. https://doi.org/10.1080/03075079.2013.842217

Duffy, R. D. (2006). Spirituality, religion, and career development: Current status and future directions. *Career Development Quarterly, 55*, 52–53.

Eagly, A. H. (1987). Sex differences in social behavior: A social-role interpretation. Lawrence Erlbaum.

Egege, S., & Kutieleh, S. (2015). Peer mentors as a transition strategy at university: Why mentoring needs to have boundaries. *The Australian Journal of Education, 59*(3), 265–277. https://doi.org/10.1177/0004944115604697

El-Abd, M., & Chaaban, Y. (2021). The role of vicarious experiences in the development of preservice teachers' classroom management self-efficacy beliefs. *International Journal of Early Years Education, 29*(3), 282–297. https://doi.org/10.1080/09669760.2020.1779669

Employability Forums from the University of Sydney (n.d.). https://educational-innovation.sydney.edu.au/teaching@sydney/national-employability-forum/

Erikson, E. H. (1968). *Identity, youth and crisis*. Norton.

Evans, D., Borriello, G. A., & Field, A. P. (2018). A review of the academic and psychological impact of the transition to secondary education. *Frontiers in Psychology, 9*, 1482–1482. https://doi.org/10.3389/fpsyg.2018.01482

Ewing, S. (2012, October). *The psychological stages of thesis writing*. https://blogs.colum.edu/marginalia/2012/10/11/the-psychological-stages-of-thesis-writing/

Eyice Karabacak, D., Demir, S., Yeğit, O. O., Can, A., Terzioğlu, K., Ünal, D., Olgaç, M., Coşkun, R., Çolakoğlu, B., Büyüköztürk, S., & Gelincik, A. (2021). Impact of anxiety, stress and depression related to COVID-19 pandemic on the course of hereditary angioedema with C1-inhibitor deficiency. *Allergy, 76*(8), 2535–2543. https://doi.org/10.1111/all.14796

Farrer, L., Gulliver, A., Bennett, K., Fassnacht, D. B., & Griffiths, K. M. (2016). Demographic and psychosocial predictors of major depression and generalised anxiety disorder in Australian university students. *BMC Psychiatry, 16*(1), 241–241. https://doi.org/10.1186/s12888-016-0961-z

Ferguson, D. (2021, April 11). UK university students struggle with stress as uncertainty grows over return date. *The Guardian*. www.theguardian.com/education/2021/

apr/11/uk-university-students-struggle-with-stress-as-uncertainty-grows-over-return-date

Ferrer, J., Ringer, A., Saville, K., A Parris, M., & Kashi, K. (2022). Students' motivation and engagement in higher education: The importance of attitude to online learning. *Higher Education*, *83*(2), 317–338. https://doi.org/10.1007/s10734-020-00657-5

Föhr, T., Tolvanen, A., Myllymäki, T., Järvelä-Reijonen, E., Peuhkuri, K., Rantala, S., Kolehmainen, M., Korpela, R., Lappalainen, R., Ermes, M., Puttonen, S., Rusko, H., & Kujala, U. (2017). Physical activity, heart rate variability-based stress and recovery, and subjective stress during a 9-month study period. *Scandinavian Journal of Medicine & Science in Sports*, *27*(6), 612–621. https://doi.org/10.1111/sms.12683

Foundation of Critical Thinking (2021). *Defining critical thinking*. www.critical-thinking.org/pages/defining-critical-thinking/766

Garcia-Ros, R., Perez-Gonzalez, F., Perez-Blasco, J., & Natividad, L. A. (2012). Academic stress in first-year college students. *Revista latinoamericana de psicología*, *44*(2), 143–154.

Gardner, H. (1983) Frames of mind: The theory of multiple intelligences. NY: Basic Books.

Gaultney, J. F. (2010). The prevalence of sleep disorders in college students: Impact on academic performance. *Journal of American College Health*, *59*(2), 91–97. https://doi.org/10.1080/07448481.2010.483708

Geddes, L. (2018). Huge brain study uncovers "buried" genetic networks linked to mental illness. *Nature (London)*. https://doi.org/10.1038/d41586-018-07750-x

Geng, G., & Disney, L. (2010). *Investigation of technical support provided by educational websites*. Proceedings of International Conference on Education Technology and Computer 2010, Shanghai. http://dx.doi.org/10.1109/ICETC.2010.5529287

Geng, G., & Midford, R. (2015). Investigating first year education students' stress level. *The Australian Journal of Teacher Education*, *40*(6), 1–12. https://doi.org/10.14221/ajte.2015v40n6.1

Geng, G. Smith, P., Black, P., Budd, Y., & Disney, L. (2019). *Reflective practice in teaching pre-service teachers and the lens of life experience*. Springer Singapore.

God, Y., & Zhang, H. (2019). Intercultural challenges, intracultural practices: How Chinese and Australian students understand and experience intercultural communication at an Australian university. *Higher Education*, *78*(2), 305–322. https://doi.org/10.1007/s10734-018-0344-0

Gomes do Rosario, C. (2017). Strategies to engage Attention-Deficit Hyperactivity Disorder (ADHD) and mainstream students in the classroom. In G. Geng, P. Smith, & P. Black (Eds.), *The challenge of teaching* (pp. 189–194). Springer.

González-Ramírez, M. T., Rodríguez-Ayán, M. N., & Hernández, R. L. (2013). The Perceived Stress Scale (PSS): Normative data and factor structure for a large-scale sample in Mexico. *The Spanish Journal of Psychology, 16*, E47–E47. https://doi.org/10.1017/sjp.2013.35

Graves, B., Hall, M. E., Dias-Karch, C., Haischer, M. H., & Apter, C. (2021). Gender differences in perceived stress and coping among college students. *PLOS One, 16*(8), e0255634. https://doi.org/10.1371/journal.pone.0255634

Greenidge, S. (2019, August). *3 tips for managing thesis writing stress.* www.ucl.ac.uk/students/news/2019/aug/3-tips-managing-thesis-writing-stress

Grossman, M., & Wood, W. (1993). Sex differences in intensity of emotional experience: A social role interpretation. *Journal of Personality and Social Psychology, 65*(5), 1010–1022.

Guo, S., Liu, F., Shen, J., Wei, M., & Yang, Y. (2020). Comparative efficacy of seven exercise interventions for symptoms of depression in college students: A network of meta-analysis. *Medicine, 99*(47), e23058–e23058. https://doi.org/10.1097/MD.0000000000023058

Gutknecht-Gmeiner, M. (2013). Experts, reviewers or amateurs: What kind of competence and training in evaluation do peers need? *Zeitschrift für Evaluation, 12*(2), 235–256.

Gyllensten, K., & Palmer, S. (2005). The role of gender in workplace stress: A critical literature review. *Health Educational Journal, 64*(3), 271–288.

Halbesleben, J., Neveu, J.-P., Paustian-Underdahl, S. C., & Westman, M. (2014). Getting to the 'COR': Understanding the role of resources in Conservation of Resources Theory. *Journal of Management, 40*(5), 1334–1364. https://doi.org/10.1177/0149206314527130

Harkness, K., & Hayden, E. P. (Eds.) (2018). *The Oxford handbook of stress and mental health.* Oxford University Press.

Harmoinen, S., Koivu, K., & Pääsky, L. (2020). University students' readiness for social activity in climate actions. *Discourse and Communication for Sustainable Education, 11*(1), 134–152. https://doi.org/10.2478/dcse-2020-0012

Harvey, L., Drew, S., & Smith, M. (2006). *The first-year experience: A review of literature for the higher education academy.* www.qualityresearchinternational.com/Harvey%20papers/Harvey%20and%20Drew%202006.pdf

Haskell, W. L., Lee, I-M., Pate, R. R., Powell, K. E., Blair, S. N., Franklin, B. A., Macera, C. A., Heath, G.W., Thompson, P. D., & Bauman, A. (2007). Physical activity and public health: Updated recommendation for adults from the American college of sports medicine and the American heart association. *Circulation, 116*(9), 1081–1093. https://doi.org/10.1161/CIRCULATIONAHA.107.185649

Healthline (2021). *Do you really burn more calories while standing?* www.healthline.com/health/fitness-exercise/calories-burned-standing

Heaney, J., Gatfield, T., Clarke, P., & Caelli, J. (2006, December). *Using action research to implement and evaluate peer learning in marketing courses:*

Engaging students through self-learning [Paper presentation]. Australian and New Zealand Marketing Academy (ANZMAC) Conference. https://anzmac.org/conference_archive/2006/documents/Heaney_Joo-Gim.pdf

Heijnen, S., Hommel, B., Kibele, A., & Colzato, L. S. (2016). Neuromodulation of aerobic exercise-A review. *Frontiers in Psychology*, 6, 1890–1890. https://doi.org/10.3389/fpsyg.2015.01890

Hellemans, K., Abizaid, A., Gabrys, R., McQuaid, R., & Patterson, Z. (2020, November). *For university students, COVID-19 stress creates perfect conditions for mental health crises*. The Conversation. https://theconversation.com/for-university-students-covid-19-stress-creates-perfect-conditions-for-mental-health-crises-149127

Helliwell, J., Layard, R., Sachs, J. D., Neve, J-E. D., Aknin, L., Wang, S., & Paculor, S. (2021). *World happiness report*. https://worldhappiness.report/ed/2021/

Henning, M. A., Krägeloh, C. U., Dryer, R., Moir, F., Billington, R., & Hill, A. G. (Eds.) (2018). *Wellbeing in higher education: Cultivating a healthy lifestyle among faculty and students*. ProQuest Ebook Central. https://ebookcentral.proquest.com

Hewitt, P., Flett, G. L., & Mosher, S. W. (1992). The Perceived Stress Scale: Factor structure and relation to depression symptoms in a psychiatric sample. *Journal of Psychopathology and Behavioral Assessment*, 14(3), 247–257. https://doi.org/10.1007/BF00962631

Hobfoll, S. (1989). Conservation of Resources: A new attempt at conceptualizing stress. *The American Psychologist*, 44(3), 513–524. https://doi.org/10.1037/0003-066X.44.3.513

Hoffman, J. A., & Miller, E. A. (2020). Addressing the consequences of school closure due to COVID-19 on children's physical and mental well-being. *World Medical and Health Policy*, 12(3), 300–310.

Holland, J., Major, D., & Orvis, K. (2012). Understanding how peer mentoring and capitalization link STEM students to their majors. *The Career Development Quarterly*, 60, 343–354. https://doi.org/10.1002/j.2161-0045.2012.00026.x

Holmgreen, L., Tirone, V., Gerhart, J., & Hobfoll, S. E. (2017). Conservation of resources theory. In C. L. Cooper & J. C. Quick (Eds.), *The handbook of stress and health: A guide to research and practice* (pp. 443–457). Wiley.

Honicke, T., & Broadbent, J. (2016). The influence of academic self-efficacy on academic performance: A systematic review. *Educational Research Review*, 17, 63–84. https://doi.org/10.1016/j.edurev.2015.11.002

Horowitz, M. J. (1976). *Stress response syndromes*. Jason Aronson.

Horowitz, M. J. (2001). *Stress response syndromes* (4th ed.). Jason Aronson.

Howe, L. C., & Krosnick, J. A. (2017). Attitude strength. *Annual Review of Psychology*, 68, 327–351. https://doi.org/10.1146/annurev-psych-122414-033600

How to perform the 4-7-8 breath to relieve unhealthy stress (2018). *The Journal of Medical Practice Management*, 33(6), 337–338.

Hunt, W., & Scott, P. (2020). Paid and unpaid graduate internships: Prevalence, quality and motivations at six months after graduation. *Studies in Higher Education*, *45*(2), 464–476. https://doi.org/10.1080/03075079.2018.1541450 www.healio.com/news/primary-care/20200623/survey-us-adults-changing-eating-habits-during-covid19

Jett, Q., & George, J. M. (2003). Work interrupted: A closer look at the role of interruptions in organizational life. *The Academy of Management Review*, *28*(3), 494–507. https://doi.org/10.2307/30040736

Ji, L-Y., Li, X-L., Liu, Y., Sun, X-W., Wang, H-F., Chen, L., & Gao, L. (2017). Time-dependent effects of acute exercise on university students' cognitive performance in temperate and cold environments. *Frontiers in Psychology*, *8*, 1192–1192. https://doi.org/10.3389/fpsyg.2017.01192

Jia, F., Krettenauer, T., & Li, L. (2019). Moral identity in cultural context: Differences between Canadian and Chinese university students. *Journal of Moral Education*, *48*(2), 247–262. https://doi.org/10.1080/03057240.2018.1499504

Jick, T. D., & Mitz, L. F. (1985). Sex differences in work stress. *Academy of Management Review*, *10*(3), 408–429.

Johnson, I. (2008). Enrollment, persistence and graduation of in-state students at a public research university: Does high school matter? *Research in Higher Education*, *49*, 776–793. https://dx.doi.org/10.1007/s11162-008-9105-8

Joubert, C., & Hay, J. (2020). Registered psychological counsellor training at a South African faculty of education: Are we impacting educational communities? *South African Journal of Education*, *40*(3), 1–9. https://doi.org/10.15700/saje.v40n3a1840

Kahn, W., Jackson, M., Kennedy, G., & Conduit, R. (2019). The effect of rotating shift schedules on sleep, mood, stress, energy expenditure and physical activity of Australian paramedics: A field study. *Sleep Medicine*, *64*, S78–S78. https://doi.org/10.1016/j.sleep.2019.11.215

Karam, F., Bérard, A., Sheehy, O., Huneau, M.-C., Briggs, G., Chambers, C., Einarson, A., Johnson, D., Kao, K., Koren, G., Martin, B., Polifka, J. E., Riordan, S. H., Roth, M., Lavigne, S. V., & Wolfe, L. (2012). Reliability and validity of the 4-item perceived stress scale among pregnant women: Results from the OTIS antidepressants study. *Research in Nursing & Health*, *35*(4), 363–375. https://doi.org/10.1002/nur.21482

Kargin, M., Aytop, S., Hazar, S., & Yüksekol, Ö. D. (2021). The relationship between gender role stress and self esteem in students of faculty of health sciences. *Perspectives in Psychiatric Care*, *57*(1), 363–370. https://doi.org/10.1111/ppc.12605

Karimshah, A., Wyder, M., Henman, P., Tay, D., Capelin, E., & Short, P. (2013). Overcoming adversity among low SES students: A study of strategies for retention. *The Australian Universities' Review*, *55*(2), 5–14.

Keshavarz, M., & Hulus, A. (2019). The effect of students' personality and learning styles on their motivation for using blended learning. *Advances in Language and Literary Studies*, *10*(6), 78–88. https://doi.org/10.7575/aiac.alls.v.10n.6p.78

Ketonen, E., Haarala-Muhonen, A., Hirsto, L., Hänninen, J. J., Wähälä, K., & Lonka, K. (2016). Am I in the right place? Academic engagement and study success during the first years at university. *Learning and Individual Differences*, *51*, 141–148. https://doi.org/10.1016/j.lindif.2016.08.017

Kift, S. (2009). Articulating a transition pedagogy to scaffold and to enhance the first-year student learning experience in Australian higher education: Final report for ALTC Senior Fellowship Program. *Australian Learning and Teaching Council*. https://transitionpedagogy.com/reports-andresources/fellowship-report/

Kim, H., Hong, A. J., & Song, H.-D. (2019). The roles of academic engagement and digital readiness in students' achievements in university e-learning environments. *International Journal of Educational Technology in Higher Education*, *16*(1), 1–18. https://doi.org/10.1186/s41239-019-0152-3

Kim, S., Park, Y., & Niu, Q. (2017). Micro-break activities at work to recover from daily work demands: Micro-break activities. *Journal of Organizational Behavior*, *38*(1), 28–44. https://doi.org/10.1002/job.2109

Kissam, B. (2021). *Take control: How to set academic goals in 2021 and beyond.* www.apu.edu/articles/take-control-how-to-set-academic-goals-in-2021-and-beyond/

Klaiber, P., Whillans, A., & Chen, F. (2018). Long-term health implications of students' friendship formation during the transition to university. *Applied Psychology : Health and Well-Being*, *10*(2), 290–308. https://doi.org/10.1111/aphw.12131

Klein, E. M., Brahler, E., Dreier, M., Reinecke, L., Muller, K. W., Schmutzer, G., Wolfling, K., & Beutel, M. E. (2016). The German version of the Perceived Stress Scale – psychometric characteristics in a representative German community sample. *BMC Psychiatry*, *16*(157).

Klemm, S. (2019). *How many calories do adults need?* Academy of Nutrition and Dietetics. www.eatright.org/food/nutrition/dietary-guidelines-and-myplate/how-many-calories-do-adults-need

Klir, G. J. (1972). Trends in general systems theory. Wiley.

Kostić, J., Žikić, O., Đorđević, V., & Krivokapić, Ž. (2021). Perceived stress among university students in south-east Serbia during the COVID-19 outbreak. *Annals of General Psychiatry*, *20*(1), 25–25. https://doi.org/10.1186/s12991-021-00346-2

Kruml, S. M., & Geddes, D. (2000). Exploring the dimensions of emotional labor. *Management Communication Quarterly*, *14*, 8–49.

Kuiper, N. A., Olinger, L. J., & Lyons, L. M. (1986). Global perceived stress level as a moderator of the relationship between negative life events and depression. *Journal of Human Stress*, *12*, 149–153.

Labrague, L. J., De los Santos, J. A. A., & Falguera, C. C. (2021). Social and emotional loneliness among college students during the COVID-19 pandemic:

The predictive role of coping behaviors, social support, and personal resilience. *Perspectives in Psychiatric Care*, *57*(4), 1578–1584. https://doi.org/10.1111/ppc.12721

Lambourne, K., & Tomporowski, P. (2010). The effect of exercise-induced arousal on cognitive task performance: A meta-regression analysis. *Brain Research*, *1341*, 12–24. https://doi.org/10.1016/j.brainres.2010.03.091

Landolt, H-P., Retey, J. V., Tönz, K., Gottselig, J. M., Khatami, R., Buckelmüller, I., & Achermann, P. (2004). Caffeine attenuates waking and sleep electroencephalographic markers of sleep homeostasis in humans. *Neuropsychopharmacology*, *29*(10), 1933–1939. https://doi.org/10.1038/sj.npp.1300526

Latham, C. (2020). Five quick brain teasers to flex those attention and working memory mental muscles. *SharpBrains* [Blog]. Newstex. https://sharpbrains.com/blog/2020/04/27/five-quick-brain-teasers-to-flex-those-attention-and-working-memory-mental-muscles

Latzman, R. D., Elkovitch, N., Young, J., & Clark, L. A. (2010). The contribution of executive functioning to academic achievement among male adolescents. *Journal of Clinical and Experimental Neuropsychology*, *32*(5), 455–462. https://doi.org/10.1080/13803390903164363

Lazarus, R. S. (1966). Psychological stress and the coping process. McGraw-Hill.

Lee, E-H. (2012). Review of the psychometric evidence of the Perceived Stress Scale. *Asian Nursing Research*, *6*(4), 121–127. https://doi.org/10.1016/j.anr.2012.08.004

Lee, W. (2017). Relationships among grit, academic performance, perceived academic failure, and stress in associate degree students. *Journal of Adolescence*, *60*(1), 148–152. https://doi.org/10.1016/j.adolescence.2017.08.006

Lee-St, J.,Walsh, M. E., Raczek, A. E., Vuilleumier, C. E., Foley, C., Heberle, A., Sibley, E., & Dearing, E. (2018). The long-term impact of systemic student support in elementary school: Reducing high school dropout. *AERA Open*, *4*(4). https://doi.org/10.1177/2332858418799085

Lemma, S., Gelaye, B., Berhane, Y., Worku, A., & Williams, M. A. (2012). Sleep quality and its psychological correlates among university students in Ethiopia: A cross-sectional study. *BMC Psychiatry*, *12*(1), 237–237. https://doi.org/10.1186/1471-244X-12-237

Lemon, N., & McDonough, S. (2020). Building and sustaining a teaching career: Strategies for professional experience, wellbeing and mindful practice. Cambridge University Press.

Leung, D., Lam, T-H., & Chan, S. S. (2010). Three versions of Perceived Stress Scale: Validation in a sample of Chinese cardiac patients who smoke. *BMC Public Health*, *10*(1), 513–513. https://doi.org/10.1186/1471-2458-10-513

Leyse-Wallace, R. (2013). *Nutrition and mental health*. CRC Press.

Li, J., Han, X., Wang, W., Sun, G., & Cheng, Z. (2018). How social support influences university students' academic achievement and emotional exhaustion:

The mediating role of self-esteem. *Learning and Individual Differences, 61,* 120–126. https://doi.org/10.1016/j.lindif.2017.11.016

Lines, R., Ducker, K. J., Ntoumanis, N., Thøgersen-Ntoumani, C., Fletcher, D., & Gucciardi, D. F. (2021). Stress, physical activity, sedentary behavior, and resilience – The effects of naturalistic periods of elevated stress: A measurement-burst study. *Psychophysiology, 58*(8), e13846. https://doi.org/10.1111/psyp.13846

Liu, S., Gallois, C., & Volčič, Z. (2019). Introducing intercultural communication: Global cultures and contexts (3rd ed.). Sage.

Liu, S., Li, S., Shang, S., & Ren, X. (2021). How do critical thinking ability and critical thinking disposition relate to the mental health of university students? *Frontiers in Psychology, 12,* 704229–704229. https://doi.org/10.3389/fpsyg.2021.704229

Loehr, J., & Schwartz, T. (2005). The power of full engagement: Managing energy, not time, is the key to high performance and personal renewal. Free Press Paperbacks.

Logan, B., & Burns, S. (2021). Stressors among young Australian university students: A qualitative study. *Journal of American College Health.* Advance online publication. https://doi.org/10.1080/07448481.2021.1947303

LoMauro, A., Colli, A., Colombo, L., & Aliverti, A. (2022). Breathing patterns recognition: A functional data analysis approach. *Computer Methods and Programs in Biomedicine, 217,* 106670–106670. https://doi.org/10.1016/j.cmpb.2022.106670

Long, M., Ferrier, F., & Heagney, M. (2006). *Stay, play or give it away? Students continuing, changing or leaving university study in first year.* Monash University – Australian Council for Educational Research Centre for the Economics of Education and Training. www.dest.gov.au/sectors/higher_education/publications_resources/profiles/stay_play_giveaway.htm.

Lopreato, J. (1977). Review of General system theory: Foundations, development, applications. *American Sociological Review, 35*(3), 543–545. https://doi.org/10.2307/2093003

Lovibond, S. H., & Lovibond, P. F. (1995). *Manual for the depression anxiety stress scales* (2nd ed.). Psychology Foundation of Australia.

Lund, H. G., Reider, B. D., Whiting, A. B., & Prichard, J. R. (2010). Sleep patterns and predictors of disturbed sleep in a large population of college students. *Journal of Adolescent Health, 46*(2), 124–132. https://doi.org/10.1016/j.jadohealth.2009.06.016

Macaskill, A. (2013). The mental health of university students in the United Kingdom. *British Journal of Guidance & Counselling, 41*(4), 426–441. https://doi.org/10.1080/03069885.2012.743110

MacCann, C., Jiang, Y., Brown, L. E. R., Double, K. S., Bucich, M., & Minbashian, A. (2020). Emotional intelligence predicts academic performance: A meta-analysis. *Psychological Bulletin, 146*(2), 150–186. https://doi.org/10.1037/bul0000219

Mahdy, D., & Zaghloul, H. (2020). The impact of practical aspects of communication and thinking skills formation on improving self-management skills in university students. *Obrazovanie i Nauka*, 22(8), 40–74. https://doi.org/10.17853/1994-5639-2020-8-40-74

Martins, A., Ramalho, N., & Morin, E. (2010). A comprehensive meta-analysis of the relationship between emotional intelligence and health. *Personality and Individual Differences, 49*, 554–564. https://doi.org/10.1016/j.paid.2010.05.029

Maymon, R., & Hall, N. C. (2021). A review of first-year student stress and social support. *Social Sciences, 10*(12), 472 (1-32). https://doi.org/10.3390/socsci10120472

McCarthy, L., & Glozer, S. (2022). Heart, mind and body: #NoMorePage3 and the replenishment of emotional energy. *Organization Studies, 43*(3), 369–394. https://doi.org/10.1177/0170840621994501

Meadows-Fernandez, R. (2017). There's such a thing as post-graduation depression. I know: I had it. *The Washington Post.* www.washingtonpost.com/national/health-science/theres-such-a-thing-as-post-graduation-depression-i-know-i-had-it/2017/08/04/4d163c6a-618d-11e7-a4f7-af34fc1d9d39_story.html

Meehan, C., & Howells, K. (2019). In search of the feeling of 'belonging' in higher education: Undergraduate students transition into higher education. *Journal of Further and Higher Education, 43*(10), 1376–1390. https://doi.org/10.1080/0309877X.2018.1490702

Meijman, T. F., & Mulder, G. (1998). Psychological aspects of workload. In P. J. D. Drenth & H. Thierry (Eds.), *Handbook of Work and Organizational Psychology. Volume, 2 Work psychology* (pp. 5–33). Hove, UK: Psychology Press.

Mercader, C., & Patel, B. P. (2013). Caffeine abuse: The phantom differential in sleep complaints/disorders? *Journal of Substance Use, 18*(3), 242–245. https://doi.org/10.3109/14659891.2012.715228

Miller, J., Krosnick, J. A., Holbrook, A. L., Tahk, A., & Dionne, A. (2016). The impact of policy change threat on financial contributions to interest groups. In J. Krosnick, I. Chiang, & T. Stark (Eds.), *Political Psychology: New Explorations* (pp. 172–202). Routledge.

Milne, A. A., & Shepard, E. H. (1959). *Winnie-the-Pooh.* Methuen.

Mimura, C., & Griffiths, P. (2004). A Japanese version of the perceived stress scale: Translation and preliminary test. *International Journal of Nursing Studies, 41*(4), 379–385. https://doi.org/10.1016/j.ijnurstu.2003.10.009

Mojza, E. J., Sonnentag, S., & Bornemann, C. (2011). Volunteer work as a valuable leisure-time activity: A day-level study on volunteer work, non-work experiences, and wellbeing at work. *Journal of Occupational and Organizational Psychology, 84*, 123–152. https://doi.org/10.1348/096317910X485737

Monash University (2022). *Introduction to literature reviews*, Research & Learning Online. www.monash.edu/rlo/graduate-research-writing/write-the-thesis/introduction-literature-reviews

Mooney, A., Moncrieff, K., & Hickey, C. (2018). Exploring pre-service teachers' experience of sport education as an approach to transition pedagogy. *Physical Education and Sport Pedagogy*, 23(6), 545–558. https://doi.org/10.1080/1740 8989.2018.1485137

Moshman, D., & Ebooks Corporation (2015). Epistemic cognition and development: The psychology of justification and truth.

Muñoz-Rodríguez, J. R., Luna-Castro, J., Ballesteros-Yáñez, I., Pérez-Ortiz, J. M., Gómez-Romero, F. J., Redondo-Calvo, F. J., Alguacil, L. F., & Castillo, C. A. (2021). Influence of biomedical education on health and eating habits of university students in Spain. *Nutrition*, 86, 111181. https://doi.org/10.1016/j. nut.2021.111181

Naylor, R., Baik, C., & Arkoudis, S. (2018). Identifying attrition risk based on the first year experience. *Higher Education Research and Development*, 37(2), 328–342. https://doi.org/10.1080/07294360.2017.1370438

Nelson, D. L., & Burke, R. J. (2002). *Gender, work stress and health*. American Psychological Association.

Nelson, D. L., & Quick, J. C. (1985). Professional women: Are distress and disease inevitable? *Academy of Management Review*, 10(2), 206–218.

Neuman, B., & Fawcett, J. (2011). *The Neuman systems model* (5th ed.). Pearson.

Newhouse, P., & Albert, K. (2015). Estrogen, stress, and depression: A neuro-cognitive model. *JAMA Psychiatry*, 72(7), 727–729. https://doi.org/10.1001/jamapsychiatry.2015.0487

Nob, R. (2021). Dimensionality of social persuasion and its relationship with academic self-efficacy. *Psychological Studies*, 66(1), 49–61. https://doi.org/10.1007/s12646-020-00588-2

O'Boyle, E. H., Jr., Humphrey, R. H., Pollack, J. M., Hawver, T. H., & Storey, P. A. (2011). The relation between emotional intelligence and job performance: A meta-analysis. *Journal of Organizational Behavior*, 32, 788–818. https://doi.org/10.1002/job.714

Ohland, M.W., Loughry, M. L., Woehr, D. J., Bullard, L. G., Felder, R. M., Finelli, C. J., Layton, R. A., Pomeranz, H. R., & Schmucker, D. G. (2012). The Comprehensive assessment of team member effectiveness: Development of a behaviorally anchored rating scale for self- and peer evaluation. *Academy of Management Learning & Education*, 11(4), 609–630. https://doi.org/10.5465/amle.2010.0177

O'Leary, Z. (2010). *The essential guide to doing your research project* (2nd ed.). Sage.

Olvera, P. M., Ledezma, J. C., Alvarado, P. V., González, A. R., González, L. G., Robles, K. A., Sandoval, K. M., González, N. T., Nava, M. A., & Vera, A. T. (2018). Academic stress, stressors and coping in dental students at the Metropolitan University Studies Center Hidalgo [CEUMH]. *Journal of Negative & No Positive Results*, 3(7), 522–530. https://doi.org/10.19230/jonnpr.2512

Ortiz-Lozano, J., Rua-Vieites, A., Bilbao-Calabuig, P., & Casadesús-Fa, M. (2020). University student retention: Best time and data to identify undergraduate students at risk of dropout. *Innovations in Education and Teaching International*, 57(1), 74–85. https://doi.org/10.1080/14703297.2018.1502090

Owens, S., Helms, S. W., Rudolph, K. D., Hastings, P. D., Nock, M. K., & Prinstein, M. J. (2018). Interpersonal stress severity longitudinally predicts adolescent girls' depressive symptoms: The moderating role of subjective and HPA axis stress responses. *Journal of Abnormal Child Psychology*, 47(5), 895–905. https://doi.org/10.1007/s10802-018-0483-x

Pannicke, B., Kaiser, T., Reichenberger, J., & Blechert, J. (2021). Networks of stress, affect and eating behaviour: Anticipated stress coping predicts goal-congruent eating in young adults. *The International Journal of Behavioral Nutrition and Physical Activity*, 18(1), 9. https://doi.org/10.1186/s12966-020-01066-8

Pearce, J. M. S. (2019). The "split brain" and Roger Wolcott Sperry (1913–1994). *Revue Neurologique*, 175(4), 217–220. https://doi.org/10.1016/j.neurol.2018.07.007

Pedler, M., Willis, R., & Nieuwoudt, J. E. (2022). A sense of belonging at university: Student retention, motivation and enjoyment. *Journal of Further and Higher Education*, 46(3), 397–408. https://doi.org/10.1080/0309877X.2021.1955844

Peel, M., Powell, S., & Treacey, M. (2004). Student perspectives on temporary and permanent exit from university: A case study from Monash University. *Journal of Higher Education Policy and Management*, 26(2), 239–249. https://doi.org/10.1080/1360080042000218285

Petty, R., & Cacioppo, J. T. (1986). Communication and persuasion central and peripheral routes to attitude change. Springer.

Pickell, D. (2021, October). *What is the data analysis process? 5 key steps to follow*. www.g2.com/articles/data-analysis-process

Planas-Lladó, A., Feliu, L., Arbat, G., Pujol, J., Suñol, J. J., Castro, F., & Martí, C. (2021). An analysis of teamwork based on self and peer evaluation in higher education. *Assessment and Evaluation in Higher Education*, 46(2), 191–207. https://doi.org/10.1080/02602938.2020.1763254

Polychronopoulou, E., Berney, M., Wuerzner, G., Tudor, L. P., Ribom, G., Satrauskiene, A., Kennedy, C., Lindroos, A., Padpavola, O., Cifkova, R., Parati, G., & Burnier, M. (2019). Effects of slow deep breathing on short-term changes in blood pressure, heart rate and o2 saturation at altitude: data from an experimental session at the Esh summer school 2018. *Journal of Hypertension, 37 Suppl 1*, e94–e94. https://doi.org/10.1097/01.hjh.0000570352.10524.2c

Popoola, S., & Fagbola, O. O. (2021). Work–life balance, self-esteem, work motivation, and organizational commitment of library personnel in federal universities in southern Nigeria. *The International Information & Library Review*, 53(3), 214–228. https://doi.org/10.1080/10572317.2020.1840244

Price-Mitchell, M. (2018). Goal-setting is linked to higher achievement. *Psychology Today*. www.psychologytoday.com/us/blog/the-moment-youth/201803/goal-setting-is-linked-higher-achievement

Prinstein, M. J., & La Greca, A. M. (2002). Peer crowd affiliation and internalizing distress in childhood and adolescence: A longitudinal follow-back study. *Journal of Research on Adolescence, 12*(3), 325–351. https://doi.org/10.1111/1532-7795.00036

Prowse, R., Sherratt, F., Abizaid, A., Gabrys, R. L., Hellemans, K. G. C., Patterson, Z. R., & McQuaid, R. J. (2021). Coping with the COVID-19 pandemic: Examining gender differences in stress and mental health among university students. *Frontiers in Psychiatry, 12*, 650759–650759. https://doi.org/10.3389/fpsyt.2021.650759

Pushkarev, G. S., Zimet, G. D., Kuznetsov, V. A., & Yaroslavskaya, E. I. (2020). The Multidimensional Scale of Perceived Social Support (MSPSS): Reliability and validity of Russian version. *Clinical Gerontologist, 43*(3), 331–339. https://doi.org/10.1080/07317115.2018.1558325

Putwain, D. W. (2019). Wellbeing and higher education. *Educational Psychology, 39*(3), 291–293.

Quality Indicators for Learning and Teaching [QILT] (2021). *Medium-term graduate: graduate outcomes in Australia.* www.qilt.edu.au/docs/default-source/default-document-library/2021-gos-l-national-report9ae5ea6b391f-45b0af9d76cc92655563.pdf?sfvrsn=d5faafb8_0

Reid, K., Flowers, P., & Larkin, M. (2005). Exploring lived experience. *Psychologist, 18*(1), 20–23.

Remor, E. (2006). Psychometric properties of a European Spanish version of the Perceived Stress Scale (PSS). *The Spanish Journal of Psychology, 9*(1), 86–93. https://doi.org/10.1017/S1138741600006004

Richardson, M., Abraham, C., & Bond, R. (2012). Psychological correlates of university students' academic performance: A systematic review and meta-analysis. *Psychological Bulletin, 138*(2), 353–387. https://doi.org/10.1037/a0026838

Rieg, S. A., Paquette, K. R., & Chen, Y. (2007). Coping with stress: An investigation of novice teachers' stressors in the elementary classroom. *Education, 128*(2), 211–226.

Rigler, K. L., Bowlin, L. K., Sweat, K., Watts, S., & Throne, R. (2017). *Agency, socialisation, and support: A critical review of doctoral student attrition* [Paper presentation]. 3rd International Conference on Doctoral Education, University of Central Florida.

Saccaro, A., & França, M. T. A. (2020). Stop-out and drop-out: The behavior of the first year withdrawal of students of the Brazilian higher education receiving FIES funding. *International Journal of Educational Development, 77*, 102221. https://doi.org/10.1016/j.ijedudev.2020.102221

Sadowski, C., Stewart, M., & Pediaditis, M. (2018). Pathway to success: Using students' insights and perspectives to improve retention and success for university students from low socioeconomic (LSE) backgrounds. *International Journal of Inclusive Education, 22*(2), 158–175. https://doi.org/10.1080/13603116.2017.1362048

Sanchez, R. J., Bauer, T. N., & Paronto, M. E. (2006). Peer-mentoring freshmen: Implications for satisfaction, commitment and retention to graduation. *Academy of Management Learning & Education*, 5(1), 25–37. https://doi.org/10.5465/AMLE.2006.20388382

Santiago, P., Nielsen, T., Smithers, L. G., Roberts, R., & Jamieson, L. (2020). Measuring stress in Australia: Validation of the Perceived Stress Scale (PSS-14) in a national sample. *Health and Quality of Life Outcomes*, 18(1), 100–100. https://doi.org/10.1186/s12955-020-01343-x

Sawatzky, R., Ratner, P. A., Richardson, C. G., Washburn, C., Sudmant, W., & Mirwaldt, P. (2012). Stress and depression in students: The mediating role of stress management self-efficacy. *Nursing Research*, 61(1), 13–21. https://doi.org/10.1097/NNR.0b013e31823b1440

Schelling, T. C. (1980). The intimate contest for self-command. *The Public Interest*, 60(60), 94–94.

Schlarb, A. A., Friedrich, A., & Claßen, M. (2017). Sleep problems in university students – an intervention. *Neuropsychiatric Disease and Treatment*, 13, 1989–2001. https://doi.org/10.2147/NDT.S142067

Science Student Services at Monash University (n.d.). www.monash.edu/science/current-students/help-and-support

Scott, G., Shan, M., Grebennikov, L., & Singh, H. (2008). Improving student retention: A University of Western Sydney case study. *Journal of Institutional Research*, 14, 1–23.

Selfhout, M. H., Branje, S. J., ter Bogt, T. F., & Meeus, W. H. (2007). The role of music preferences in early adolescents' friendship formation and stability. *Journal of Adolescence*, 32(1), 95–107. https://doi.org/10.1016/j.adolescence.2007.11.004

Selye, H. (1936, July 4). A syndrome produced by diverse nocuous agents. *Nature*, 138(3479), 32.

Seyal, A., Siau, N. Z., & Suhali, W. S. H. (2019). Evaluating students' personality and learning styles in higher education: Pedagogical considerations. *International Journal of Learning, Teaching and Educational Research*, 18(7), 145–164. https://doi.org/10.26803/ijlter.18.7.10

Shah, M., Kift, S., & Thomas, L. (2021). Student retention and success in higher education : Institutional change for the 21st century. Palgrave Macmillan.

Shamoo, A. E., & Resnik, D. B. (2009). *Responsible conduct of research* (2nd ed.). Oxford University Press.

Shaw, M. P., Peart, D. J., & Fairhead, O. J. W. (2017). Perceived stress in university students studying in a further education college. *Research in Post-Compulsory Education*, 22(3), 442–452. https://doi.org/10.1080/13596748.2017.1362534

Sherman, T., & Kurshan, B. (2005). Constructing learning. *Learning & Leading with Technology*, 32(5), 10–39.

Sibley, B. A., Hancock, L., & Bergman, S. M. (2013). University students' exercise behavioral regulation, motives, and physical fitness. *Perceptual and Motor Skills*, 116(1), 322–339. https://doi.org/10.2466/06.10.PMS.116.1.322–339

225

Silva, P., Lopes, B., Costa, M., Melo, A. I., Dias, G. P., Brito, E., & Seabra, D. (2018). The million-dollar question: can internships boost employment? *Studies in Higher Education, 43*(1), 2–21. https://doi.org/10.1080/03075079.2016.1144181

Simpson, P., & Stroh, L. K. (2004). Gender differences: Emotional expression and feelings of personal inauthenticity. *Journal of Applied Psychology, 89*(4), 715–721.

Siqueira, R., Rodrigo, F. H., Adriano, A., & Romélio Rodriguez Añez, C. (2010). Perceived stress scale. *Journal of Health Psychology, 15*(1), 107–114. https://doi.org/10.1177/1359105309346343

Skari, L. (2014). Community college alumni: Predicting who gives. *Community College Review, 42*(1), 23–40. https://doi.org/10.1177/0091552113510172

Small, L., Shaw, A., & McPhail, R. (2021, March 29). *1 in 4 unemployed Australians has a degree. How did we get to this point?* The Conversation. https://theconversation.com/1-in-4-unemployed-australians-has-a-degree-how-did-we-get-to-this-point-156867

Smith, J. A., & Osborn, M. (2015). Interpretative phenomenological analysis as a useful methodology for research on the lived experience of pain. *British Journal of Pain, 9*(1), 41–42. https://doi.org/10.1177/2049463714541642

Sonnentag, S., & Fritz, C. (2007). The recovery experience questionnaire: Development and validation of a measure for assessing recuperation and unwinding from work. *Journal of Occupational Health Psychology, 12*(3), 204–221. https://doi.org/10.1037/1076-8998.12.3.204

Sproesser, G., Schupp, H. T., & Renner, B. (2014). The bright side of stress-induced eating: Eating more when stressed but less when pleased. *Psychological Science, 25*(1), 58–65. https://doi.org/10.1177/0956797613494849

Stacey, V. (2022, January 28). Canada: survey points psychological, academic and financial stress. *ThePieNews*, https://thepienews.com/news/survey-points-psychological-academic-and-financial-stress-in-canada/

St. Hilaire, M. A., & Lockley, S. W. (2015). Caffeine does not entrain the circadian clock but improves daytime alertness in blind patients with non-24-hour rhythms. *Sleep Medicine, 16*(6), 800–804. https://doi.org/10.1016/j.sleep.2015.01.018

Stallman, H. M. (2010). Psychological distress in university students: A comparison with general population data. *Australian Psychologist, 45*(4), 249–257. https://doi.org/10.1080/00050067.2010.482109

Student Accommodation in Melbourne, Australia (n.d.). www.unilodge.com.au/student-accommodation-melbourne/royal-melbourne/rooms-apartments

Students' Union at UCL (2021). *10 ways to make friends at university*. https://studentsunionucl.org/articles/10-ways-to-make-friends-at-university

Sundram, B. M., Dahlui, M., & Chinna, K. (2014). 'Taking my breath away by keeping stress at bay' – An employee assistance program in the automotive assembly plant. *Iranian Journal of Public Health, 43*(3), 263–272.

Swanepoel, A., & van Heerden, S. (2018). An exploration of the roles and the effect of role expectations on the academic performance of first year occupational therapy students:

A University of the Free State case study. *South African Journal of Occupational Therapy*, *48*(1), 16–21. https://doi.org/10.17159/2310-3833/2017/vol48n1a4

Swintopia (2020). www.swinburne.edu.au/news/2020/08/swinburne-unveils-swintopia/

Talsma, K., Robertson, K., Thomas, C., & Norris, K. (2021). COVID-19 beliefs, self-efficacy and academic performance in first-year university students: Cohort comparison and mediation analysis. *Frontiers in Psychology*, *12*, 643408. https://doi.org/10.3389/fpsyg.2021.643408

Thomas, L., & Herbert, J. (2014). *'Sense of belonging' enhances the online learning experience*. The Conversation. https://theconversation.com/sense-of-belonging-enhances-the-online-learning-experience-30503

University of Sydney Career Portal for Students (2022). www.sydney.edu.au/about-us/careers-at-sydney.html

Vaccarino, V., Feekery, A., & Matanimeke, V. (2021). Birds of a feather end up flocking together when studying abroad. Can a university bridge the cultural differences that challenge friendships between Pacific Island students and New Zealand students? *International Journal of Intercultural Relations*, *81*, 204–213. https://doi.org/10.1016/j.ijintrel.2021.01.012

van Assche, K., Valentinov, V., & Verschraegen, G. (2019). Ludwig von Bertalanffy and his enduring relevance: Celebrating 50 years General System Theory. *Systems Research and Behavioral Science*, *36*(3), 251–254. https://doi.org/10.1002/sres.2589

van Gigch, J. (1974). *Applied general systems theory* (3rd ed.). Harper and Row.

van Hooff, M., Flaxman, P., Söderberg, M., Stride, C., & Geurts, S. A. (2018). Basic psychological need satisfaction, recovery state, and recovery timing. *Human Performance*, *31*(2), 125–143. https://doi.org/10.1080/08959285.2018.1466889

van Hooff, M., & Geurts, S. (2014). Need satisfaction during after work hours: Its role in daily recovery. *Stress & Health*, *30*, 198–208. https://doi.org/10.1002/smi.2595

van Rooij, E., Jansen, E., & van de Grift, W. (2018). First-year university students' academic success: The importance of academic adjustment. *European Journal of Psychology of Education*, *33*(4), 749–767. https://doi.org/10.1007/s10212-017-0347-8

Vandeleur, C. L., Jeanpretre, N., Perrez, M., & Schoebi, D. (2009). Cohesion, satisfaction with family bonds, and emotional well-being in families with adolescents. *Journal of Marriage and Family*, *71*(5), 1205–1219. https://doi.org/10.1111/j.1741-3737.2009.00664.x

Vierkant, T. (2013). Mental muscles and the extended will. *Topoi*, *33*(1), 57–65. https://doi.org/10.1007/s11245-013-9188-5

Volet, S., & Ang, G. (2012). Culturally mixed groups on international campuses: An opportunity for inter-cultural learning. *Higher Education Research and Development*, *31*(1), 21–37. https://doi.org/10.1080/07294360.2012.642838

Volpato, C., & Contarello, A. (1999). Towards a social psychology of extreme situations: Primo Levi's If This Is a Man and social identity theory. *European*

Journal of Social Psychology, 29(2–3), 239–258. https://doi.org/10.1002/(SICI)1099-0992(199903/05)29:2/3<239::AID-EJSP926>3.0.CO;2-O

Vowels, L.M., Francois-Walcott, R. R. R., Carnelley, K. B., & Checksfield, E. L. (2022). Adapting to change: How has COVID-19 affected people's work and personal goals? *PloS One, 17*(2), e0262195–e0262195. https://doi.org/10.1371/journal.pone.0262195

Wadsworth, W. (2020). *EXTREME study routine secrets for ambitious students.* https://examstudyexpert.com/study-routine/

Wallace, L., Patton, K. M., Luttrell, A., Sawicki, V., Fabrigar, L. R., Teeny, J., MacDonald, T. K., Petty, R. E., & Wegener, D. T. (2020). Perceived knowledge moderates the relation between subjective ambivalence and the 'impact' of attitudes: An attitude strength perspective. *Personality & Social Psychology Bulletin, 46*(5), 709–722. https://doi.org/10.1177/0146167219873492

Walsh, G., & Bartikowski, B. (2012). Employee emotional labour and quitting intentions: Moderating effects of gender and age. *European Journal of Marketing, 47*(8), 1213–1237. https://doi.org/10.1108/03090561311324291

Wardle, T. (Director) (2018). *Three identical strangers* [Documentary]. CNN Films.

WebMD (2022). www.webmd.com/balance/stress-management/stress-relief-breathing-techniques

Will, M. (2018). The long-term impact of systemic student support in elementary school: reducing high school dropout. *Education Week, 38*(8), 5.

Willcox, B. J., Yano, K., Chen, R., Willcox, D. C., Rodriguez, B. L., Masaki, K. H., Donlon, T., Tanaka, B., & Curb, J. D. (2004). How much should we eat? The association between energy intake and mortality in a 36-year follow-up study of Japanese-American men. *The Journals of Gerontology. Series A, Biological Sciences and Medical Sciences, 59*(8), B789–B795. https://doi.org/10.1093/gerona/59.8.B789

Willcoxson, L., Cotter, J., & Joy, S. (2011). Beyond the first-year experience: The impact on attrition of student experiences throughout undergraduate degree studies in six diverse universities. *Studies in Higher Education, 36*(3), 331–352. https://doi.org/10.1080/03075070903581533

Williams, C., Dziurawiec, S., & Heritage, B. (2018). More pain than gain: Effort-reward imbalance, burnout, and withdrawal intentions within a university student population. *Journal of Educational Psychology, 110*(3), 378–394. https://doi.org/10.1037/edu0000212

Yachnin, P. (2020, January). *Humanities PhD grads working in non-academic jobs could shake up university culture*. The Conversation. https://theconversation.com/humanities-phd-grads-working-in-non-academic-jobs-could-shake-up-university-culture-127298

Yu, Y., Yang, X., Yang, Y., Chen, L., Qiu, X., Qiao, Z., Zhou, J., Pan, H., Ban, B., Zhu, X., He, J., Ding, Y., & Bai, B. (2015). The role of family environment in depressive symptoms among university students: A large sample survey in China. *PLOS One*, *10*(12), e0143612. https://doi.org/10.1371/journal.pone.0143612

Zander, L., Brouwer, J., Jansen, E., Crayen, C., & Hannover, B. (2018). Academic self-efficacy, growth mindsets, and university students' integration in academic and social support networks. *Learning and Individual Differences*, *62*, 98–107. https://doi.org/10.1016/j.lindif.2018.01.012

Zhang, Q., Tong, J., & Huo, D. (2018). Development of the energy management scale. *Social Behavior and Personality*, *46*(12), 2081–2095. https://doi.org/10.2224/sbp.7426

Zhou, Y., Jindal-Snape, D., Topping, K., & Todman, J. (2008). Theoretical models of culture shock and adaptation in international students in higher education. *Studies in Higher Education (Dorchester-on-Thames)*, *33*(1), 63–75. https://doi.org/10.1080/03075070701794833

Zimet, G. D., Powell, S. S., Farley, G. K., Werkman, S., & Berkoff, K. A. (1990). Psychometric characteristics of the multidimensional scale of perceived social support. *Journal of Personality Assessment*, *55*(3–4), 610–617. https://doi.org/10.1080/00223891.1990.9674095

Zografova, Y. (2019). Identities and everyday interethnic relationships. *Qualitative Sociology Review*, *15*(2), 26–43. https://doi.org/10.18778/1733-8077.15.2.03

Appendix A
How to use Perceived Stress Scale-10

PSS-10 is a self-report questionnaire. The items are easy to understand, and the response alternatives are simple to grasp. The questions are general in nature and relatively free of content specific to any sub-population group (Cohen et al., 1983). The PSS-10 can be used to determine whether 'appraised' stress is an aetiological factor in behavioural disorders or disease. Items of the PSS were designed to tap how unpredictable, uncontrollable, and overloaded respondents find their lives (Cohen & Williamson, 1988). PSS-10 has been found to provide better predictions for psychological symptoms, physical symptoms and utilisation of health services than other similar instruments (Cohen & Williamson, 1988). In a cross-sectional study, higher PSS scores were associated with greater vulnerability to stressful life-event-elicited symptoms (Kuiper et al., 1986). PSS-10 scores are obtained by reversing the scores on the four positive items, e.g. 0=4, 1=3, 2=2, etc. and then summing across all 10 items. Items 4, 5, 7 and 8 are the positively stated items. PSS-4 scores are obtained by reverse coding items # 2 and 3.

PSS-14 scores are obtained by reversing the scores on the seven positive items, e.g. 0=4, 1=3, 2=2, etc., and then summing across all 14 items. Items 4, 5, 6, 7, 9, 10 and 13 are the positively stated items.

An example of using PSS-10

To calculate the PSS-10 score, the scores of the Items 1, 2, 3, 6, 9, and 10 are summed up firstly. Then the scores of Items 4, 5, 7 and 8 are re-calculated by using reversing the scores. Thirdly, all the four reversed scores are summed. Finally, both sums are scored in total. A student who scored 25 in PSS-10 provided a self-reflection about her mental health status.

Last month we were in the examination weeks, which means we had a lot of examinations, and many assignments were due to be submitted. It was the busiest time before the completion of the semester. Yes, I could see myself under a lot of stress, and that's why the score was high. I am not surprised, though, as it is quite normal at the end of the semester. I was not this stressed earlier in the semester, but getting myself tested does give me a clear view of my mental health and wellbeing.

This example of PSS-10 shows this university student has a high level of stress, support should be sought, and positive energy should be built for this student.

Appendix B
Energy building strategies and evaluation sheet for wellbeing

The Appendix includes a hands-on sheet for you to develop and use. The sheet was developed based upon Full Engagement Training Systems (Loehr & Schwartz, 2005). The following sheet also includes some examples for your references.

This sheet has four sections and procedures for you to follow. While it is not a clinical instrument, it is strongly recommended you complete the sheet regularly and reflect on the usefulness of your strategies.

Energy Building Strategies and Evaluation Sheet for Wellbeing

Name: _____

Date:_____

Step One: Evaluation and reflection about myself

My Strengths:	My Values:
1. _honesty_____	1. ____integrity_____
2. _high organisation skills____	2. ____respect and care to others___
3. _innovative_____	3. ____health_____
4. _____	4. _____
5. _____	5. _____

Think of someone you respect and admire and list three qualities of this person.

1. gentleness and caring
2. high achievement despite facing challenges
3. always respect for others

Who am I at my best?

hard-working, easy going, and high achiever

What is my personal vision, including my work/career visions?

At university, I would like to be a high academic achiever. As a university student, I would also like to be kind and have empathy and integrity for others. As a future employee, I would like to be confident with capabilities that others trust.

Step Two: List top study/work-related barriers

Barriers	Examples
1. Lack of concentration	Cannot be engaged on one task. Hard to meet the due date.
2. Little patience	Had negative feelings towards others and myself. Had low confidence in myself and others.
3. Negative thinker in relationships	Had no or limited connections/communication to family and friends.
4. Lack of passion	Life is grey and cannot generate any excitement.

Step Three: Energy building strategy (can be repeated based upon the barriers)

Barrier: Lack of concentration

Values driving change: high achiever

Expected outcome: positive energy for full engagement

	Strategies to support change	Starting date
Physical	Go to bed before 11 p.m. and ensure 7–8 hours of sleep. Eat and drink every 2 hours to maintain physical energy.	February 1
Emotional	Have a long phone call to a friend or a long conversation with family once a week. Have a reading session with the children.	March 1
Mental	Have a half an hour walk alone every day.	March 1
Spirituality	Treat other people with respect and kindness.	February 1

Barrier:

Values driving change:

Expected outcome:

Strategies to support change	Starting date
Physical	
Emotional	
Mental	
Spirituality	

Barrier:

Values driving change:

Expected outcome:

Strategies to support change	Starting date
Physical	
Emotional	
Mental	
Spirituality	

Step Four: Rate the strategies using the scale (add any notes if needed)

Strategies	Sun	Mon	Tue	Wed	Thu	Fri	Sat	Notes
Go to bed before 11 p.m. and ensure 7–8 hours of sleep. Not useful ◄────────► very useful		x	x	x	x			Difficult to apply for weekends. Have higher energy and be better engaged in the performance.
Eat and drink every 2 hours to maintain physical energy. Not useful ◄────────► very useful	x	x	x		x	x	x	
_____ Not useful ◄────────► very useful								
_____ Not useful ◄────────► very useful								
_____ Not useful ◄────────► very useful								
_____ Not useful ◄────────► very useful								

237

Appendix C
'Colourful' life at universities

Introduction

This Appendix is to provide an overview of university support for their students across the UK, Australia and the United States. In order to present authentic examples, we use a university in the UK, a university in Australia and a university in the US as examples to show you the support their students receive during their studies. We are also acknowledging there are differences (including names and terminologies) across various universities, depending on the location, demographic background of the university, public or private, and funding resources. Therefore, we strongly recommend you check your university's websites and student services facilities for detailed support.

An example from the United Kingdom

The university provides a lot of student services to its students, including their 18 specialist libraries with millions of books and journal subscriptions, courses in 17 languages offered by its language and international education centre, and home to three museums. Other than these facilities, it also offers many sports centres and production theatres and study facilities.

In particular, the Students' Union at the university has numerous facilities and support for its students. For example, students can take advantage of study places, computers and group workspaces. In addition, there are cafes, shops, event venues, a gym and a hair salon. In fact, its Students' Union is a registered charity that all of its students have access to. Through the Students' Union (https://studentsunionucl.org/), students have access to various support provided by the university, including housing, employment, academic and financial support. Students are also provided with safety support, including understanding and protection from scams, sexual violence, and wellbeing. Advisors are available to students by appointment.

There are also over 200 clubs and societies in the Students' Union, including sporting, cultural and artistic activities. These clubs and societies include culturally based societies, such as the Afghan Society, Malaysian Society and American Society, sported-related clubs, such as the Amateur Boxing Club, American Football Club and Golf Club, and many other hobby clubs and societies, such as the Graphic Novels and Comic Society, Music Society and TEDx Society. And MORE! These clubs and societies provide excellent opportunities for students to participate in activities and events organised by other students, to socialise with other students with similar habits and backgrounds and to seek support (if needed).

Moreover, students have volunteering opportunities to engage with the local community. Students have access to newsletters and learn about their local communities. Moreover, they can also work on building their career goals while working in the Student Club, and can come with research initiatives for further studies.

An example from Australia

When you are browsing through the website of an Australian university, you will notice the support offered by the university is similar to the UK university example. For example, this university offers support and facilities in the areas of health and welfare, career and employability, academic learning, and other forms of support (https://services.unimelb.edu.au). Support in health and welfare includes health and counselling services, an eye care clinic and dental clinic. Academic support covers use of the university library, academic skills advice and overseas learning experience support. There are also career offices to help students build their skills and experience while studying at the university. Finally, other extra support includes student housing support, childcare services, scholarships and financial support, etc. Other than the support and facilities from the university, students can join Student Life, and there are also over 200 student clubs and societies for students to join and participate in, ranging from spiritual, cultural and musical to political and other special hobbies. Student Life at the university also offers mentoring programmes, the Students' Union and Graduate Student Association facilities.

There are some differences in university support between the different countries. For example, the university offers a clearer information page for students in relation to COVID and safety updates. Moreover, academic support is emphasised in the support and facilities offered by the university.

An example from the United States

The university in the US emphasises student success and has also provided a lot of support and facilities to students. More than half of its students pay no tuition fees. Other than services similar to those provided by the universities in the UK and Australia, this university has a strong reputation as advocate for students who are the first generation in their families to attend higher education, and they concentrate on community engagement as well. Different from the UK and Australian higher education institutions, this university's outward facing website does not list all the support and services at the university. Instead, it appeals to students' academic values and their experience as a whole, including their pathway or transfer experience.

Summary

In summary, each university has their values embedded in their education, and all students and staff are working towards these goals with commitment to the university values and involvement in their university communities. If you feel challenged or stressed, feel free to ask for assistance and support from your university. Each university will offer unique contributions to your wellbeing, so ensure you investigate everything that is on offer to you. Overall, there are many ways to ensure your wellbeing during your studies. Enjoy the discovery process.

Index

Page numbers in *italics* refer to Figures and Tables.